Straight to ADVANCED

Student's Book
with Answers

Richard Storton
Zoltán Rézműves

Contents

Unit	Language focus	Vocabulary	Writing
1 Aspire and inspire Page 6	1 Past and present perfect simple and continuous 2 Inversion	Inspiration and success **Word formation:** Adjectives	Part 1: Essay
2 Working together Page 15	1 Modals 2 Relative clauses	Relationships	Part 2: Letter/email
Review Units 1 and 2 Page 24	Reading and Use of English Part 4: Key word transformation Reading and Use of English Part 3: Word formation		
3 A sense of wonder Page 26	1 Gerunds and infinitives 2 Reported speech	1 Travel 2 The senses **Word formation:** Nouns 1	Part 2: Review
4 Living in the past Page 35	1 Adverbs of degree 2 Comparisons	1 Memory 2 Rooms and spaces	Part 2: Report
Review Units 3 and 4 Page 44	Reading and Use of English Part 4: Key word transformation Reading and Use of English Part 1: Multiple-choice cloze		
5 Pushing the limits Page 46	1 Conditionals 2 Unreal time, wishes	1 Work 2 Health **Word formation:** Verbs	Part 2: Proposal
6 Changing times Page 55	1 Passives 2 Passives of reporting verbs	1 Change 2 Figurative language	Part 1: Essay
Review Units 5 and 6 Page 64	Reading and Use of English Part 4: Key word transformation Reading and Use of English Part 3: Word formation		
7 Brave new worlds Page 66	1 Future forms (review) 2 Future in the past	1 Verbs with *up-*, *down-*, *over-* and *under-* 2 Science and research	Part 2: Review
8 Getting through Page 75	1 Conjunctions 2 Discourse markers	1 Expressing feelings 2 Onomatopoeic words **Word formation:** Nouns 2	Part 2: Letter/email
Review Units 7 and 8 Page 84	Reading and Use of English Part 4: Key word transformation Reading and Use of English Part 2: Open cloze		
9 To the market Page 86	1 Determiners and pronouns 2 Reference, substitution and ellipsis	1 Money 2 Describing trends	Part 2: Proposal
10 School of thought Page 95	1 Emphasis with cleft sentences 2 Participle clauses	1 Academic language 2 The mind and brain **Word formation:** Affixes review	Part 2: Report
Review Units 9 and 10 Page 104	Reading and Use of English Part 4: Key word transformation Reading and Use of English Part 3: Word formation		

Additional Material	Grammar Reference	Writing Bank	Wordlist
Page 106	Page 115	Page 130	Page 137

Reading and Use of English		Listening	Speaking
Part 8: Multiple matching	Part 2: Open cloze	Part 1: Multiple choice	Part 2: Long turn Part 1: Interview
Part 7: Gapped text	Part 1: Multiple-choice cloze	Part 2: Sentence completion Part 4: Multiple matching	Part 3: Collaborative task Part 4: Discussion
Part 6: Cross-text multiple matching	Part 3: Word formation	Part 3: Multiple choice	Part 2: Long turn
Part 5: Multiple choice		Part 2: Sentence completion Part 1: Multiple choice	Part 3: Collaborative task Part 4: Discussion
Part 7: Gapped text	Part 1: Multiple-choice cloze	Part 4: Multiple matching	Part 2: Long turn
Part 6: Cross-text multiple matching	Part 2: Open cloze	Part 3: Multiple choice	Part 3: Collaborative task Part 4: Discussion
Part 5: Multiple choice	Part 1: Multiple-choice cloze	Part 4: Multiple matching Part 1: Multiple choice	Part 3: Collaborative task Part 4: Discussion
Part 7: Gapped text	Part 3: Word formation	Part 2: Sentence completion	Part 2: Long turn
Part 8: Multiple matching	Part 1: Multiple-choice cloze	Part 3: Multiple choice	Part 3: Collaborative task Part 4: Discussion
Part 6: Cross-text multiple matching	Part 2: Open cloze	Part 4: Multiple matching Part 2: Sentence completion	Part 2: Long turn Part 3: Collaborative task Part 4: Discussion

Listening scripts
Page 141

Answer key
Page 152

Introduction

About the course

Straight to Advanced is an intensive preparation course for students taking the *Cambridge English: Advanced (CAE)* examination, equivalent to level C1 in the Council of Europe's Common European Framework Reference for Languages. The course has been designed to help you develop the skills required for the *Advanced* exam and to improve your overall language level.

The Student's Book

The **Student's Book** has ten units with fresh and engaging topics, which are also pertinent to the exam. Each unit contains in-depth preparation and practice for the *Advanced* exam, with the following boxes guiding you to the best strategies for success in the exam:

- In the earlier units there are regular **Help** boxes, which give advice on how to deal with the different task types in the four papers of the *Advanced* exam.
- In later units **Remember** boxes remind you of the key points presented in the Help boxes.
- **Useful language** boxes appear in the Speaking sections and contain vocabulary and grammatical structures that would be most beneficial to use when doing that particular part of the Speaking exam.

Each unit has at least one **Vocabulary** section. The words and phrases have been carefully chosen with the exam in mind and will also help to boost your word store and language level. Throughout the book, collocations (pairs or groups of words that are often found together) are highlighted in **bold** for you to record. There is also a **Wordlist** on pages 137–140 for your reference. In Units 1, 3, 5, 8 and 10 there are **Word formation** sections which are designed to help improve your vocabulary and to assist you in preparing for Reading and Use of English Part 3.

There are two **Language focus** sections in each unit which will help to review and build upon your existing grammatical knowledge. All of the language points covered are those you are expected to demonstrate at this level. Each Language focus section refers you to the **Grammar Reference** on pages 115–129, which explains the grammatical point in more depth.

All **skills** (reading, writing, speaking and listening) are given full coverage throughout each unit. There is also a **Writing Bank** on pages 130–136, which includes a sample question and model answer for each of the possible writing tasks in the exam. Important features in each model answer have been highlighted. For each task type there is also a Useful language box and a further writing task for you to do.

There are five two-page **Review** sections, one every two units, which allow you to further practise the vocabulary and grammatical structures presented in the preceding two units. Each of the Review sections also contains two Reading and Use of English tasks, one of which is always Reading and Use of English Part 4: Key word transformation.

The Student's Resource Centre

The **Student's Resource Centre**, which can be accessed using the code provided on the inside front cover of this book, provides several additional resources. There are videos of two candidates performing all four parts of the Speaking paper of the *Advanced* exam. These come with accompanying worksheets and will allow you to see how the Speaking exam is carried out whilst thinking about best practice and strategy for answering the questions. There are also Extra Language Practice Worksheets for each unit, which provide you with the opportunity to further practise the language covered in the Student's Book. The Wordlist is also available here with definitions, example sentences and phonetic script for each word or phrase.

The Workbook

The **Workbook**, which contains ten units, is a useful companion to the Student's Book. Each unit gives further practice for the Vocabulary and Language focus sections from the corresponding unit of the Student's Book. In every unit there is also one each of the following exam tasks: Reading and Use of English, Listening and Writing. The exam tasks in the first four units of the Workbook are the same as those in the Student's Book, which allows you to consolidate the strategies covered in the Help boxes.

The Cambridge English: Advanced (CAE) examination

The *Advanced* examination is made up of four papers. The Writing, Listening and Speaking papers are each worth 20% of the total marks, while the Reading and Use of English paper is worth 40%. The scores from all four papers are averaged to give you an overall result for the examination. A breakdown of each paper in the *Advanced* exam is provided on the next page.

Reading and Use of English — 1 hour 30 minutes

This paper has eight parts: Parts 1 to 4 are grammar and vocabulary tasks; Parts 5 to 8 are reading tasks. Each correct answer in Parts 1 to 3 receives one mark; each question in Part 4 carries up to two marks. For Parts 5 to 7, each correct answer receives two marks, and there is one mark for each question in Part 8.

Part	Task type	Number of questions	What you have to do
1	Multiple-choice cloze	8	There is a text with eight gaps. For each gap decide on the best answer from a choice of four. The main focus is on vocabulary.
2	Open cloze	8	There is a text with eight gaps. Complete each gap with one word. The main focus is on grammar, with some focus on vocabulary.
3	Word formation	8	There is a text with eight gaps. Complete each gap with the correct form of a given word. The main focus is on vocabulary.
4	Key word transformation	6	Complete a gapped sentence with three to six words, included the word which you are given. The completed sentence must have the same meaning as the lead-in sentence. The focus is on grammar, vocabulary and collocation.
5	Multiple choice	6	Decide on the best answer from a choice of four.
6	Cross-text multiple matching	4	Read across four texts to match questions or 'prompts' to parts of the texts.
7	Gapped text	6	Replace paragraphs which have been removed from a text.
8	Multiple matching	10	Match questions or 'prompts' to the correct text or part of a text.

Writing — 1 hour 30 minutes

This paper has two parts, each of which carries the same number of marks. There is one Part 1 question, which must be answered by all candidates, and in Part 2 you write an answer to one question from a choice of three. You are required to write between 220 and 260 words for each part.

Part	Task type	Number of tasks	What you have to do
1	Essay	1 (compulsory)	Write an essay based on two points given in the task.
2	From the following: report, review, proposal, letter/email.	3 (choose one)	Write your answer according to the task instructions and in an appropriate style.

Listening — approximately 40 minutes

This paper has four parts with a total of 30 questions. Each part contains one or more recorded text, which is heard twice. Recordings may be monologues, such as speeches, lectures or announcements, or they may be conversations, radio interviews or discussions. You are tested on your ability to understand, for example, opinions, attitudes, specific information, gist or detail. There is one mark for each correct answer.

Part	Task type	Number of questions	What you have to do
1	Multiple choice	6	Listen to three short extracts, and answer two three-option multiple-choice questions for each.
2	Sentence completion	8	Listen to one speaker for three to four minutes and complete gaps in sentences with words or phrases from the recording.
3	Multiple choice	6	Listen to an interview or an exchange between two speakers for approximately four minutes and answer six four-option multiple-choice questions.
4	Multiple matching	10	Listen to five short, related monologues, each lasting for approximately 30 seconds. There are two tasks for which you are required to choose the correct option from a list of eight.

Speaking — approximately 15 minutes

This paper has four parts. There are usually two candidates and two examiners, one of whom conducts the test and assesses, while the other assesses but does not take an active part in the test.

Part	Task type	Time	What you have to do
1	Interview	2 minutes	Answer questions from the interviewer with information about yourself.
2	Long turn	4 minutes	Talk about a set of photographs for one minute, and comment for 30 seconds after the other candidate's turn.
3	Collaborative task	4 minutes	You are given instructions with written prompts which you use in a two-minute discussion, followed by a one-minute decision-making task.
4	Discussion	5 minutes	Participate in a discussion which is related to the topic of Part 3.

1 Aspire and inspire

Vocabulary and Speaking
Inspiration and success

1 💬 The photographs show people who have been inspired and inspired others. Work with a partner. Discuss who or what you find inspiring.

2 Complete the phrases in 1–6 below using the correct form of the words in the box.

> get set push encounter reach achieve
> keep make follow overcome

Six top tips for success

1 To _____ it in the hyper-competitive world we live in, you'll need plenty of _____ **up and go** to keep you motivated.

2 Don't be put off if you _____ **obstacles**. The road to _____ **your goals** will be fraught with challenges.

3 Think about people who you admire; _____ **in your hero's footsteps** can provide direction.

4 You must _____ **the fear** of failure. Try to view failing as an opportunity to learn.

5 _____ yourself manageable **targets**; small accomplishments can _____ you **driven and focused**.

6 Keep _____ **yourself**, people don't _____ **the pinnacle of their careers** by standing still.

3 💬 Discuss with a partner. To what extent do you agree with the advice given in exercise 2?

Reading and Use of English Part 8
Multiple matching

1 💬 Work in pairs. You are going to read a magazine article about books that inspired people to change their lives. Look at the book titles (A–D). How do you think they might have inspired the person writing about them?

2 For questions **1–10**, choose the correct book (A–D). The books may be chosen more than once.

Which person mentions the following?	
an appreciation of the author's skill for writing	1
the idea of reading as a form of escapism	2
an aspect that makes the book different from others of its genre	3
the inspiration that the book provided to follow a particular career	4
a change in how the reader viewed their belongings	5
how hard work was rewarded with satisfaction	6
how the book prevented the reader from making a certain decision	7
an assumption challenged by the book's style	8
the suggestion of pleasure coming from a sense of nostalgia	9
how the reader's profession attracted them to a particular theme	10

Unit 1 Aspire and inspire

BOOKS THAT CHANGED YOUR LIFE

We asked four people to share which books inspired them.

Help
- Read the whole text to get a general sense. You do NOT need to understand every word.
- Underline key words in the questions. The first two have been done for you.
- Scan each section (A–D) to look for information that matches the underlined key words.

3 💬 Has a book or film ever inspired you in similar ways to the writers in the article?

A Harry Potter and the Philosopher's Stone

I was studying literature at university, drowning in a sea of essays on critical thought with a pile of dusty classics stacked precariously on my desk – my assigned reading for the year. As a child, my parents instilled a love of reading in me with nightly bedtime stories. Throughout my teens, I could always be found with my head buried in a book, exploring unknown worlds. This passion had been the inspiration for my choice of degree, a decision that had seemingly back-fired. Then my friend Luca lent me *Harry Potter* and urged me to read it. The joy I felt as a child reading magical tales came flooding back. Without this book reawakening my love of reading, I probably would have dropped out and wouldn't now be working at my local newspaper. Even now a stray thought sometimes comes into my head: 'Do not be like Rita Skeeter', the dastardly reporter in the books.

B Into the Wild

I first read this book when I was 17 years old, and have read it every year since. It's the true story of Chris McCandless, a young man from a well-to-do family who gave up all of his possessions, abandoned his car, donated his savings to charity and went to live a sparse existence in the wilderness north of Mt. McKinley, Alaska. Reading the book did not inspire me to follow suit, as I'm not the most outdoorsy of people at the best of times. Nonetheless, it fascinated me that someone had heard Chris's story and felt the need to relate it to the world. I wanted to be able to tell stories like that, subtle yet powerful, each sentence perfectly crafted. Ten years on, I edit human interest stories for a national magazine. The experiences that people go through in their everyday lives are far more captivating than anything I could dream up myself.

C The Hitchhiker's Guide to the Galaxy

The Hitchhiker's Guide to the Galaxy is special because I didn't expect it to have any effect on me, let alone one so enduring. I don't even remember exactly when I read it, except that it was in the first few years of my arrival in Britain as a graduate student. I remember being intrigued by the description of it as a piece of comedy science fiction and, as a financial analyst, I was especially delighted by the economic theories. I'd been reading sci-fi since I was 10 or 11 and the books were rather serious stuff. Sci-fi wasn't supposed to be comical, yet this book was hilarious. And I guess that's the lasting effect it had on me. It made me understand that serious didn't have to be sombre.

D The Life-Changing Magic of Tidying Up

When you walk into my suburban cottage, the first thing that strikes you isn't, 'Wow, look at this stark minimalist paradise!'. Yet I am now a certifiable de-cluttering freak, having recently got rid of around 65 per cent of my possessions. The reason is Marie Kondo's blockbusting book. You may have heard of it. You may even have bought it. And then, as with all good self-help books, you probably wedged it back on your (overcrowded) bookshelf. Not me. It took me a whole year of stress, confusion, humiliation, heavy lifting and determination, but I did it. A big lesson has been the realisation that the less you have, the easier it is to see the items that you haven't been using for years. We gave an old pram, which I was initially loath to part with for sentimental reasons, to a charity and after they told me about the family receiving it, I felt a warm glow of pride.

Unit 1 Aspire and inspire

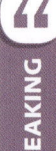

Speaking Part 2
Long turn

1   Look at the photographs below. They show **people taking part in different activities.**

Student A: Compare **two** of the pictures and say **why the people might be doing the activities,** and **who might have inspired them.**

Student B: When your partner has finished, answer the following question.

Which activity do you think would be the most interesting to do?

- Why do you think these people might be doing these activities?
- Who might have inspired them?

2   Now change roles. Look at the photographs on page 106 and follow the instructions.

Help

Student A
- When you compare the two pictures you selected, talk about the similarities as well as the differences between them.
  Both pictures show …, but this one …, whereas the other …
- Speculate about what the pictures show or suggest. Don't simply describe what you can see.
  I imagine/suppose/expect/think …
  It's possible/likely that …
  They might/could/may be …
- You need to talk for about one minute.

Student B
- Develop your answer by giving reasons and examples.
- You need to talk for about thirty seconds.

Language focus 1
Past and present perfect simple and continuous

1a Sentences **1–4** below are taken from the reading text on page 7. Underline and name the perfect tense being used in each sentence.

1 This passion had been the inspiration for my choice of degree …
2 … the less you have, the easier it is to see the items that you haven't been using for years.
3 I'd been reading sci-fi since I was 10 or 11 …
4 I first read this book when I was 17 years old, and have read it every year since.

1b Now match sentences **1–4** to uses **a–d**. Use the options only once.

a emphasising the duration of an action which started in the past and continues to be relevant in the present
b showing that a past event or situation occurred before another past event or situation
c describing a situation which started in the past and continues in the present
d emphasising the duration of an action up to another time in the past

⚙ Read more about perfect tenses in the Grammar Reference pages 115–116.

2 Complete each sentence with the correct form of the verb in brackets. Use the perfect tenses.

1 Angela _____ (work) for the BBC, but I'm not sure if she's still working for them now.
2 We _____ (paint) the bedroom for three hours and we are nowhere near finished.
3 Julian _____ (know) about the problem since I first told him two weeks ago.
4 When I met Michael in Nairobi, he _____ (live) there for several years.
5 Luckily, when Richard reached the airport, the flight _____ (not take off) and he managed to board the plane.
6 I remember the 14 July celebrations in 2000. That was the first time I _____ (visit) Paris.
7 Lately, I _____ (take) piano lessons so I can surprise my wife on her next birthday.
8 Susan _____ (watch) television right until the power was cut off.
9 Once I _____ (check) the instructions, the procedure became quite clear.
10 It's no surprise I'm hungry. I _____ (not eat) all day.

3 We can use different adverbs and time expressions to be more precise about past experiences. Match sentences **1–4** to their meanings **a–d**.

1 I haven't been to Japan <u>yet</u>.
2 I've been to Japan <u>recently</u>.
3 I haven't been to Japan <u>for some time</u>.
4 I've been to Japan six times <u>so far</u>.
a I've been a lot and will probably go again.
b I've been in the last year or so.
c I've never been there but intend to in the future.
d I've been there but it was quite a few years ago.

4 For sentences **1–6**, decide which ending is not correct, **A**, **B** or **C**.

1 I think I've asked you not to play that song
   A a hundred times.
   B already.
   C so far.
2 Mr and Mrs Peters have lived in Geneva
   A for a long time.
   B when they were younger.
   C all their lives.
3 Have you completed all your assignments
   A all afternoon?
   B already?
   C yet?
4 Katya had been living in Hong Kong
   A since she was a kid.
   B for some time.
   C last year.
5 My sister hasn't been feeling very well
   A all morning.
   B yet.
   C lately.
6 I asked Nell if she had been waiting
   A long.
   B recently.
   C for some time.

5a Complete each sentence so that it is true for you.

Since I was young, I've …
I had never … until …
Before I started learning English, I'd …
… is the best … I've ever …
All my life I've been …

5b 💬 Compare your sentences with a partner.

Unit 1 Aspire and inspire

Speaking Part 1
Interview

1. 💬 In Part 1 of the Speaking test, the examiner asks you and your partner questions about yourselves. Ask and answer these questions with a partner.

   1. Where are you from? What do you do there?
   2. How long have you been studying English?
   3. What do you enjoy most about learning English?

2. 💬 After asking some simple questions, the examiner will ask you about things like your childhood, your plans for your future, your home and your interests.

   Work with a partner. Decide who is the examiner and the candidate. Ask and answer the questions opposite.

Help
- Answer the examiner's questions as fully as possible. Avoid one-word answers.
- Keep your responses natural and spontaneous.
- Use a variety of structures and vocabulary.

Word formation
Adjectives

1a Look at these examples of answers students have given to the questions in Speaking Part 1. <u>Underline</u> the adjective in each example. Then write down the word from which each adjective is formed.

> In the summer, I'm going to do some voluntary work at a school in Serbia.

> This time last year I started exercising more and changed my diet. Nowadays I feel much more energetic.

> Seeing as I'm quite a restless person I tend to exercise quite a lot.

> One of my most memorable travel experiences was when I visited my brother who lives in Shanghai.

1b Use the suffixes in exercise **1a** to form adjectives from these words. Use the same suffix for all the words in each group. You may need to make other spelling changes.

1 imagine	compliment	necessity
2 science	drama	specify
3 break	like	knowledge
4 count	doubt	care

THE PAST
1. What do you consider to be your greatest achievement?
2. What are your earliest childhood memories?
3. What have been the happiest moments in your life so far?
4. What were your ambitions when you were ten years younger than now?
5. How was your life different from now this time last year?

3. 💬 Change roles. Use the questions on page 107 and repeat the Speaking Part 1 exam practice activity with different topics.

2. Complete each gap with an adjective using the word in capital letters and one of the suffixes in the box. You may need to add a negative affix and make other spelling changes.

   -ent   -ative   ~~-ial~~   -ory   -ous   -ant   -y

The Life Coaching industry is becoming increasingly **(0)** _influential_ , as more and more people turn to 'experts' for advice on everything from schedule management to ways to make **(1)** _____ changes in their lives.	INFLUENCE SIGNIFY
It seems that people are more open to making big changes in their lives no matter how **(2)** _____ they may seem at first glance. One of the main reasons people hire coaches is that they feel that they are making **(3)** _____ progress at work and need an outsider's perspective. Coaches can talk you through strategies to become more **(4)** _____ with your colleagues and methods to make your point of view more **(5)** _____ .	RISK SATISFY COOPERATE APPEAR
Sounds too good to be true, right? Well, due to lack of regulations, the quality of coaching can vary, so be **(6)** _____ and do your homework before selecting the right coach for you.	CAUTION

Unit 1 Aspire and inspire

Listening Part 1
Multiple choice 🔊 1.01–1.03

1 💬 **Discuss these questions with a partner.**
   1 How much do you know about your family history?
   2 Is there anyone in your family you consider to be your role model? Why?

2 🔊 **You will hear three different extracts. For questions 1–6, choose the answer (A, B or C) which fits best according to what you hear. There are two questions for each extract.**

Extract One
You hear two friends talking about role models.
1 <u>What</u> is it about the man's role model that <u>inspires</u> him?
   A his ability to <u>keep</u> his <u>personal life private</u>
   B his <u>dedication</u> to achieving <u>business success</u>
   C his <u>relationships</u> with members of his <u>family</u>
2 What is the woman's main concern about role models?
   A People have unreasonable expectations of what examples they can show us.
   B It is impossible to choose role models who lead exemplary lives.
   C Sometimes we select role models in order to live up to others' expectations about us.

Extract Two
You overhear two students discussing their impressions after a class.
3 What do both speakers agree was problematic about the lecture?
   A The talk focused on people who didn't play an important role in history.
   B The lecture turned out to be significantly longer than advertised.
   C The title of the lecture was misleading.
4 Why does the woman mention the battle of Waterloo?
   A to give an example of a historical turning point the lecturer failed to cover
   B to refer to an eye witness' account of the event
   C to support how relevant personal histories are in discussing historical events

Extract Three
You hear part of an interview on a television programme.
5 What reason does the man give for not doing research online?
   A The registry office he contacted was unhelpful.
   B There was no information available in connection with his family.
   C He lacked the necessary skills.
6 How far back has the man managed to trace his family origins so far?
   A He has found several living relatives on the Polish side of his family.
   B His grandparents are the oldest generation he knows anything about.
   C He has managed to trace where his great-grandparents had come from.

Help

- Underlining key phrases in the questions will help focus your attention when you listen. Question **1** has been done for you.
- The key phrases may be paraphrased in the recording. Think of one or two different ways of saying the same information.
- The first time you listen to the recording, locate the information and select the most likely answer.
- The second time you listen, check your initial choices and finalise your answers.

3 Check your answers by reading the listening script on page 141. <u>Underline</u> the parts of each extract which guided you to the correct answers. The first extract has been done for you.

4 💬 **Discuss these questions with a partner.**
   1 What do you think was the most significant turning point in your country's history?
   2 How do you think it affected ordinary people at the time?
   3 If you could invite five people from the past or present for dinner, who would you choose? Why?
   4 If you could go back in time, which period of history or historical event would you most like to visit/see? Why?

Unit 1 Aspire and inspire

Language focus 2
Inversion 🔊 1.04

1a 🔊 **Listen to the following three extracts from the listening and complete the gaps.**

1 I _____ anything about the other aspects of his life until I saw the film.
2 I _____ a footballer as my role model!
3 I _____ close to tears …

1b Now look at how the extracts are expressed below using inversion. How has the original word order changed? What other effect does inversion have on the sentence?

1 **Not until** I saw the film did I know anything about the other aspects of his life.
2 **Under no circumstances** would I choose a footballer as my role model!
3 **Rarely** do I come close to tears …

2 Complete this text about inversion by choosing the correct word in *italics*.

We can put a **(1)** *negative/positive* adverb or certain other expressions at the start of a sentence for emphasis. When we do this, there is inversion of the **(2)** *subject/noun* and the **(3)** *main/auxiliary* verb. We use inversion to make sentences **(4)** *more/less* emphatic and more **(5)** *formal/informal*.

⚙ Read more about inversion in the Grammar Reference page 116.

3 Rewrite sentences **1–7** using inversion and starting with the words given. Make any other necessary changes.

0 I'm sick and tired of his attitude; he won't speak to me like that again.
   Never again _will he speak to me like that; I'm sick and tired of his attitude._
1 Vanessa only realised her purse had been stolen when she tried to take it out to pay.
   Only when _____
2 You should not share the contents of this document with anyone else.
   On no account _____
3 He is really clever and incredibly funny.
   Not only _____
4 You've never mentioned any reservations about getting married before.
   At no time _____
5 I wouldn't have made that satay dip if I'd known Jared was allergic to nuts.
   Had I _____
6 We rarely see players with such natural ability.
   Seldom _____
7 I'd just arrived home when they called me back to the office.
   No sooner _____

4 💬 Work in pairs. Using the phrases in **bold** in exercises **1b** and **3**, write three sentences of your own, using inversion. Then swap sentences with your partner and rewrite your partner's sentences without inversion.

Reading and Use of English Part 2
Open cloze

1 💬 Work with a partner. Do you recognise the people in the photos? What are their achievements?

2 Read the text, ignoring the gaps. Do any of the stories surprise you?

3 💬 For each gap **1–8**, try to decide what type of word is missing (main verb, auxiliary verb, preposition, etc.). Compare your ideas in pairs.

4 Read the text again. Think of the word which best fits each gap. Use only **one** word in each gap. There is an example at the beginning (0).

Fail first to succeed

It is logical to assume that famous people who achieved worldwide success **(0)** _HAD_ clearly been born lucky. Astonishingly, **(1)** .... often than not, the opposite is true. It seems that the road to outstanding achievements is frequently paved with disappointments. Take, for example, Michael Jordan, often regarded **(2)** .... the most talented basketball player in history. But talent doesn't guarantee immediate success. In his teens, his coach decided to drop him **(3)** .... the high-school squad. Or consider Akio Morita, **(4)** .... name may sound unfamiliar, although you've undoubtedly heard about his company, Sony. Their first product was a rice cooker, which, disappointingly, was not very good at cooking rice and often managed to burn it. **(5)** .... surprisingly, Sony sold fewer than 100 rice cookers. It was, all **(6)** .... all, an abject failure. But it didn't prevent Akio Morita from fulfilling his ambition for Sony. Today, the brand is a household name **(7)** .... over the globe. Or what about Stephen King, one of the most successful authors that ever lived? His first book, *Carrie*, received 30 rejections, and King lost his motivation to continue. He even threw the book in the bin. Fortunately his wife took it **(8)** .... and encouraged him to try again. The rest, as they say, is history.

Help

- Read the text first, ignoring the gaps, to get a general idea of what it is about.
- You may be able to fill in some gaps just by looking at the words immediately before and after them. For others, you will need to understand a longer passage or the whole text.

Writing Part 1
Essay

1 Read the task below, and answer these questions.
1. **Who** are you writing for?
2. **What** are you writing about? How many of the listed factors do you need to include?
3. **How** are the opinions quoted related to the points in the notes? Do you have to use these opinions in your essay?

Your class has recently listened to a podcast on how images in the media shape young people's future ambitions. You have made the notes below.

Factors in how media images influence young people's ambitions
- celebrities presented as role models
- limited choice of possible careers shown
- fame and wealth as goals

Some opinions expressed in the podcast:

'Media celebrities are often inappropriate role models for young people.'

'There is only a narrow selection of careers shown in the media – those that most closely reflect the target audience.'

'The media plays an ambiguous role in shaping what people see as key factors in happiness.'

Write an essay for your tutor discussing **two** of the factors mentioned in your notes. You should explain **which factor has the more significant impact** on young people's ambitions, **giving reasons** in support of your opinion.

You may, if you wish, make use of the opinions expressed in the podcast, but you should use your own words as far as possible.

Unit 1 Aspire and inspire

2 Read the model answer below. Which two factors has the writer chosen to include? What is the purpose of each paragraph? Complete the plan below.

> Essay Plan
> Paragraph 1: Introduction — to engage interest and present the topic of the essay.
> Paragraph 2:
> Paragraph 3:
> Paragraph 4:

How images in the media shape young people's future ambitions

Statistics show that people aged 14–21 spend over 2.5 hours each day watching television and as much as 27 hours a week online. They are exposed to more media images than ever before and this can have lasting effects on their aspirations.

Firstly, it should be pointed out that media companies decide what professions are represented; these are decided upon the basis of viewing figures and the profit they generate. Those that do not appeal to a broader audience are rarely shown. Some would argue that, as a result, young people are less likely to consider occupations they are seldom exposed to. However, other sources of inspiration should not be overlooked. A recent survey amongst students revealed that friends, family, college or real-life role models have a far greater influence on what careers young people pursue than the media.

On the other hand, few people would dispute that the vast majority of younger people perceive success as wealth. The main reason for this opinion is the glamorous lifestyles given substantial coverage in the media. This has led many teens and young adults to view fame and fortune as the primary sources of happiness. Consequently, other more worthwhile life goals may be overlooked.

In conclusion, whilst the media generally only ever present certain types of jobs, there are other influences which outweigh the effect this has. A much more significant aspect in forming adolescent goals is how media images link being rich and famous to success, as in today's society this seems to be a widespread belief.

3 Read the model answer again and complete the following tasks.

a Complete the table below with phrases from the model answer.

Giving your opinion	... should not be overlooked.
Stating other people's views	
Widely held beliefs	
Providing sources	

b Circle the linking words and phrases in the model answer.

4 Write an answer to the following Part 1 task in **220–260** words.

Your class has recently listened to a lecture on how college shapes young people's future ambitions. You have made the notes below.

> **Factors in how college shapes young people's ambitions**
> - limited availability of subjects
> - attitude of peers towards work
> - testing and assessment

> **Some opinions expressed in the lecture:**
> 'Some people panic in exams and do not achieve good results.'
> 'You are more likely to trust advice from people you know well and believe in.'
> 'Colleges do not always have a wide range of subjects to suit the needs of their students.'

Write an essay for your tutor discussing **two** of the factors mentioned in your notes. You should **explain which factor has the more significant impact** on young people's ambitions, **giving reasons** to support your opinion.

You may, if you wish, make use of the opinions expressed in the lecture, but you should use your own words as far as possible.

Help

- Read the question carefully to ensure you understand all the requirements.
- Plan your essay and organise your ideas into paragraphs.
- Use a wide range of expressions to link and structure your sentences into a cohesive essay.
- Make sure you support your opinions with reasons.

More information in the Writing Bank pages 130–131.

2 Working together

Vocabulary
Relationships

1 💬 Work in pairs. What do you think the relationship between the people in the photographs might be?

2a Complete each phrase in **bold** with the correct option, A, B or C.

1 Do you often ___ **with friends or family over pointless things**? How quickly do you normally make up?
   A differ   B quarrel   C dispute

2 Were you ___ **in the city** or **in the countryside**? Was it a good place to spend your childhood?
   A brought up   B grown up   C raised up

3 Do you usually ___ **with your colleagues/classmates**? How does this positive/negative relationship affect your work?
   A see eye to eye   B get back together
   C rub shoulders

4 Have you ever met someone who you **immediately** ___ **with**? Are you still friends now?
   A hit it off   B set up   C fell out

5 Do you ___ **anyone in your family**? If so, is it a physical trait or a characteristic that you share with them?
   A take to   B take in   C take after

6 Is there anyone in your life who you **have** ___ who you would like to get back in contact with?
   A kept in touch with   B drifted apart from   C put up with

7 Do you think it is important for friends **to be** ___ or is it OK to have a different outlook on life?
   A kept at arm's length   B moving in the same circles
   C on the same wavelength

2b 💬 Discuss the questions in exercise **2a** with your partner.

3a In sentences 1–4, circle the adjective in *italics* which is NOT used with the noun in **bold**.

1 Gregory's a *fair-weather/lifelong/mutual/committed* **friend**.
2 They have a *strained/complicated/nuclear/stable* **relationship**.
3 Farah had a very *conventional/close/unusual/strict* **upbringing**.
4 Sophia has a large *close-knit/sheltered/extended/immediate* **family**.

3b Look at exercise **3a** again. Make collocations using the adjectives you circled and the nouns in **bold**. More than one answer may be possible.

4 💬 Work in pairs. Use the adjective + noun collocations in exercises **3a** and **3b** to talk about your own relationships.

Unit 2 Working together

Listening Part 2
Sentence completion 🔊 1.05

1 💬 Work in pairs. When you meet new people, how do you try to get to know them better? What kinds of questions do you ask?

2 💬 Read the following dictionary entry and discuss the questions with your partner.

> **network** VERB
> to meet and talk to people in order to receive or give information, especially about business opportunities

1 In which ways can people network for study or work? Which ways are best?
2 Have you become close friends or colleagues with someone you have met through networking?

3 🔊 You will hear a business expert called Anthony Conrad talking about effective ways to network. For questions **1–8**, complete the sentences with a word or short phrase.

NETWORKING – SOME USEFUL ADVICE

Anthony states that the way people feel about networking can have a **(1)** .... on how they get on at work.
Anthony asserts networks are important for promotion as they offer access to **(2)** .... and information.
Personal networking describes day-to-day social behaviour and grows with **(3)** ....
The Harvard study results suggest employees in **(4)** .... are unaffected by the stress of networking.
Anthony says providing employees with chances to network more often would build their **(5)** .... in doing it.
Psychologists and business experts report that the best way to build a strong connection with a new contact is to find **(6)** ....
Anthony states that understanding a person's **(7)** .... will encourage them to offer help.
Anthony concludes that if networking is given time, it will bring **(8)** ....

Help

- Look at each gap before listening and decide what type of word or phrase is missing.
- Use the sentence context to help you with grammatical clues – sometimes you will need to use plural forms.
- Write down the exact word or phrase that you hear. These are often single or compound nouns.
- For some questions you will hear distractors. These are words which at first seem relevant, but do not complete the sentence correctly. Listening carefully to the context surrounding a question should help you select the most appropriate answer.
- Check your answers. Incorrect spelling and grammar will lose marks.

4 💬 Work in pairs. Is networking in your country more common now than in the past? Why do you think that might be?

5 💬 Think of an example of two people you know who would benefit from being introduced to one another. Tell your partner.

Speaking Part 3
Collaborative task

1a 💬 Work in pairs. Here are some things which could help you to advance your career and a question for you to discuss. Talk to each other about how useful these ways of networking could be.

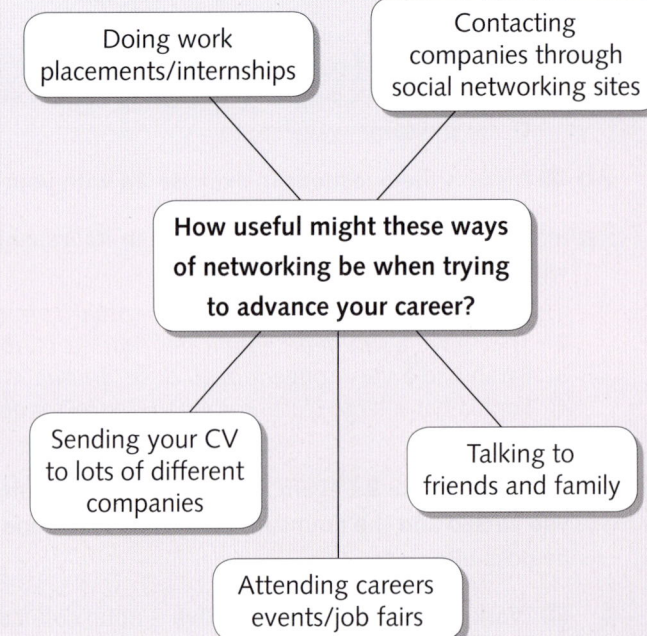

16

1b Now decide which type of networking would be most effective.

Help

- There are two phases in Part 3 of the Speaking test. First, you discuss a question with your partner(s) by referring to some written prompts. The focus is on exchanging ideas, expressing and justifying opinions, speculating and evaluating.
- In the second phase, the examiner asks another question related to the written prompts you have already discussed. The focus here is on negotiating towards a decision.
- Show the examiner you can keep a discussion going by asking relevant questions, allowing your partner(s) time to respond and by commenting on or extending their contribution.

Useful language

Make suggestions:
Have you considered …? In their position I'd … What would you say to …?

Explain and clarify:
That's the reason why … What I mean is … What I'm trying to say is …

Refer to your partner's comments:
You mentioned …, could you explain that in more detail? Do you have you any thoughts on …?

Agree/Disagree:
*I think we agree (that) …
Well, we seem to disagree. You think that …, while I'm of the opinion (that) …*

Speaking Part 4
Discussion

 Discuss these questions with your partner.

1. Do you think that companies should pay people for work experience/internships? Why/Why not?
2. Do you think that it's important to consult your friends and family when you make important decisions? Why/Why not?
3. Some people believe that online relationships are less important than relationships with people you see regularly. Do you agree? Why/Why not?
4. If you have a problem, do you often approach other people to help you solve it? Why/Why not?
5. Do you think that businesses should provide more opportunities for employees to develop social relationships? Why/Why not?
6. Some people say that nowadays we are more interested in looking after ourselves than others. What do you think?

Help

- In Part 4, you will be asked a series of questions related to the topic in Part 3. You will hear the questions, but not see them. Ask the examiner to repeat the question if necessary.
- The focus here is on your ability to express opinions using a range of structures. Try to develop your ideas as much as possible by giving examples or supporting evidence.

Unit 2 Working together

Language focus 1
Modals

1 **Look at the messages people have sent others in their network. <u>Underline</u> the correct modal verbs in *italics*.**

1 Hi Andy, sorry about the late response to your invitation to connect. I *should have/must have* missed it when you first contacted me. I *would/should* love to become part of your network. All the best, Saïd.

2 Hi Sara, just a quick message to let you know that you *needn't/couldn't* complete the questionnaire attached to my last email, it wasn't meant to be on there! Rachel.

3 Aidan, you really *shouldn't have/mustn't have* posted that video without asking permission. *Can't you have/Haven't you* heard of copyright laws?

4 Hi Ciara, I *won't/can't* seem to find that website that you recommended I post my CV on. Please *can/may* you forward a link? Thanks, Mark.

2 **Look at these possible uses of modal verbs. Match the modal verbs you underlined in exercise 1 with the correct use.**

ability/inability   criticism
annoyance   habit
asking for/giving permission
obligation/necessity
lack of obligation/necessity
logical deduction   possibility
concession   offer   refusal
request   willingness

⚙ Read more about modals in the Grammar Reference pages 116–118.

3 **Choose the sentence (A or B) that is closest in meaning to the sentence given.**

1 The alarm doesn't come on automatically.
   A You don't have to turn the alarm on.
   B You should turn the alarm on.

2 You needn't phone her if you don't want to.
   A You mustn't phone her if you don't want to.
   B You don't have to phone her if you don't want to.

3 Using their online booking system couldn't be easier.
   A You may as well use their online booking system.
   B You should find their online booking system simple to use.

4 It's possible that the results of the test will be available later today.
   A The results should be available later today.
   B The results might be available later today.

5 We can't not invite him.
   A We'd better invite him.
   B We'd better not invite him.

6 Although I try hard, I can never explain this clearly.
   A Try as I may, I can never explain this.
   B Try as I can, I may never explain this.

4 💬 **Work in pairs. Look at photographs A and B and answer these questions.**

1 What do you think the relationships between the people and animals might be?
2 How might their relationship develop in the future?

Unit 2 Working together

Reading and Use of English Part 1
Multiple-choice cloze

> **Help**
> - This part of the Reading and Use of English paper is primarily a test of vocabulary. Questions typically focus on fixed phrases, collocations, idioms and phrasal verbs.
> - Look at the choice of words and select the one which fits in terms of meaning and grammar.

1 For sentences 1–3, <u>underline</u> the correct option. Then match each sentence to the appropriate description **a–c**.
  1 Dutch police have ___ an innovative way to tackle illegal drones – eagles!
    A imagined   B realised   C invented   D discovered
  2 The authorities are working out how to effectively ___ with nuisance drones.
    A deal   B fight   C get   D break
  3 The eagles will wear ___ armour to ensure they are not hurt.
    A safety   B defensive   C protective   D precaution

  a The selected option is the only word with the correct meaning.
  b The selected option is part of a collocation or other common word pattern.
  c The selected option is the correct part of a phrasal verb.

2 Look at the title of the text from a newspaper. What do you think it is about? Read the text, ignoring the gaps, to check your ideas.

3 Read the text again. For questions **1–8**, decide which answer (**A**, **B**, **C** or **D**) best fits each gap. There is an example at the beginning (**0**).

A bird's eye view on tackling waste

The vulture is (0) _D_ unloved but Peruvian environmental authorities are attempting to change (1) ..... . Wearing GPS trackers and mini video cameras, ten vultures have been (2) ..... to lead authorities to illegal dumps whose run-off (3) ..... the rivers and Pacific coastline of the capital, Lima.
The city (4) ..... 2.1 million tonnes of rubbish per year and according to officials an estimated 20 per cent of this ends up in dumps which are unregulated and can be the (5) ..... of diseases. These areas are renowned for the flocks of vultures that feed there.
The vultures are playing an important role in a programme which aims to raise (6) ..... about the issue. The birds fly to the sites in search of food and in doing so identify locations where there are large volumes of organic matter and rubbish. The GPS coordinates are checked to (7) ..... whether the sites are legal and the video footage is posted online. This forms part of a social media campaign encouraging local residents to confirm illegal sites, (8) ..... ensure that they are closed before they harm surrounding communities.

0	A rarely	B seldom	C usually	D <u>often</u>
1	A thoughts	B options	C attitudes	D ideas
2	A uncovered	B abandoned	C detected	D dispatched
3	A spoils	B damages	C pollutes	D stains
4	A generates	B builds	C develops	D makes
5	A start	B origin	C source	D beginning
6	A understanding	B realisation	C knowledge	D awareness
7	A verify	B study	C predict	D guess
8	A assisting	B helping	C aiding	D improving

4 💬 Work in pairs. Can you think of any other situations where animals are used to help humans in a task? Do you think that people should use animals for potentially dangerous tasks or activities? Why/Why not?

Unit 2 Working together

Reading and Use of English Part 7
Gapped text

1 💬 Discuss these questions with a partner.
   1 Is it important to understand how animals exist in the wild? Why/Why not?
   2 Why do you think that people have such strong relationships with some kinds of animals and not others?
   3 Is it important to protect endangered species? Why/Why not? What are the possible benefits?

2 Read the title and the first line of the text. What do you think the text is about? Who would enjoy reading this kind of text?

3 Read the body of the text and check the predictions you made in exercise 2. Do not read paragraphs A–G yet.

4 You are going to read an extract from an article. Six paragraphs have been removed from the extract. Choose from the paragraphs A–G the one which fits each gap (1–6). There is one extra paragraph which you do not need to use.

A fine balance – managing the relationships between animals and humans

Ecotourism, where travellers visit natural environments with an eye toward funding conservation efforts or boosting local economies, has become increasingly popular in recent years. In many cases it involves close observation of, or interaction with, wildlife, such as when tourists swim with marine animals. However, during a recent project life scientists analysed large volumes of studies on how ecotourism affects vulnerable animals and concluded that such experiences can be detrimental to a range of species.

1

They found that while ecotourism could be instrumental in ensuring that groups of animals in the highest risk categories avoid extinction, there were definite drawbacks. Ecotourism, by its very nature, tends to focus tourist activity on specific sites of interest. And whilst taking an interest in the world around you is all well and good, the numbers may surprise you.

2

One way it is causing this is by the simple fact that the presence of humans changes the way animals behave. It makes them more vulnerable — to poachers, for one — but also in less obvious ways. When animals interact in seemingly benign ways with humans, they may let their guard down. As animals learn to relax in the presence of humans, they may become bolder in other situations. If this transfers to their interactions with predators, they are more likely to be injured or killed.

3

In fact, researchers have pointed out that ecotourism has effects similar to those of animal domestication and urbanisation. In all three cases, regular interactions between people and animals may lead to habituation. Domesticated animals become more docile and less fearful due to regular interactions with humans. Domesticated fish are less responsive to simulated predatory attacks. Mammals and birds which live in urbanised areas are slower to flee from danger.

4

A case in point is the New Zealand sea lion, which is found around the southern mainland, and the dangers it faces. Fisheries are the main threat to sea lion populations as they reduce pup survival rates by affecting the supply of food. However, ecotourism also tends to impact on this stage too. Tourists, keen to photograph pups, often get too close to the animals, causing them to retreat to the sea. In turn this means that young seals miss feeding opportunities.

Unit 2 Working together

Help

- Summarise each paragraph in a few words. Try to predict what the writer will say next.
- Read all the missing paragraphs and try to identify the purpose of them. Are they explaining a point, illustrating an example or showing contrast?
- Read the information before and after the gaps to help you identify any reference links, e.g. *Them → People*.
- Check your answers by reading the whole article again to ensure that it makes sense. Check that the extra paragraph does not fit any of the gaps.

A Having said this, researchers have identified a threshold effect where ecotourism displaces activities conventionally seen as harmful to wildlife. When more money is generated by tourism, attitudes change regarding primary industries. Although whether this results in action tends to depend on those who own or directly benefit from such businesses.

B Conversely, in other cases, the food chain is also affected by natural predators being discouraged by an abundance of humans in the ecosystem. The sum total of all this is that prey species become less alert and increasingly tame.

C The major outcome of this research is that the findings were integrated into established computer models which calculated the viability of a threatened species. The research teams then quantified the impacts of ecotourism operations on habitats, population change and migration patterns.

D However, it's not all bad news. Other species such as the cheetah have greatly benefited from increased tourist numbers. With this interest has come an awareness regarding the threat from poaching. Furthermore, local communities have seen that tourism revenue outweighs their reward from any involvement in hunting the animals.

E Protected areas around the globe receive in the region of 8 billion visits each year and this is beginning to take its toll. Ecotourism can now be added to the growing list of drivers of human-induced rapid environmental change.

F It has been estimated that direct spending through ecotourism is worth approximately $600 billion annually. This far surpasses the $10 billion which is spent each year safeguarding and managing areas which contain protected or endangered species.

G Indeed, interacting with people can cause significant change in the characteristics of various species over time. If individual animals selectively habituate to humans – particularly tourists – and if invasive tourism practices enhance this habituation, ecotourism may be creating traits which have unintended consequences.

5

The economic benefits of ecotourism are, however, very much dependent upon scale. This is clearly demonstrated in Indonesia, where small-scale ecotourism has focused on orang-utans. While interest in this species has helped it secure a protected status, the positive effects have not been able to overcome the problem of habitat loss. This is due to the financial importance of logging, which so far surpasses interest in animal conservation as a source of income.

6

Whatever the future for ecotourism, the hope is new analysis will encourage more research into the interactions between people and wildlife. It is essential to develop a more comprehensive understanding of how various species in various situations respond to human interaction. We now know that even minimal interaction could affect the behaviour or biology of a species and influence its function within its community. However, it is also important to acknowledge that without this interaction, some species may no longer exist at all.

5 💬 **Discuss the following questions:**
1. What kind of ecotourism happens in your country? Do the tourists always behave responsibly?
2. Do you think that there should be limits on the types of interaction people have with wild animals? Why/Why not?

6 💬 **Work in small groups. Imagine you are the government ministers in charge of wild animals in your country. What policies would you introduce to protect them and control their interaction with humans?**

Unit 2 Working together

Language focus 2
Relative clauses

1 **Look at sentences 1–4 from the reading text. Match them to explanations a–d.**
   1 Mammals and birds which live in urbanised areas are slower to flee from danger.
   2 … the hope is new analysis will encourage more research into the interactions between people and wildlife.
   3 A case in point is the New Zealand sea lion, which is found around the southern mainland, and the dangers it faces.
   4 This is due to the financial importance of logging, which so far surpasses interest in animal conservation as a source of income.

   a non-defining relative clause containing non-essential information
   b defining relative clause with pronoun omitted
   c defining relative clause containing essential information
   d non-defining relative clause referring to the whole clause

2 **In exercise 1, in which sentences can a pronoun be replaced with *that*? Why? Which relative pronouns can be omitted completely? Why?**

 Read more about relative clauses in the Grammar Reference pages 118–119.

3 **Complete each gap with a word from the box.**

   | where | which | who | whom | whose | why |

   1 Patrick's been doing voluntary work with young people, some of _____ have learning difficulties. He does it at the youth centre _____ he has boxing lessons.
   2 During the late 90s he worked in Midland, Texas, _____ at that time was a relatively small city _____ main industry was oil and gas. Since then it has grown rapidly in size.
   3 We went to a gig this weekend, _____ is something _____ we haven't done for ages.
   4 I spoke to a woman _____ said she used to live near us when we were younger but I really can't remember her.
   5 The reason _____ so many people are moving there is that it's a city _____ offers a lot of opportunities.
   6 After university, Katy, _____ had hated living in London, returned to the town _____ she had grown up in and _____ most of her school friends still lived.

4 **Look at your answers in exercise 3 again. Decide which of the words you have written: a) can be replaced with *that*, b) can be omitted.**

Listening Part 4
Multiple matching 1.06–1.10

You will hear five short extracts in which people are talking about the challenging places where they have lived.

While you listen you must complete both tasks.

TASK ONE

For questions **1–5**, choose from the list (**A–H**) the main challenge being described.

A the loneliness
B the lack of open spaces
C the lack of support from the local community
D the difficulty in finding food
E the language barrier
F the extreme weather conditions
G the threat from humans
H the wildlife

Speaker 1 [1]
Speaker 2 [2]
Speaker 3 [3]
Speaker 4 [4]
Speaker 5 [5]

TASK TWO

For questions **6–10**, choose from the list (**A–H**) how each speaker responded to the problem.

A They became more confident.
B They felt depressed.
C They grew closer to their family.
D They expanded their social circle.
E They left the area.
F They took the opportunity to explore new subjects.
G They felt a stronger connection to old friends.
H They gained a better perspective on life.

Speaker 1 [6]
Speaker 2 [7]
Speaker 3 [8]
Speaker 4 [9]
Speaker 5 [10]

Help

- Read both Task One and Task Two before the recording begins so that you can predict the language you are going to hear.
- Underline the important words in options **A–H** and think about what the speaker might talk about.

Writing Part 2
Letter/email

1 Read the following Part 2 task and model answer. For numbers **1–8** in the model answer, cross out the word or phrase which does not fit the sentence for reasons of meaning, grammar or register. There is an example at the beginning (**0**).

> You have received a letter from the HR department of a zoo about an ex-colleague of yours who is applying for a job there.

> I would be grateful if you could provide us with some details on the candidate's work experience, any relevant personal skills and qualities, and explain why they might be a suitable person for the role of Qualified Animal Keeper.
> Thank you in advance.

Write your **letter**.

> TO (0) <u>WHOM</u>/<s><u>WHO</u></s> IT MAY CONCERN
> I am writing with (1) <u>reply</u>/<u>reference</u> to your letter asking for information to support Georgia Suarez's application for the post of Qualified Animal Keeper at San Diego Zoo. I had the pleasure of working with Georgia for two years as a volunteer at the Wilderness Nature Reserve in Kenya and would not hesitate to recommend her for this role.
> (2) <u>Whilst</u>/<u>During</u> working at the nature reserve, Georgia received training on the health and safety of animals. She learnt a great deal about the care and behaviour of wild animals and seemed to have a particular affinity for the big cats. (3) <u>In addition</u>/<u>However</u>, the role included helping formerly captive animals adjust to the wild and working closely with experts on the breeding programme for endangered animals. I am sure you will see the benefit of such skills at your zoo.
> (4) <u>Aside from</u>/<u>Moreover</u> her considerable experience, Georgia is a tremendously hard-working and driven individual who will always go that extra mile for the job. (5) <u>I feel I must also point out</u>/<u>I reckon</u> that she is a very personable and diplomatic person, which was essential when working in such a close-knit team in Kenya. These were (6) <u>also</u>/<u>furthermore</u> extremely useful qualities to have when it came to showing tour groups around the reserve.
> For these reasons, I have no doubt that Georgia will be an excellent employee. I very much (7) <u>wish</u>/<u>hope</u> that you will consider her for the position. I am certain that you will not regret the decision.
> Yours (8) <u>faithfully</u>/<u>sincerely</u>,
> Alessandro Medina

2 Read the letter again. What is the purpose of each paragraph?
Paragraph 1: reference to letter received and reason for writing

3 Look at the letter again and find examples of the following features:
   a expressions for stating opinions: *I am sure …*
   b relative clauses: *who will always go that extra mile …*
   c a range of language for describing characteristics: *tremendously hard-working*

4a Read the following Writing Part 2 question.

> You have received a letter from the director of the Amazon Research Centre in Brazil about an ex-colleague of yours who is applying for a job there.

> Dear …
> Please could you provide some information on the applicant's personal qualities, what qualifications and experience they possess, and whether or not you feel they would be suitable for the role of Conservation Research Assistant at our remote Amazon centre.
> Kind regards,
> Dr Kimberley Schmidt

4b 💬 Work in pairs. Discuss what qualities might be suitable for the job and what experience or qualifications may be necessary.

5 Write your letter in **220–260** words in an appropriate style.

Help

Plan what you are going to write. Note down your ideas then organise the best ones into logical paragraphs. When you write your formal letter
- be persuasive, but not aggressive. Write in an appropriate formal register.
- remember to use appropriate opening and closing formulae, e.g. *Dear Dr Schmidt*.
- check your answer for grammar and spelling mistakes before revising if necessary.

More information in the Writing Bank page 135.

Review | Units 1 and 2

Reading and Use of English Part 4
Key word transformation

For questions **1–6**, complete the second sentence so that it has a similar meaning to the first sentence, using the word given. **Do not change the word given**. You must use between **three** and **six** words, including the word given. Here is an example (**0**).

> **0** It's impossible that people lived like that in the past.
> **POSSIBLY**
> People _COULDN'T POSSIBLY HAVE LIVED_ like that in the past.

1 You really shouldn't underestimate the German team's ability.
ACCOUNT
On .... underestimate the German team's ability.

2 I managed to finish just before the teacher told the class to stop writing.
HAD
No .... the teacher told the class to stop writing.

3 It wasn't necessary for Tom to speak at the wedding – he barely knows the couple.
NEED
There was .... a speech at the wedding – he barely knows the couple.

4 It's a school rule that pupils can't take phones into class.
ALLOW
The school .... take phones into class.

5 I really don't want you to contact him again.
CIRCUMSTANCES
Under .... to contact him again.

6 George and Paul were acquaintances for a long time before they worked together.
KNOWN
George and Paul .... many years before they worked together.

Help
- The given word must not be changed in any way.
- Pay close attention to tenses, verb patterns and prepositions as you rewrite the sentence.

Reading and Use of English Part 3
Word formation

For questions **1–8**, read the text below. Use the word given in capitals at the end of some of the lines to form a word that fits in the gap **in the same line**. There is an example at the beginning (**0**).

Getting cultural in Berlin

Museum Island in Berlin is one of the most attractive (**0**) _CULTURAL_ sites in Europe, housing five world-renowned museums. Central to the site is the Pergamon Museum, whose collection contains perhaps the most (**1**) .... examples of Islamic art in the world and reflects the connection between Eastern and Western (**2**) ....
As numbers of visitors have grown, there has been a need for (**3**) .... to the existing structures. In 2000, an architectural competition was held to design an (**4**) .... extension. Somewhat controversially, the winning design proposed large-scale (**5**) .... to a set of buildings unchanged since 1930. However, these changes will (**6**) .... visitors to enjoy a broader range of collections. The new building will also incorporate conservation studios. These will allow archaeological students to study previously (**7**) .... objects and encourage an (**8**) .... approach to preserving the past.

CULTURE
SIGNIFY
CIVIL
MODIFY
INNOVATE
ALTER
ABLE
ACCESS
INTERACT

Vocabulary

Underline the correct alternative in *italics*.

1 We're a really *close-knit/immediate* family – we overcome any *fears/obstacles* that get in our way together.
2 We really *drifted apart/hit it off* when we first met. I admire her *get/set* up and go attitude.
3 I'm afraid that he takes *after/to* his father – his fear of *failure/mistakes* stopped him from starting out on his own in business.
4 As a group, it's so important to *make/set* manageable targets. That way you're less likely to *differ/quarrel* with one another when the going gets tough.
5 Although I was *brought/raised* up in the city, I always wanted to *reach/follow* in my grandfather's footsteps and work at sea.
6 When we were teenagers we were in a band. I thought one day we'd *get/make* it, but it came to nothing, and we soon *drifted apart/got back together*.
7 They don't really *see eye to eye/put up* with one another. Both of them are so *driven/pushed* to succeed – perhaps they are too alike.
8 Michelle didn't *keep/reach* the pinnacle of her career through standing still. She worked hard and knew the benefit of *rubbing shoulders/falling out* with the right people.

Language focus

1 **In the text below, decide whether the underlined verbs are correct or incorrect. Correct any mistakes.**

I (1) <u>could</u> as well admit it – the time when I'm the happiest is when I'm hanging off the side of a frozen waterfall by near-frost-bitten fingers.

It's not something you (2) <u>would</u> necessarily admit to your loved ones, who (3) <u>have to</u> be a bit offended, but I (4) <u>won't</u> think of a situation when I feel more alive. You're probably thinking I (5) <u>shouldn't</u> be a bit irresponsible, and you (6) <u>might</u> be right I suppose. I (7) <u>need</u> to admit that when I first started ice-climbing I felt it was reckless, too.

However, while it (8) <u>may</u> look incredibly dangerous, with careful preparation the risk is minimal. I (9) <u>would</u> have spent hours checking and double checking my equipment over the years. I (10) <u>must</u> climb whole mornings and afternoons in some pretty grim conditions because it's something that I love.

2 **Complete the text with a perfect form of the verb in brackets.**

It is 15 May and at the age of 18 years and 228 days, Max Verstappen **1** _____ (become) the youngest driver to win a Formula One race by triumphing at the Spanish Grand Prix. His family **2** _____ (have) a long association with motor sports that continues to this day. Verstappen's father drove for many different teams and his uncle, Anthony Kumpen, **3** _____ (be) involved in NASCAR racing since 2014.

Verstappen's career began early. By the age of 14, he **4** _____ (beat) drivers regularly on the international stage. This soon led to a move to Formula One. In fact, Verstappen **5** _____ (drive) for more than half a season at the top level before obtaining a normal driver's licence on his 18th birthday.

Verstappen **6** _____ (live) in Monaco since October 2015. He **7** _____ (say) that the reason for this is that many racing teams are based there. From this location he **8** _____ (plan) his path to becoming a future World Champion.

3 **Complete each gap in the text below with a relative pronoun. More than one answer may be possible.**

You might not have heard of oxytocin, **1** _____ is a hormone normally produced and stored in the human brain, but it is increasingly being used to improve relationships. Researchers, some of **2** _____ have been trialling the hormone for years, report that subjects **3** _____ are given oxytocin in nasal sprays display a greater sense of trust. This was tested by playing a trust game in **4** _____ participants were given cash and had to decide whether to lend to people described as trustworthy, untrustworthy or neutral. The subjects **5** _____ inhaled oxytocin gave more money to both trustworthy and neutral 'trustees'. This could be because oxytocin reduces the fear of betrayal. However, neither group gave money to the untrustworthy individuals, **6** _____ implies that oxytocin only increases trust **7** _____ there is no reason to be distrustful. Whatever the reason, scientists, **8** _____ research may have implications for the future of social interaction, should further explore uses of the hormone.

3 A sense of wonder

Vocabulary and Speaking
Travel

1 💬 **The photos show people on holiday in another country. Discuss these questions with a partner.**
   1 Have you had similar travel experiences in your life?
   2 What kind of person do you think would go on each type of holiday?
   3 What do you think might be the most/least enjoyable thing about each experience?

2 **For questions 1–5, decide which answer (a, b or c) best fits each gap.**

   1 When Roger travels, he prefers to _____ rather than stick to obvious touristy spots.
      a hit the road
      b go off the beaten track
      c be on the road

   2 Julia always travels _____ – she flies with budget airlines and stays in hostels.
      a on a shoestring
      b luxuriously
      c economy

   3 Whenever John's travelling abroad he always negotiates to get the best possible price; he _____ .
      a goes with the flow
      b gets taken for a ride
      c drives a hard bargain

   4 Maria and Jo really enjoyed the _____ of Tokyo; they found the fast pace of life really exciting.
      a laid-back atmosphere
      b hustle and bustle
      c peace and tranquility

   5 Samuel likes to _____ when they're on holiday, whereas Antonia is much more spontaneous and happy to decide what they're doing on the day.
      a get an upgrade
      b follow an itinerary
      c take in the sights

3 💬 **Work with a partner. Discuss which person in exercise 2 most closely reflects your attitude to travelling. Use the vocabulary in exercise 2 to describe your ideal holiday.**

Word formation
Nouns 1

1 Underline the noun with a suffix in each sentence **1–5**, then identify what suffix is being used.

growth → -th

> **0** Environmentally friendly forms of transport have experienced a significant <u>growth</u> in recent years. **1** In many cities around the world there is no shortage of people riding bicycles. **2** Nowadays, more and more people in this country are beginning to see the wisdom in this. **3** At first, you may see the physical exercise as an unnecessary hardship, but you will soon discover its joys. **4** With more and more daily practice comes cycling proficiency – when you're so good at it, it no longer feels like a burden. **5** And cycling also reduces noise, which might even make you more popular in your neighbourhood. So, what are you waiting for? Hop on your bike!

2 Use the suffixes in the box to form nouns from the pairs of words. Use the same suffix for both words in each pair. You may also need to make other spelling changes.

-ity	-ure	-er	-or	-(s)ion	-ation	-ness

0 foreign/travel → *foreigner, traveller*
1. cancel/publish
2. confuse/collide
3. proceed/sign
4. senate/investigate
5. punctual/diverse
6. fair/tidy

3 Write the correct form of the words in brackets using suffixes from exercises **1** and **2**. The noun you use may also require a plural ending.

0 The government is reducing corporation tax to attract foreign <u>*investors*</u> (invest).
1. I can't imagine Sara living somewhere so cut off. She'd go mad with _____ (bored).
2. The receptionist rang to tell Kerry there were several _____ (pack) waiting for her at the front desk.
3. I just can't get over his _____ (selfish) – it would have been a goal if he had passed the ball.
4. Julia has lots of great ideas on how to maximise _____ (efficient) in your day-to-day life and stop wasting time.
5. There is every _____ (likely) that road tax will increase next year.
6. He develops _____ (apply) for a well-known software company.
7. Lake Baikal has a _____ (deep) of 1,637 metres, making it the world's largest lake in terms of volume.
8. The price of _____ (member) for the golf course was way more than Tom could afford.

Reading and Use of English Part 3
Word formation

1 For questions **1–8**, read the text below. Use the word given in capitals at the end of some of the lines to form a word that fits in the gap **in the same line**. There is an example at the beginning (**0**).

Visiting new (**0**) <u>*LOCATIONS*</u> is always a thrilling experience, but sometimes the journey can be even more (**1**) _____ than the destination. The Trans-Siberian Express is (**2**) _____ acknowledged to be the longest single train ride in the world. You travel over 9,000 kilometres and it takes seven whole days after your (**3**) _____ from Moscow to arrive in Vladivostok in the Russian Far East. What makes the experience really (**4**) _____ is seeing the immense Russian landscapes roll past and realising the (**5**) _____ of the country. Travelling on the Trans-Siberian is also a chance to build (**6**) _____ friendships with fellow visitors or Russian locals. Unless you travel with your own friends, you have to share a compartment with (**7**) _____ , which may prove to be a significant challenge in communication. However, once these language barriers are overcome, it can also be a great chance to improve your (**8**) _____ with different cultures from around the world.	LOCATE ENJOY UNIVERSE DEPART FORGET VAST LAST STRANGE FAMILIAR

2 💬 Work in pairs. Discuss what you think makes a journey memorable.

Unit 3 A sense of wonder

 Listening Part 3

Multiple choice 🔊 1.11

1 Look at the picture above. What do you think is happening? What is the cause of this?

2 Look at exercise **3**. <u>Underline</u> the key words in the questions and options to help you focus on the important information when you listen to the recording. Question **1** has been done for you.

Help

- Think about what attitude or opinion is suggested by the options.
- Listen for ideas, not exact words (for example, instead of *very important*, you may hear *really vital, of paramount importance, absolutely key*, etc.).
- Never leave a question unanswered. Eliminate obviously wrong options, then select the answer that seems the most likely to be correct.

3 🔊 You will hear an interview with a university researcher called Dr Susan Cullnean talking about her book. For questions **1–6**, choose the answer (**A**, **B**, **C** or **D**) which fits best according to what you hear.

1 In Dr Cullnean's opinion, what does <u>communicating</u> with people from other cultures <u>enable us to do</u>?
   A help <u>avoid</u> cross-cultural <u>confrontations</u>
   B <u>increase</u> our global <u>awareness</u>
   C <u>travel</u> to foreign countries more <u>frequently</u>
   D understand the challenges of multiculturalism

2 Dr Cullnean says it leads to failure in cross-cultural communication when people
   A feel uncertain about what their cultural values and attitudes are.
   B are unaware of the rules for correct behaviour in a different environment.
   C prove incapable of viewing situations from the perspective of others.
   D start judging their own beliefs as strange.

3 How does Dr Cullnean feel about cultural stereotypes?
   A She accepts that they may serve a role in helping us understand another culture.
   B She is concerned that people in power can misuse them for their own purposes.
   C She is undecided whether they are more beneficial than harmful.
   D She is often confused by them in more complex situations.

4 The key to the 'active listening' technique Dr Cullnean mentions is to
   A identify who is responsible for communication breakdowns.
   B translate words into one's own language to eliminate misunderstanding.
   C summarise and regularly check what the other person has just said.
   D consider issues from all perspectives.

5 Dr Cullnean mentions Julia as an example for communication breakdown because of
   A misinterpreted gestures.
   B lack of awareness of preferred distances.
   C her level of English proficiency.
   D different sensitivity to how loudly speakers should talk.

6 What is the advice Dr Cullnean gives the interviewer?
   A Never use stereotypes to inform behaviour.
   B Stand closer to people from the Mediterranean.
   C Let people try to understand you better.
   D Review assumptions as you communicate.

Unit 3 A sense of wonder

Language focus 1
Gerunds and infinitives

1a Write the correct form of the verb in brackets to complete these extracts from the recording.

1. People **tend** _____ (view) their own beliefs and attitudes as ...
2. We should try to **avoid** _____ (stereotype).
3. We must be prepared to **continue** _____ (observe) people's behaviour.
4. We**'d be better off** _____ (find) ways to **make** it _____ (work).
5. I couldn't **imagine** her _____ (have) any communication problems with me.
6. That **led** me _____ (discover) the problem was with ...
7. I should **remember** _____ (stand) a bit closer.

1b Which verbs in **bold** in exercise **1a** could be followed by more than one verb form? Would it change the meaning of the sentence? How?

Read more about gerunds and infinitives in the Grammar Reference pages 119–121.

2 Read the short text below. Find one mistake in the use of gerunds or infinitives in each sentence and correct it.

> **My trips to the market**
>
> **1** A market I really enjoyed to visit was in Muara Kuin, Indonesia. **2** To watch traders selling fruit and vegetables from their boats is mesmerising. **3** I was a bit disappointed that I didn't manage trying fried locusts. **4** I wasted quite a bit of time to look for them before someone informed me Indonesians didn't eat them. **5** It's definitely worth to research what is on offer at markets before going.
>
> **6** If you ever find yourself in Basel, Switzerland in December, you should definitely to check out the market in the Old Town. **7** I remember to go there a few years ago with my sister – it was wonderful. **8** There was so much food trying and handmade gifts to buy. **9** We ending up spend a fortune as it is quite expensive. **10** I'd love going again but I'd need to save up some money first!

Vocabulary
The senses

1 💬 Discuss these questions with a partner.
1. What is your favourite smell? Does it remind you of anything?
2. What food do you associate most with your country? What does it taste like?
3. What's the most unattractive landmark in your country?

2 For sentences **1–8**, underline the adjective in *italics* which is **not** possible.

1. The peanuts were so *salty/tasty/dry*, they made me terribly thirsty.
2. Good, ripe cheese often smells quite *pungent/smelly/subtle* – some people find it too strong.
3. The flavours in the vegetable risotto were really *delicate/faint/overpowering* – I could hardly taste them, but they enhanced the experience.
4. The banquet table at the wedding looked *rich/breathtaking/spectacular* – all the dishes were presented beautifully.
5. The meal was not bad, but it was so *bland/flavourless/delicious*! I like my food with a bit more kick.
6. The air in the bazaar was full of the *fragrant/foul/aromatic* scent of spices – it was delightful but quite intense.
7. The cupcakes Tina made looked *appetising/dreadful/vile* but to be fair, they didn't taste too bad.
8. The stew was *revolting/disgusting/mouth-watering*. It tasted awful and made us quite ill.

3 💬 Work in pairs. Tell your partner about a time when you visited an interesting or unusual place. Describe the sights, flavours and smells that you associate with your visit.

Unit 3 A sense of wonder

Reading and Use of English Part 6
Cross-text multiple matching

1 💬 Work with a partner. Look at the photo of an exhibition. Discuss what you think makes it special.

2 Skim read the four reviews to check your ideas. Which option, **A**, **B**, **C** or **D**, best summarises what makes the exhibition unusual?

   A It is organised by Tate Britain at a venue outside the art gallery.
   B The exhibition requires visitors to use all five of their senses.
   C People have to experience the works of art without using their sight.
   D Every exhibit is accompanied by a special meal.

3 You are going to read four reviews of an unusual exhibition. For questions **1–4**, choose from reviews **A–D**. The reviews may be chosen more than once.

Which reviewer	
shares reviewer A's experience of feeling distracted from seeing the works of art?	1
disagrees with the others about whether the exhibition is an enjoyable experience?	2
makes a similar comment to reviewer C about the use of sounds and noises?	3
has a different view from the others about whether the aims of the exhibition were achieved?	4

Help

- Read the rubric, title and subtitle carefully to find out what the central theme is.
- For each question, identify the key information to look for.
- Read the four extracts quickly to get a general idea.
- Locate the information that you need in order to answer each question in the text.
- Identify each reviewer's opinion and compare it to the others'.

4 💬 Discuss in groups. Would you like to visit the Tate Sensorium Exhibition? Why/Why not? Have you ever heard about or seen any other unusual art exhibitions or stage performances?

THE TATE Sensorium Exhibition

A

The show's ambition is to trigger responses to a selection of artworks, not just from your eyes, but from all the senses. As it says in the press release: 'Galleries are overwhelmingly visual. But people are not'.

Each of the four chosen paintings is accompanied by a different selection of sensual stimuli. For the Bacon, aromas of 'an animalistic horse-like scent' drift across the space to remind you of the picture's setting in Hyde Park, and you eat the salty chocolate 'to bring out the painting's dark nature'.

It's quite good fun. And even now, a couple of days later, I can still remember the taste of that salty chocolate. What I can't remember is the Bacon painting. Weirdly, it's become a blank. Instead of adding to the visual experience, the Tate Sensorium has managed somehow to obliterate it and replace it with all the other guff.

Of course galleries need to be 'overwhelmingly visual'. They're devoted to something called the visual arts.

B

'If their interest is flagging, give them chocolate' is a rule that can be applied to just about any situation, and it certainly worked with the final painting, Francis Bacon's *Figure in a Landscape*. A large chocolate – intense, bitter and slightly salty – beautifully complemented the sinister painting, to the extent that a musky perfume and yet more rattling noises were barely noticed.

This is a well-meaning project, falling somewhere between branding, architecture and art, which added up to considerably less than the sum of its parts. But then 'creative studios' don't perhaps lend themselves to single powerful, defining visions. A circular graph based on my wrist-band responses was completely neutral except for sharp surges in rooms 2 and 4.

From these I decide that I was alarmed at the prospect of being deafened in the first instance, and that I like looking at Francis Bacon paintings while eating good chocolate in the second. I don't think I needed to go all the way to Tate Britain to learn this.

Unit 3 A sense of wonder

Four reviewers give an account of their experience visiting the art gallery.

C

Bacon's *Figure in a Landscape* (1945) was heavily influenced by sensorial stimulus, this time the taste of a grainy ball of chocolate. The texture led me to focus on the top-left corner of the painting, which looked as 'dusty' as the sounds I was hearing.

The overall experience of Tate Sensorium was compelling and exciting, and I would have little to add to it. My only concern with Tate Sensorium was the predominance of often extremely loud sounds. While the other senses were present only once or twice, sounds were never absent, perhaps as they are the easiest to insert into a gallery space. I would have preferred to have had moments of silence, to be able to perceive the difference between experiencing a painting with or without sounds. But the exhibition succeeds in its intended purpose, namely to trigger new and fresh interpretations of paintings by appealing to different senses, and to see the ways in which smell, touch, taste, and hearing can contribute to our appreciation of art.

D

The final section has a spot-lit tray with four bite-sized chocolates in front of *Figure in a Landscape* (1945) by Francis Bacon. Eating in the gallery space is the only time I feel a little apprehensive about the whole experience. While smell, touch and hearing are often unnoticed by-products of looking at art, taste is a sense usually reserved for the ubiquitous gallery café.

If you are not expecting great artistic revelations, then the entire experience is an unusual way of spending 20 minutes in a gallery. But it probably won't make you look at the paintings afresh, because you stop seeing them even when your eyes are fixed on them. The voice at the beginning asks you to seek 'your own interpretation' and as you are whizzed through the dark gallery, with props and wafts to play to your senses, there is little to no time to contemplate the works. Still, my sense of sight was piqued. The Tate Sensorium made me look at the collection in a new way – by not allowing me to see it properly.

Language focus 2
Reported speech
Tense changes and reporting verbs

1 The following sentence reports what a reviewer has written about the Tate Sensorium. What changes have been made to the original statement in reported speech?

'What I can't remember is the Bacon painting … it's become a blank.'

The reviewer **remarked** that what he couldn't remember was the Bacon painting, and **added** that it had become a blank.

2 How do the following tenses and verbs change after a past reporting verb in reported speech?

~~present simple~~	present continuous
present perfect	past simple	past perfect
will	be going to	can	should	must

present simple → past simple

3 Compare the following two questions with the way they are reported. Then rewrite questions 1–4 as reported questions.

'How much time did you spend at the exhibition?'
The interviewer asked the woman how much time she had spent at the exhibition.

'Did you enjoy it?'
The interviewer asked her if/whether she enjoyed it.

1 'What was the most unusual thing about your visit yesterday?'
2 'Did being offered chocolate in a gallery surprise you?'
3 'Do you think young people would enjoy the experience?'
4 'How often do you visit museums or galleries?'

⚙ Check your answers to exercises 2 and 3, and read more about tense changes in the Grammar Reference page 121.

4 Rewrite the direct speech in sentences 1–8 in reported speech. Use a suitable reporting verb from the box.

offered	~~claimed~~	queried	argued
demanded	reminded	admitted	stressed
predicted			

0 'The exhibition succeeds in its intended purpose.'
The reviewer *claimed that the exhibition succeeded in its intended purpose.*

1 'Of course galleries need to be "overwhelmingly visual".'
The reviewer …

2 'Don't get a taxi, I'll pick you up from the airport.'
Her friend …

3 'You're not finished! What have you been doing all day?'
His tutor …

4 'Remember, everyone – whatever you decided last week can't be changed now.'
The staff manager …

5 'I can't emphasise enough how important the next few months will be.'
The team leader …

6 'This may turn out to be the best year for all of us.'
The optimist …

7 'Are you sure that Alice will be able to get to the interview on time?'
The chief editor …

8 'I have made some mistakes during the reform process.'
The minister …

5 Complete each gap with the missing preposition.

1 Joan congratulated us _____ completing the course successfully.
2 The manager told me off _____ forgetting about the planning meeting.
3 You've never objected _____ having your photo taken before!
4 The workers protested _____ the company introducing longer weekend hours.
5 His colleagues accused him _____ delaying the project.
6 My sister discouraged me _____ entering the competition this year.

⚙ Check your answers to exercises 4 and 5 in the Grammar Reference pages 121–122.

6a 💬 Discuss the following with your partner. Note down their answers.
- something you regret
- something you weren't allowed to do as a child
- a decision you made recently
- a place you would recommend visiting
- a promise you made to someone

6b 💬 Work with a different partner and report your original partner's answers from exercise 6a.

Unit 3 A sense of wonder

Speaking Part 2
Long turn

1. 💬 Look at photographs 1–3. They show **people trying different cultural experiences abroad**.

   Student A: Compare **two** of the pictures, and say **what the people might be learning about the country's culture**, and **how they might be feeling**.

   Student B: When your partner has finished, answer the following question.

   Which of the cultural activities in the photographs would you be most interested in doing?

   - What might these people be learning about the country's culture?
   - How might they be feeling?

2. 💬 Now change roles. Look at photographs 4–6 on page 108 and follow the instructions.

Help

- You should compare the similarities and differences in the photos rather than describe them.
- Use a wide range of vocabulary. For example, when answering **How might they be feeling?**, try to use more complex language than *happy*, *sad* or *worried*.
- Use the full amount of time available to you; ensure you fully answer all aspects of your task.
- Try not to go off-topic.

Useful language

Use your dictionary to help you match the words below to photographs **1–3** on this page and **4–6** on page 108. You may use some words more than once and others not at all.

*exhilarated   intrigued   engrossed   enthralled
captivated   inspired   energised   stressed
anxious   hassled   content   composed   glum
queasy   unsettled   overwhelmed   miserable*

33

Unit 3 A sense of wonder

Writing Part 2
Review

1 **Work in pairs. Discuss these questions.**
   1 Would you describe yourself as an artistic person?
   2 Do you have a favourite piece of art or artist?
   3 Do you think it is important for governments to encourage the arts? Why/Why not?

2 **Read the following Part 2 question and discuss with your partner how you might answer it.**

> You have seen the following announcement in an art magazine.

> **Reviews wanted**
> Have you seen a memorable exhibition in a museum or art gallery recently? If so, tell us about your experience, what you feel makes it memorable and whether you would or would not recommend it to other people.

> Write your **review**.

3 **Read the model answer and answer the following questions.**
   1 What made the exhibition memorable?
   2 What was the writer's opinion? Was it generally positive or negative?
   3 Would they recommend it?

4 **Identify the purpose of the four paragraphs.**

   Paragraph 1: brief summary of what the exhibition is – where it is and who it's by

5 **Find examples of the following features of reviews in the model answer.**
   1 commenting positively
      extraordinary art experience
   2 commenting negatively
   3 expressions for making recommendations

6 **Write an answer to the Part 2 task in exercise 2 in 220–260 words.**

Help

- <u>Underline</u> the key words in the question to ensure you include all the points.
- Plan your review and divide your answer into clear paragraphs.
- Use a range of language.
- When you have finished, check your writing carefully for spelling and grammatical errors.

More information in the Writing Bank page 136.

Dismaland

Do you think that theme parks are just for kids and that art galleries are dull and tedious? I certainly thought so until I visited Banksy's Dismaland in Weston-super-Mare in the UK. Banksy has once again shocked and intrigued the art world by transforming a run-down, disused seaside fairground into the venue for this extraordinary art experience.

As you arrive at the park you are 'welcomed' by glum greeters and slightly threatening security guards who direct you through what looks like an airport security zone. Once inside you see a crumbling fairytale castle and a distorted-looking Little Mermaid. These are the images that have come to characterise the park but there are plenty of other sculptures and installations. The depressing nature of the exhibition is strangely compelling and the ability of the staff to keep up the miserable act is impressive.

Overall though, I must say that the experience wasn't an enjoyable one – the atmosphere is deliberately gloomy and rather unsettling. Even though you are given three-and-a-half hours to look around, an hour was more than enough time for me before I made a swift exit. The messages behind the art are easy enough to interpret but were too cynical for my taste.

Dismaland is a definite must-see for Banksy fans and I highly recommend it to anyone interested in having a truly unique and unforgettable experience – it's just not one I wish to repeat anytime soon!

Dismaland

4 Living in the past

Vocabulary and Speaking
Memory

1 💬 Read the quotations about memory and discuss these questions with your partner. Give reasons for your opinions.
1 What is each quotation trying to say?
2 Do you agree or disagree with it?
3 Which is your favourite quote?

> We don't remember days; we remember moments.
> **Cesare Pavese**

> Forgetfulness is a form of freedom.
> **Kahlil Gibran**

> Always have old memories and young hopes.
> **Arsène Houssaye**

> I don't understand people who hide from their past. Everything you live through helps to make you the person you are now.
> **Sophia Loren**

2a Complete each sentence with the correct form of a verb from the box. Use each verb only once.

| haunt   have   bring   jog |
| reminisce   spark   stick   share |

1 Whenever I hear that song by Jack Johnson, it _____ **back memories of** summer holidays spent surfing in Varazze.
2 Seeing her again _____ **my memory** and all the good times we'd had came flooding back.
3 One thing he told me that has always _____ **in my mind** was to keep trying no matter what.
4 David _____ **a memory like a sieve**. He can never remember where he's left his keys.
5 Sheila often _____ **about** her old schooldays with friends; they _____ so many happy **memories**.
6 Certain smells can suddenly _____ **a memory** and transport you back to different times in your life.
7 I'm still _____ **by the memory** of the last time we went on holiday together. The hotel was awful!

2b 💬 Look at the the phrases in **bold** in exercise **2a**. Work with a partner to think of a different way of expressing them.

3a Use the phrases in **bold** from exercise **2a** to write three sentences that are true for you.

3b 💬 Work in pairs. Discuss your sentences and ask questions to get more information about what your partner has written.

4 In sentences **1–5**, decide whether the expressions in **bold** describe a clear or an unclear memory. Use a dictionary if necessary.
1 She had the **distinct impression** that she'd been in this room at some time in the past.
2 I think I've seen this film before. I have a **faint recollection** of the story.
3 He didn't seem to have **the foggiest idea** who Paul was.
4 Oh, I remember her from my **dim and distant past**.
5 It wasn't Adele's most **memorable performance** – but she's still a world-class singer.

5 💬 Work in pairs. Discuss the following questions.
1 What's the most memorable film you've seen recently? Why was it memorable?
2 Can you recollect what you were doing this time last year? Where were you?
3 Has anything particularly memorable happened to you this year? What was it?

35

Unit 4 Living in the past

Listening Part 2
Sentence completion 🔊 1.12

1. 💬 Look at photographs 1–4. Can you remember any similar childhood experiences? How did you feel at the time? Tell your partner.

2. 🔊 You will hear Dr Natasha Drake talking about research into childhood memory and its potential uses. For questions 1–8, complete the sentences with a word or short phrase.

Remembering and forgetting

Dr Drake suggests that for many people, their earliest memories follow (1) .... that are similar to stories.

Dr Drake describes how brain activity is at its highest before (2) .... and in the first stages of a child's development.

The Canadian research has concluded that when neurons develop (3) .... declines.

Dr Drake claims that research shows that memories from early childhood are often completely (4) .... as new abilities are being learnt.

Dr Drake says that psychologists used to associate lack of childhood memories with (5) ....

As the way we feel at the moment affects our memories, we often create (6) .... of what has happened.

Dr Drake uses the phrase 'jumping the queue' to explain how some memories stand out during (7) ....

Dr Drake states that making changes or removing memories might result in an (8) .... on the way parts of the brain communicate and operate.

Help
- Read the exam task carefully before you listen. Think about the type of word that could be missing. After you have completed the task, check your answers to make sure they make sense grammatically.
- Write down the exact word or phrase that you hear. These are often single or compound nouns, which are sometimes accompanied by an adjective. You will not be required to write more than three words for each answer.
- If you are not sure whether a word is singular or plural, check the rest of the sentence to see which is grammatically correct.

3. 💬 Work in pairs. Do you agree with Dr Drake's suggestion that our ability to remember things changes over time? Which of your memories would you like to preserve in detail? Why?

Language focus 1 🔊 1.13
Adverbs of degree
extremely, very, absolutely, completely, etc.

1a 🔊 Complete the sentences from Listening Part 2 with a suitable adverb. Listen and check.
1. One would assume that such significant events would be retained or at least _____ **difficult** to forget.
2. Certain memories will become _____ **vague**, many others forgotten altogether.
3. However, the new research suggests that memory loss is _____ **inevitable** as the brain develops.

1b The adverbs *a bit* and *very* could be used in sentences **1** and **2**, but not **3**. Why is this?

2 Underline the adjective which does **not** collocate with the adverb in **bold**.
0. **extremely** challenging/<u>impossible</u>/hard/difficult
1. **terribly** boring/important/upset/usual
2. **perfectly** acceptable/adequate/understandable/gifted
3. **severely** damaged/limited/unnecessary/weakened
4. **utterly** qualified/ridiculous/false/impossible
5. **badly** hurt/injured/needed/inadequate
6. **enormously** clear/influential/popular/powerful

⚙ Read more about adverbs of degree in the Grammar Reference page 122.

3 Complete each sentence with an appropriate phrase from exercise **2**.
1. The entry test was _____. Most people think they've failed.
2. Have you read this story? I can't believe it. It's _____.
3. The building was _____, during the last storm.
4. He's an _____ figure in the art world. Many people listen to his opinion.
5. You don't need to apologise, it's _____ that you wouldn't want to stay.
6. I found his latest film _____ – I actually walked out in the end.
7. Fortunately nobody was _____ in the crash.

quite

4a *Quite* has two meanings: to a particular degree (= *fairly*) and to a large degree (= *really*). What is the meaning of *quite* in these two sentences?
1. I was quite happy with his answer.
2. The fireworks at the festival were quite spectacular.

4b 💬 Work in pairs. Which meaning of *quite* from exercise **4a** is used in sentences **1–4**? Discuss how true the sentences are for you.
1. I work long hours so I'm usually quite exhausted by the evening.
2. I quite enjoy spending time by myself.
3. The last meal that I cooked was quite delicious.
4. On the whole, I'm quite a positive person.

⚙ Read more about *quite* in the Grammar Reference page 122.

5a 💬 Work in pairs or small groups. Write sentences describing a time when you:
- ate something really disgusting
- were extremely confused
- felt absolutely delighted
- were terribly bored

5b Read your sentences to your partner(s) who should respond using an adverb of degree.

> I once ate a piece of raw chicken which was really disgusting. I thought it was sushi!

> That's absolutely horrible! How did you feel afterwards?

Unit 4 Living in the past

Listening Part 1
Multiple choice 🔊 1.14–1.16

1 💬 Work in pairs. Discuss what kind of things you tend to remember easily, for example, people, events, places, details about books or films, facts and figures. Have you any special way of doing this?

2 🔊 You will hear three different extracts about memory and the past. For questions **1–6**, choose the answer (**A**, **B** or **C**) which fits best according to what you hear. There are two questions for each extract.

Extract One
You hear part of a film review show.
1 The woman recommends a film which
   A is based on a science-fiction novel.
   B does not have a fixed genre.
   C has won many awards.
2 The woman says that some parts of the film are
   A too repetitive.
   B very confusing for viewers.
   C shown out of sequence.

Extract Two
You hear a radio interview about how the past is used to sell products.
3 The woman says that the music used in advertising is designed to
   A stimulate memory.
   B be memorable.
   C work alongside visuals.
4 The woman says that businesses use old-fashioned packaging because it reflects
   A modern tastes.
   B good design.
   C tradition and trust.

Extract Three
You hear a brother and sister talking about their childhood home.
5 What view does the man express about his parent's current home?
   A He feels nostalgic when he thinks about it.
   B He's indifferent to its modern design.
   C He finds it too overcrowded.
6 The man and woman both agree that people
   A form an attachment to their childhood homes.
   B have memories which are often more positive than the reality.
   C should choose houses based on their size.

Help
- One of the focuses of this task type is determining feeling, attitude or opinion. Consider the different ways that speakers will express these to one another. They could use fixed expressions such as *In my opinion*, *I reckon that*, etc.
- You are often asked to identify whether speakers agree or not. Consider fixed expressions which may reflect this, e.g. *exactly*, *precisely*, *true*, *I'd go along with that*, *on the contrary*, *I'm not so sure about that*, etc.

3 Check your answers by reading the listening script on pages 144–145. Underline the parts of the extract which guide you to the correct answer.

4 💬 Do you agree with the idea mentioned in Extract One that people often reconstruct or change their memories? Why/Why not?

Unit 4 Living in the past

Vocabulary
Rooms and spaces

1 　Work in pairs. Describe the house or apartment that you grew up in. What do you remember about it? Which of the photos **1–4** most closely resembles it?

2 　Work in pairs. Student A: Look at photographs **1** and **2**. Student B: Look at photographs **3** and **4**. Note down ideas on how to describe them. Use the words and phrases below and your own ideas.

| bright and cheerful | cramped and cluttered | old-fashioned | dark |
| light and airy | retro | spacious | tasteful | sparsely decorated |

3 　Complete the gaps in each sentence with two of the answers **A–D**.
  1 They have a lovely wooden cabin in the hills. It's really _____ **built** and in the living room there's a wood-burning stove, so it's always **warm and** _____ .
    A solidly　　B cosy　　C airy　　D minimally
  2 My brother's apartment is near the station. It's _____ **located** for commuting. He's really into modern design so it's _____ **furnished**.
    A simply　　B dimly　　C pleasingly　　D conveniently
  3 Your room is always so **neat and** _____ . Do you never let it **get** _____ ?
    A shabby　　B tidy　　C messy　　D smart
  4 The palace is _____ **decorated** with expensive rugs and paintings. To be honest, with all the gold picture frames and chandeliers it **looks a little** _____ .
    A modestly　　B elegant　　C lavishly　　D gaudy
  5 I know you like all these _____ **lit** corners to make the place seem cosy, but I think it makes the room look **dark and** _____ .
    A softly　　B dingy　　C brightly　　D tasteless

4 　Using the language in exercises **2** and **3**, describe your ideal home to your partner.

39

Unit 4 Living in the past

Reading and Use of English Part 5
Multiple choice

1. Do most people in your country prefer to live in the city, the suburbs or the countryside?

2. Skim read the article and check if any of your ideas from exercise **1** were mentioned.

3. Read the article again. For questions **1–6**, choose the answer (**A**, **B**, **C** or **D**) which you think fits best according to the text.

A PLACE OF GREAT BEAUTY?

The simplest of activities such as a brisk walk in the countryside or a stroll along the beach are well-known mood-boosters, and health experts have long recommended getting out of the city to improve physical and mental well-being. But a new study by the University of Warwick suggests that beautiful urban architecture, the sweep of docklands, or a gritty suburban river bank can have just as much impact on health and happiness levels. It seems more and more people are starting to realise that it is 'scenery' not just 'greenery' which is important when determining what makes a positive environment.

To find out what kind of landscapes made people feel healthier, academics used a broad-ranging online questionnaire to identify how visually appealing respondents found images of Britain. They then cross-referenced the resulting 1.5 million ratings with reports on how residents already living in those areas felt about their health. This data was gathered from existing sources, most notably the 2011 Census. Crucially, the researchers found that the areas which rated as the most scenic and uplifting were often not green ones.

This seems to contradict much previous research, which has found that living in green areas makes people live longer and feel happier. A notable piece of research from the University of Illinois concludes that greenery is 'essential to our physical, psychological and social well-being.' The more green space that people are surrounded by, the more relaxed they tend to be. Green spaces, especially those located in urban areas, are often associated with improved quality of life. This is in part because nature tends to calm people and help them to psychologically rejuvenate.

The Illinois study suggested that long-term exposure to nature, or more natural landscapes, meant that people were better able to handle life challenges. As a result, people residing near green spaces reported having happier interpersonal relationships, and better cognitive function.

This phenomenon certainly seems to have a global reach. Research from Japan, as in many other countries, found that older people lived longer when their homes were within walking distance of a park or other green space. In comparative studies, it was found that the less elderly people had access to nature, the less well they performed in memory tests. They also tended to have relatively poorer levels of attention and memory, and reduced impulse control. Furthermore, a number of published reports from the United States have shown that planting trees in residential areas and creating more extensive green spaces in existing urban environments correlates with a lowering of crime rates. It seems that leafy suburban streets help in some way to generate a more 'civilised' atmosphere in our cities.

According to Dr Suzy Moat, Associate Professor of Behavioural Science at Warwick University, the research team had expected to identify a strong connection between green space and health. While their analysis confirmed that people do report their health to be better in areas with more green land cover, they also found that the visual appeal of a person's immediate environment had positive effects. In fact, the British team found that the photographs in their study that rated the most scenic did not contain the highest proportion of the colour green. Instead, photos which were deemed by respondents to be 'very scenic' tended to contain large proportions of grey, brown and blue. This suggests that urban environments, with their more cramped and cluttered views, have a place in our understanding of beauty.

The findings imply that it is the overall cohesion of architecture, design and the environment which boosts people's health and happiness, not just the number of parks and trees. According to this data, the beauty of our everyday environment might have more practical importance than was previously believed. In future, urban planners and policymakers might find it valuable to consider aesthetics when embarking upon large projects such as housing developments or transport networks – as opposed to prioritising utility or profit. Such findings also imply that simply introducing greenery, without considering the beauty of the resulting environment, might not be enough. Sites which visually engage the viewer, rather than providing a well-maintained, but ultimately dull backdrop, are more likely to have positive impacts on well-being. It seems now we have to be increasingly careful about where and how we build, more than ever before.

Unit 4 Living in the past

Help

- For each question, identify and underline the key information to look for.
- Identify the writer's attitude by noting any evaluative language which is used. Try to categorise this as positive or negative, and then think of a term to describe their attitude in general, e.g. *optimistic, critical*.

1 In the first paragraph, what does the writer imply about the research from Warwick University?
  A It supports existing ideas about the positive benefits of rural life.
  B It highlights the importance of architectural design on happiness.
  C It contradicts a number of existing assumptions about environment and well-being.
  D It finds a strong correlation between environment and long-term health.

2 The conclusions of the Warwick University research were based on
  A previously published data generated by academics.
  B a comparison of newly researched information with published data.
  C information the research team collected through a national census.
  D data found on verified online sources.

3 According to the writer, existing research about the positive effects of green spaces
  A contains a number of contradictions.
  B tends to highlight the mental effect only.
  C is based on limited data.
  D seems to share conclusions worldwide.

4 The writer mentions crime rates in order to illustrate
  A an area where nature seems to have a positive effect.
  B the main focus of previous research.
  C a social problem that affects urban environments.
  D the way in which cities and rural spaces differ.

5 The report undertaken by Warwick University shows that people
  A are mentally healthier when surrounded by plenty of green land.
  B have positive attitudes when they live in conventionally attractive places.
  C find both rural and urban environments visually stimulating.
  D respond negatively to living close to neighbours.

6 The writer suggests that much current urban design
  A overlooks the visual importance of new projects.
  B adds considerable value to an area.
  C has many practical uses.
  D does not include enough green spaces.

4 💬 Work in pairs. What are your views on the area where you live? How could it be improved?

Language focus 2
Comparisons

1a Complete each gap in sentences 1–4 with the correct word from the article.
  1 _____ simplest _____ activities such as a brisk walk in the countryside …
  2 It seems _____ and _____ people are starting to realise that it is 'scenery' not just 'greenery' which is important …
  3 _____ more green space that people are surrounded by, _____ more relaxed they tend to be.
  4 It seems _____ we have to be increasingly careful about where and how we build, **more than** _____ before.

1b Check your answers in the article.

2 Match the sentences in **1a** to uses **a–d** below.
  a to compare the present with the past
  b when one thing is the result of another
  c to emphasise an increasing amount
  d to put one thing or action above all others in the same category

⚙ Read more about comparisons in the Grammar Reference pages 122–123.

3 Correct the mistakes or replace the incorrect comparative in the underlined sections (1–9) in the text below. There is an example at the beginning (0).

Opened in 1997, the Guggenheim Museum in Bilbao is **0** one of ~~more~~ *the most* inspiring buildings **1** <u>out of</u> the world. Many commentators have pointed out how much **2** <u>it looks as</u> a boat, which is quite appropriate seeing as the architect took his inspiration from the Basque port. A few people have criticised the design as being **3** <u>not nearly</u> more contemporary than the traditional buildings in the surrounding area. However, for many others, it is **4** <u>a great deal</u> the most striking landmark in the city.
The architect, Frank Gehry has designed several other buildings which are **5** <u>just like</u> imaginative, making him **6** <u>one of the best well-respected</u> architects of his generation. Some would even say **7** <u>the most</u> he designs, **8** <u>a bit better</u> he gets. In terms of his influence, Gehry has inspired others to use similar building materials and forms with spectacular but **9** <u>little</u> less unique results.

4 💬 Look at the picture of the Guggenheim Museum on page 40. Discuss with a partner how it compares with the buildings in your area.

Unit 4 Living in the past

Speaking Part 3
Collaborative task

1a Work in pairs. Here are some factors which affect where people choose to live, and a question for you to discuss. Talk to each other about how these factors affect where people choose to live.

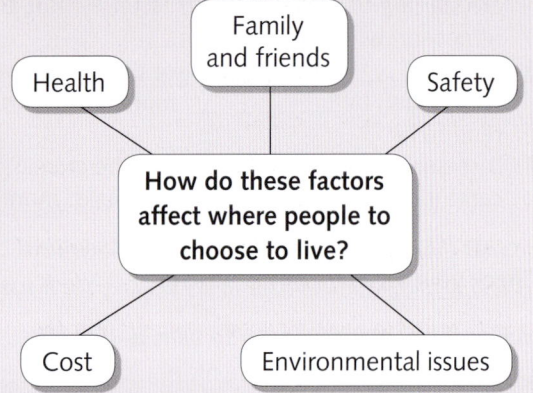

1b Now discuss and decide which two factors are the most important when deciding where to live.

Useful language

Use a range of structures to speculate, compare and provide examples. You also need to use a range of structures to show that you are working collaboratively.

Speculate:
I imagine that a lot of people think (that) …
It could be that people believe …
Some people might …
It's possible that …

Compare:
If you compare … with …
I'd say that … is more important because …
Compared to …, … is more important because …
I might be wrong, but I'd say that this factor is the most important because …

Provide examples:
For example …
For instance …
An example of this is …

Active listening:
That's an interesting point.
So, when you say …, do you mean …?

Conclude the discussion:
So, to sum up, …
So, what we're saying is …
So, basically we agree …

2 Now do the Speaking Part 4 task on page 109.

Writing Part 2
Report

1 Read the following Part 2 task. Discuss with your partner what some of the advantages and disadvantages of the location might have been.

> You are studying at an international college. Recently you attended an intensive residential summer course. The course was based in an old house in the countryside, where students prepared for a week before taking an English exam.
> The College Principal has asked you to write a report evaluating to what extent the accommodation was suitable for the course, areas where improvements could be made, and make recommendations for next year's event.

Write your **report**.

2 Now read the model answer and compare the advantages and disadvantages the writer mentions with those you discussed in exercise **1**.

3 💬 Read the model answer again and discuss the following questions with your partner. Give examples from the report to justify your answers.

Content	Is the information given relevant? Is the target reader fully informed? Have all the required points been covered?
Communicative achievement	Is the register appropriate? Does the report communicate both straightforward and more complex ideas effectively?
Organisation	Is the report organised into logical paragraphs? Is the report clear?
Language	Is there a sufficient range of grammatical structures and vocabulary?

4 Linkers are used in the report for cohesion. Match the underlined linkers to the functions a–d.

a adding information _____, _____
b ordering points/sequencing ideas _____, _____
c showing contrast _____
d summing up _____

5 Reports should outline their purpose at the beginning. It is important that there is evaluation in the report and that a recommendation is given if required. Complete the table with words and phrases from the model answer.

Outlining the purpose of the report	
Evaluating	+ *pleasantly situated,*
	− *not particularly convenient to get to,*
Making recommendations	

6 Write an answer to the following Part 2 task. Write **220–260** words in an appropriate style.

You are on the Students' Committee at the college where you study. Last year the college organised a leisure break, where students went to a house near the coast to do sports and social activities. The Principal has asked you to write a report evaluating the location and property, and saying whether it should be chosen in the future.

Write your **report**.

Unit 4 Living in the past

The main purpose of this report is to evaluate the suitability of the property used for student accommodation during the recent intensive exam preparation course. <u>Additionally</u>, recommendations regarding future courses will be outlined.

The accommodation was based in a pleasantly situated farmhouse on the outskirts of town. While the house itself was simply furnished, it was comfortable and roomy. Students had access to all necessary facilities and the rooms for sleeping were spacious.

It is clear from student feedback that the general view of the location was wholly positive. <u>However</u>, it should be noted that the property was not particularly convenient to get to. <u>Furthermore</u>, while the living areas of the house were well-suited to domestic needs, some felt that the house was not quite right for the purposes of study. A few of the rooms allocated for study were a bit dark, and this impacted on students' well-being.

If the accommodation is to be used in the future, certain considerations need to be taken into account. <u>Firstly</u>, study sessions should be held in the larger reception rooms, which are brighter and more stimulating. <u>Secondly</u>, some of the furniture could be removed to make the house neater and increase space.

<u>In conclusion</u>, to best address the concerns raised in the above report, it may be worthwhile considering a more modern location for any similar future events. This should perhaps also be based closer to the town to ensure ease of access. It is felt that these improvements will contribute to the on-going success of the course.

Help

- Note down your ideas then organise the best ones into logical paragraphs.
- Include a brief introduction outlining your purpose.
- Use a range of linking words and phrases.
- Use a range of verbs and phrases to evaluate and to make suggestions and recommendations.
- Ensure that your writing is in a formal/neutral style.
- Check your answer for grammar and spelling mistakes before revising it if necessary.

More information in the Writing Bank page 132.

Review | Units 3 and 4

Reading and Use of English Part 4
Key word transformation

For questions **1–6**, complete the second sentence so that it has a similar meaning to the first sentence, using the word given. **Do not change the word given.** You must use between **three** and **six** words, including the word given.

1 'Well done Mary, you've done a good job,' said Jon.
   CONGRATULATED
   Jon .... a good job.

2 'Don't come here alone at night, will you?' said my sister.
   THERE
   My sister tried to discourage me .... own at night.

3 'I had paid a fortune by the end of the holiday,' said Tamsin.
   UP
   Tamsin said that .... a fortune for the holiday.

4 The museum didn't impress me as much as the one I visited in Paris.
   NOTHING
   The museum was .... as the one I visited in Paris.

5 'Where are you thinking of heading to on holiday this summer?' the travel agent asked Sandra.
   MIND
   The travel agent asked Sandra where .... for a summer holiday.

6 The documentary was far less interesting than I expected.
   NEARLY
   The documentary .... I expected.

Reading and Use of English Part 1
Multiple-choice cloze

For questions **1–8**, read the text below and decide which answer (**A, B, C** or **D**) best fits each gap. There is an example at the beginning (**0**).

Feeding demand

Maintaining high levels of food production in times of growing populations is cause for (**0**) ..*A*.. in many countries. Perhaps a better way to sustain these populations is to (**1**) ..... traditional crops. Many common staples, such as the potato, require a massive amount of energy to provide sufficient quantities to meet global (**2**) ...... Yet throughout the world there's an abundance of native root vegetables which can be grown using less water, poorer soil and (**3**) ..... less effort. One challenge of making these crops commercially viable is that they often require (**4**) ..... conditions that are not commonly found on agricultural land. A further (**5**) ..... is that the knowledge on how best to grow them may have been lost over time. To address this (**6**) ....., growers in Australia are working with aboriginal groups to collectively pool their understanding. By (**7**) ..... up this information for future use, perhaps they will be better prepared to feed (**8**) ..... generations.

0	A <u>concern</u>	B appeal	C outrage	D reflection
1	A reconstruct	B release	C reconsider	D renovate
2	A consumption	B congestion	C consensus	D conservation
3	A eventually	B ultimately	C secondly	D firstly
4	A specific	B partial	C dedicated	D typical
5	A controversy	B disaster	C crisis	D complication
6	A item	B story	C topic	D issue
7	A seizing	B storing	C drawing	D taking
8	A subsequent	B nearby	C immediate	D progressive

Vocabulary

1 Match each sentence beginning **1–8** with an appropriate ending **a–h**.

1 My wife bought this for a really good price. She knows how to **drive**
2 Marco said that the aromatic scent **sparked**
3 I don't really fancy travelling in economy. Let's see if we can **get**
4 I love this tune, it really **brings back**
5 If you get the chance, **take**
6 We've followed their blog since they **hit**
7 Kate thinks that it was seeing you again that **jogged**
8 We're not really big spenders. If possible, we **travel**

a **an upgrade** to first class.
b **her memory** of last summer.
c **on a shoestring** by staying in hostels.
d **a memory** of his visits to the spice markets in Marrakech.
e **the road** early last year.
f **a hard bargain** when it's needed.
g **in the sights** in Lucca. It's such a tranquil city.
h **memories** of my last year at school. It was always playing on the radio.

2 Complete each gap with the correct form of one of the adjectives in blue. Two of the words in each group are not needed.

1 cosy   shabby   fragrant   overpowering   ~~tasteful~~
Her parents have a _tastefully_ decorated farmhouse with a big open fire. It's so _____ in the winter and there's always the lovely _____ smell of burning pine.

2 flavourless   gaudy   lavish   mouth-watering   vile
The wedding reception was held in such a _____ looking place. It's a pity the food wasn't as nice. It looked _____, but tasted _____.

3 aromatic   bland   bright   dim   spectacular
Have you ever eaten there before? It's a _____-lit, fairly cluttered little place – you can barely see where you're going – but the food is _____. They use lots of _____ spices – the scent of which fill the room.

4 breathtaking   convenient   cramped   spacious   old-fashioned
We bought a place near the metro because it was _____ located for the commute to work. There's only a small kitchen and living room so it's a bit _____ for the two of us. Also the décor looks a bit _____, but we'll make the best of it.

5 airy   delicious   dingy   pungent   revolting
We wandered into a dark and _____ basement shop, which sold cheese. Some of them were unbelievably _____ but they tasted _____.

Language focus

Complete each gap with the correct form of the word in brackets.

Working as a photographer for a travel magazine, I really enjoy **0** _seeing_ (see) the world through a creative lens. You have to work hard at **1** _____ (analyse) your surroundings constantly, especially when that means having to **2** _____ (find) a shot that nobody else has considered.
My profession is regarded by many **3** _____ (be) one of the best in the world. Certainly there is plenty of competition these days. Most people imagine **4** _____ (travel) around the globe, **5** _____ (take) snapshots of exotic locations. They forget you're required **6** _____ (fulfil) the editor's brief. That might mean **7** _____ (stand) for hours in a pungent swamp **8** _____ (photograph) the wildlife or waiting for hours for the sun **9** _____ (set). Having said that, once you adjust to working in those kinds of conditions you can't help **10** _____ (feel) sorry for people with office jobs. I suppose there is a tendency **11** _____ (complain) about the job you do, but realistically I couldn't contemplate **12** _____ (do) anything else.
My advice for people considering **13** _____ (apply) for similar work? Well, the best way to begin is by **14** _____ (check) out what kind of images the magazines are currently using. Send in an example of your own work in a similar style but which shows your identity. Showing people your own take on things never fails **15** _____ (make) a positive impression.

5 Pushing the limits

Vocabulary and Speaking
Work

1 💬 **The pictures below show people in different work and study situations. Discuss these questions with a partner.**
   1 How can the people and things in the photos influence us at work or college?
   2 Are these influences good or bad?
   3 Whose life do you think is the most/least stressful?

2 For sentences **1–5**, underline the correct words in *italics* to complete the different phrases in **bold**.
   1 Maria has really impressed her managers and is already **in the** *running/racing* **for a promotion** after only six months.
   2 We currently have four **positions to** *fill/hire* within the department. It will certainly take a while for the new recruits to *go/get* **up to speed** and understand how the company works.
   3 Charlie has no social life at the moment – he is completely **snowed** *under/over* with assignments for his Masters and he has recently **taken** *on/in* **more responsibility** at work.
   4 After Claire graduates, she wants to follow her passion and *be/go* **into** politics.
   5 I just don't think that Marcel is **cut** *out/around* **to be** a doctor – he wouldn't be able to handle the stress.

3 💬 **Discuss these questions with your partner.**
   1 Would you be willing to take an **unpaid internship** for a year if there was the prospect of getting a full-time job at the end of it?
   2 Would you ever apply for a job that you knew your friend had already applied for?
   3 Would you rather have a **low-paid job** that you love doing or a job which you don't enjoy but comes with lots of **perks** such as 30 **days' paid holiday**, a **company car** and a **pension**?

4 💬 **Use the vocabulary in exercises 2 and 3 to discuss the following with your partner.**
   • your dream job
   • your present work/study situation
   • a time you felt very stressed whilst studying/working

Unit 5 Pushing the limits

Listening Part 4
Multiple matching 🔊 1.17–1.21

1 💬 Work in pairs. What makes you stressed? What do you usually do about it?

2 🔊 You will hear five short extracts in which people are talking about stress.

While you listen you must complete both tasks.

TASK ONE

For questions **1–5**, choose from the list (**A–H**) what each speaker mainly feels stressed about.

A staying away from home
B addressing large groups of people
C a lack of respect from co-workers
D an academic rival
E lack of financial security
F meeting deadlines
G arguing with a friend
H health problems

Speaker 1 [1]
Speaker 2 [2]
Speaker 3 [3]
Speaker 4 [4]
Speaker 5 [5]

TASK TWO

For questions **6–10**, choose from the list (**A–H**) how each speaker usually deals with stress.

A having a change of scenery
B confronting the issue directly
C doing something else for a short time
D going for a coffee with a friend
E taking an extended holiday
F sharing their problems with someone
G doing intense physical exercise
H adopting an optimistic attitude

Speaker 1 [6]
Speaker 2 [7]
Speaker 3 [8]
Speaker 4 [9]
Speaker 5 [10]

3 💬 Work in pairs. Which technique mentioned in the listening do you think would be most effective in typical stressful situations in your own life? Why?

Remember
- You don't need to understand every word.
- Try to identify the speaker's main points, feelings, attitudes or opinions.

Language focus 1
Conditionals

1 Match sentences **1–5** to the different uses of conditionals **a–e**.

1 If you work for yourself, you can hardly ever say no.
2 If you carry on exercising so much, you'll do yourself an injury.
3 Things would be less tense now if I hadn't been promoted.
4 If we asked a hundred people, sixty-five of them would say standing up in front of an audience is their biggest fear.
5 I would have enjoyed university more if I'd got on better with my fellow students.

a a situation that is always or generally true (**zero conditional**)
b the predicted result of a possible future situation (**first conditional**)
c a hypothetical imaginary situation in the present/future (**second conditional**)
d an imaginary situation entirely in the past (**third conditional**)
e an imaginary situation in the past with a probable result in the present (**mixed conditional**)

Other uses of conditionals  1.22

2a Look at these further uses and explanations of different conditional forms. Complete the gaps with one word.

1 To emphasise more strongly how hypothetical the situation is that you are describing:
   If I **were** _____ work longer hours, I'd go crazy.

2 To describe a past event which depends on another event:
   If it **hadn't been** _____ me, she wouldn't have even heard about it!

3 To talk about something which may be possible but not likely:
   If I _____ **to** see him later today, I'll ask him out for a coffee.

4 We can replace *if* with this word:
   I've only got one more year left until I get my law degree … _____ I complete my dissertation on schedule.

2b 🔊 Listen and check your answers.

⚙ Read more about conditionals in the Grammar Reference pages 123–124.

47

Unit 5 Pushing the limits

3 For sentences **1–6**, <u>underline</u> the correct alternative in *italics*.

1. If your company *would/were to/will* transfer you to another office, would you accept the promotion?
2. If Jess hadn't started piano lessons as a child, she *won't play/wouldn't be playing/wouldn't have played* in opera houses all over the world these days.
3. I would never have climbed that rock if it *weren't/hadn't/wouldn't* been for the encouragement of my friends.
4. *Provided/Suppose/Unless* the car doesn't break down, we'll make it to Berlin on time.
5. If you *should/would/might* follow me, I'll show you where the various departments are located.
6. Could you ask Richard to call me if you *chance/happen/had* to see him later today?

Speaking Part 2
Long turn

1. 💬 Work in pairs. Look at the photographs. They show **people in different kinds of professions**. Do you know anyone who does this type of work? Would you like to do any of the jobs shown? Why/Why not?

2. Look at the photographs again.
   Student A: Compare **two** of the pictures, and say **why the people might have chosen their professions**, and **what risks they might face in their work**.
   Student B: When your partner has finished, answer the following question.
   Which of these professions do you think is most appealing to young people?

   - Why might the people have chosen their profession?
   - What risks might they face in their work?

Useful language

Try to think of alternative ways of saying what attracted people to a profession/sport and what risks they might face.
… might have been tempted by …
… may have found the … irresistable/appealing
… risk/(be) in danger of + gerund (e.g. risk injuring themselves)
run the risk of …

3. 💬 Now change roles. Look at the photographs on page 110 and follow the instructions.

Word formation
Verbs

1 💬 Work in pairs. What affixes have been used to form the underlined verbs?

- I imagine that the team <u>socialise</u> together after practice.
- Regular exercise helps them <u>strengthen</u> their muscles.
- It's a sport that seems to <u>captivate</u> a lot of people.
- As matches reach their conclusions, players' emotions often <u>intensify</u>.
- They <u>endanger</u> their own lives to help save others.

2 💬 We also use prefixes to change the meaning of a verb. Discuss the meaning of the prefixes in **bold**.

1 **re**fuel
2 **dis**agree
3 **mis**calculate
4 **un**pack
5 **de**frost
6 **out**number

3 Complete the gaps in sentences 1–8. Use a verb formed with the word in brackets and an affix from exercise **1** or **2**.

A QUICK GUIDE TO LIVE BY

1 Drink more water. It's important to _____ (hydration) throughout the day.
2 Stretching will help to _____ (straight) out your posture.
3 Try to do at least 20 minutes of intense exercise every morning. You'll feel _____ (energy) for the day ahead.
4 Detoxing is a good way to _____ (pure) your system and kick-start your metabolism.
5 A great way to _____ (stress) after a busy week at the office or college is to spend time with friends and NOT talk about work!
6 _____ (minimal) clutter in your house. A tidy home is a tidy mind.
7 Have at least one day a week when you _____ (connect) from technology. Turn off your phone, computer and TV, and get back to basics!
8 Participating in team sports can _____ (rich) your life in many ways – from helping you to relax to improving your communication skills.

Reading and Use of English Part 1
Multiple-choice cloze

For questions **1–8**, read the text below and decide which answer (**A, B, C** or **D**) best fits each gap. There is an example at the beginning (**0**).

Getting back in the saddle

Growing up on a farm (0) ..C.. me to spend most of my adolescence riding at full gallop. Every spare moment was (1) ..... to grooming, mucking out and honing my skills. (2) ....., in my eagerness I had little time for anything else. Giving up would have been (3) ....., I'd never have believed it. That all changed one fateful day when I was thrown from the saddle, dislocating my shoulder in the (4) ...... My trainer tried to (5) ..... me to get back riding as soon as possible, listing a myriad of reasons why. But my (6) ..... of riding had shifted – the mere thought of it made me incredibly anxious. Time passed and the memory of the accident grew more distant. The (7) ..... notion that I risked further injury by riding again began to seem ridiculous. So last month I finally (8) ..... at the decision to go riding for the first time in five years. As soon as I got up on the horse the old adrenaline rush and joy that I used to feel came flooding back.

	A	B	C	D
0	supported	ensured	<u>enabled</u>	aided
1	dedicated	engaged	employed	appointed
2	Furthermore	Nonetheless	However	Indeed
3	inconceivable	irrelevant	untrustworthy	imperfect
4	course	action	process	manner
5	stimulate	reassure	motivate	comfort
6	vision	perception	insight	awareness
7	misapplied	misbehaved	misused	misguided
8	arrived	accomplished	achieved	attained

Unit 5 Pushing the limits

Reading and Use of English Part 7
Gapped text

1 💬 **Discuss these questions with a partner.**
  1 What do you do to keep fit? How often do you exercise?
  2 What motivates you to keep exercising?
  3 What do you think drives professional athletes to succeed?

2 Quickly read the article about a British runner, ignoring the missing paragraphs. Answer the following questions.
  1 What makes her achievements special?
  2 Why is her sport becoming more popular?

3 Six paragraphs have been removed from the article. Choose from the paragraphs **A–G** the one which fits each gap (**1–6**). There is one extra paragraph which you do not need to use.

Lizzy Hawker:
What you can learn from Britain's greatest ultra-marathon runner

'Why?' Lizzy Hawker asked herself, lying on her back in total darkness on a strip of road leading into Kathmandu, with the wild beauty of Everest above her, and the bustling chaos of Kathmandu just 15 km below. 'Why, already hours into the third night, am I still asking my body to run?' More than 60 hours have passed since Hawker left Everest Base Camp for the 320 km run down to the Nepalese capital, a journey with over 10,000 m of ascent and 14,000 m descent.

[1]

She manages to pull herself to her feet and begins to put one in front of the other, moving through the heavy rain to the stadium finish line where a few friends are waiting with hot, sweet tea. There Hawker discovers her time – 63 hours 8 minutes compared to her previous 71 hours 25 minutes. She's done it. Is she happy? She feels relief at the end of the race but also a 'loss of purpose'.

[2]

Hawker is one of the world's best ever ultra and endurance athletes. Anyone who even dabbles in this type of sporting event will know her name and her exploits well. She has always loved running and exploring mountains, but a surprise win in the renowned Ultra-Trail du Mont-Blanc (UTMB) in 2005 revealed her aptitude for extreme events.

[3]

She has been slowed by injury over the past few years, but is tentatively coming back into form and completed an 80 km race in Nepal earlier this year. She has also been using her time to plan her own ideal race, the Ultra Tour Monte Rosa (UTMR), a 116 km trail across the Italian and Swiss Alps, her favourite training ground when she was preparing for the Mont Blanc races. Hawker runs to find balance rather than to take herself to extremes. 'Endurance is really more a way of living than just a sport,' she explains from Kathmandu, a city she has come to know well.

[4]

Hawker is unique of course, but participants in ultra-running and extreme endurance events are becoming less rare. Over the decade in which she's been competing, the sport has grown exponentially: the UTMB started in 2003 with a few hundred runners but this year 2,300 hopefuls will be waved off from Chamonix's town square, along with thousands more taking part in variations of the full event.

50

Unit 5 Pushing the limits

Remember
- Look for logical clues: information that is repeated or thematically connected.
- Grammatical clues can also help you decide where the missing paragraphs fit. Look at time expressions, linking words, pronouns or verb tenses.

A She went on to win this race five times, a gold at the World Championships in Korea in 2006 and in 2011 set a new record for the greatest distance covered in 24 hours on the road. To name but a few of the achievements she racked up in the subsequent decade.

B In the wake of the Nepal earthquake, she spends much of her time here, raising money for charity and living peripatetically between races, training and being wherever she needs to be to earn some money to keep her feet on those trails. Before running took over, she worked as an environmental scientist for the British Antarctic Survey.

C There is a dawning realisation that a new, bigger, challenge awaits her: to run there and back. Her dream now is to race from Kathmandu up to Everest Base Camp, and down again. 'The threefold challenge of altitude, distance and time. Bonkers,' she admits in her exhilarating memoir, *Runner*.

D The length of the race is never exactly the same, this year it will reach 170 km – the equivalent of four marathons – which must be completed within 47 hours. There is support along the way, but the idea is the runners are semi self-sufficient.

E Fancy your chances? Hawker shares her advice for getting started: 'Just start! Build up slowly and do what you enjoy. Whatever body type you are, you can train so that you can perform to the best of your own personal ability. The important thing is to do it because you love it, then more is possible than you realise.'

F This is her third attempt in six years. There are no other competitors, no one to beat but herself, no prize money or podium moment – only the breaking of her own records on a trail which has come to hold a special significance for the British ultra-runner.

G But is this sort of challenge actually good for us? Bashing our feet against hard surfaces and dragging our lungs up to high altitudes only to bring them crashing back down again sounds like torture.

[5]

Who is fuelling this boom in endurance running? 'I think the reasons that people take up ultra-running are as diverse as the trails and roads we run on,' says Hawker, 'and are the same reasons that people run at all levels. Perhaps the more comfortable our daily lives become, the more we need to look for something that challenges us in a very immediate way. Some people find this challenge in endurance events. It's great to see how it has grown widely and throughout the world. The sport now also receives far greater media coverage.'

[6]

'Anything taken to extremes can be unhealthy,' admits Hawker, adding sagely, 'but as it is said, "everything in moderation, including moderation". We were made to be active and to be constantly moving. So it could also be argued that running long distances is more natural than being sedentary and sitting for most hours of the day.'

4a Write down some questions you would like to ask an ultra marathon runner.

What encouraged you to take up running?
What do you do if you lose your motivation during a race?

4b 💬 Taking it in turns with a partner to be the interviewer and the interviewee, ask your questions.

Unit 5 Pushing the limits

Language focus 2
Unreal time, wishes

1 Look at these examples of what the interviewed athlete may have said. Do they use the underlined verb to refer to a present, future or past situation here? What tense do they use?

1 **I wish** I'd trained harder before the race – I wasn't fully prepared.

2 **If only** I'd taken some spare trainers with me last week. The ones I wore weren't comfortable.

3 **I'd rather** we trained in small groups more. It would be so much easier to organise.

2 The following sentences have the same meaning as the examples in 1 but use a different expression for wishes. What verb forms are used after the expressions in **bold**?
1 **I'd like to** have trained harder before the race.
2 **I regret** not taking some spare trainers with me last week.
3 **I'd prefer** it if we trained in small groups more.

⚙ Read more about the use of unreal time and wishes in the Grammar Reference page 124.

3 Rewrite these sentences using the words in brackets.
0 I'd prefer it if my neighbours didn't play their music so loudly. (rather)
 I'd rather my neighbours didn't play their music so loudly.
1 I've never learnt to ski properly. (wish)
2 I'd like to take up an apprenticeship rather than go to university. (sooner)
3 I can't ride a motorcycle but I wish I could. (if only)
4 I visited Paris on a package tour – I knew it was going to be a bad idea. (rather)
5 In my school it was compulsory to learn English but I'd sooner have learnt Spanish. (preferred)
6 My parents think I should exercise a lot more. (would like)

4a Which of the wishes in exercise 3 do you share?

4b 💬 Compare your answers with a partner. How much do you have in common?

5 💬 Work in pairs or groups. Use conditionals or the expressions for wishes to talk about your own experiences. Discuss these topics or your own ideas.
- learning a new skill
- going travelling
- dealing with stress in your life
- maintaining your health and fitness
- doing sports

Vocabulary
Health

1 💬 Work in pairs. Describe the situation in photos **1** and **2**. How do you think the people in the photos are feeling?

2 Read the text below. Use the context to work out the meaning of the expressions in **bold**.

> I was feeling **under the weather** but had to go to college as I had a test that I couldn't miss. I must have **caught** the flu **from** my friend Jessica – she had been feeling **run-down** all week. She kept almost falling asleep in class and was coughing and sneezing all over the place! I hadn't slept well so I felt really **worn out** before I even got to the exam hall. Luckily I'm **on the mend**. I just have a bit of a cold now, so my other exams should go much better!

1

3 Underline the adjectives in *italics* that can be used with the body part in **bold**. More than one adjective may be possible. Use a dictionary if necessary.
   a *dislocated/fractured/torn* **muscle**
   b *sprained/fractured/broken* **rib**
   c *blistered/pulled/swollen* **feet**
   d *twisted/sprained/torn* **ankle**
   e *pulled/dislocated/sprained* **shoulder**
   f *sore/blocked/bruised* **throat**

4 Tell your partner about a time you injured yourself or felt ill. Use the language in exercises **2** and **3**.

WRITING

Writing Part 2
Proposal

1 Work in pairs. Discuss these questions.
   1 What facilities or services exist in your area that contribute to the health and fitness of local residents?
   2 Who typically uses them?
   3 How often do you use them?

2a Read the following Part 2 exam task, and underline key phrases in the instructions.

> Your town council made an announcement that they are planning to increase investment in the health and fitness of local residents. They have invited proposals for projects from members of the public.
>
> You have decided to submit a proposal:
> • suggesting a facility or service the council should invest in.
> • outlining ways in which the proposed facility or service will have benefits for the health and fitness of residents.

Write your **proposal** in **220–260** words.

2b What facilities or services do you think should be invested in where you live? Why?

Unit 5 Pushing the limits

3 Read the model answer and circle the information which matches the key phrases you underlined in exercise **2a**. Were any of the same ideas you discussed in exercise **2b** mentioned?

4 💬 Discuss these questions with your partner.
1 Do you think the writer has fully answered the task?
2 Can you think of any other benefits the writer didn't mention?
3 Do you think these benefits should be included?

Proposal for health and fitness project

Introduction

The council has recently announced its intention to increase spending on health and fitness projects, and issued a public appeal for proposals. My proposal outlines one possible project for the council to invest in.

General recommendation

Firstly, I believe the increased investment should mostly focus on creating new facilities for residents, rather than on maintenance or upgrading existing facilities, which might have a much less significant impact. I strongly feel that undertaking a larger-scale single project may attract more attention than spreading the investment across a number of initiatives.

An outdoor gym

Although the town boasts generous green spaces as well as several playgrounds for children, there are very few outdoor facilities for physical activities for adult users. Installing an outdoor gym would encourage more people to visit and use our public parks than before.

Health and fitness benefits

The gym equipment would facilitate physical exercise, which should contribute positively to people's well-being. Furthermore, by placing the outdoor gym near existing, and possibly upgraded, children's playgrounds, we could encourage families to spend more time actively together with the adults setting a good example. If the gym facilities were available free of charge to the public, the project would also appeal to people who previously never used existing indoor facilities because of their high costs.

In conclusion, I believe it would be to our advantage to concentrate on one large-scale useful project, which would undoubtedly justify the investment. Therefore I am putting forward my proposal for your consideration.

---

5 Complete the table below with examples from the model answer.

Introducing points	*one possible (project)*
Making a comparison	*rather than*
Introducing a contrasting idea	
Adding a new idea or example	
Summarising	
Making a recommendation	

6 Either
a write your own answer to the question in exercise **2a**.
or
b write an answer to the following question.

> Your college is planning to organise a sports event to appeal to young people in the area. The student representative on the college board has asked you to draft a proposal
> - outlining ways in which young people could be encouraged to participate in the planned sports event.
> - suggesting suitable activities for the event that would attract as many young people as possible.

Write your **proposal** in **220–260** words.

Help

- Include all the key points from the task.
- Use headings to help you highlight the key parts of your proposal.
- Use appropriate phrases to link and sequence your text.

More information in the Writing Bank page 133.

6 Changing times

Vocabulary and Speaking
Change

1 💬 Discuss these questions with a partner.
   1 What kinds of changes are shown in pictures 1–4? Have they affected you in any way?
   2 Do you think that these changes are positive or negative? Why/Why not?

2 In sentences 1–6, underline the adjective in *italics* which is very different in meaning to the other two. In each case say in what way it is different.
   1 It **made a** *significant/pleasant/refreshing* **change** to do something practical rather than just sit at my desk all day.
   2 The board have just announced plans **to make** *sweeping/far-reaching/subtle* **changes** to how the company conducts business internationally.
   3 When she took over the company she **made a few** *cosmetic/radical/minor* **changes** – mostly regarding marketing, like changing the company logo.
   4 This year there was **a/an** *sudden/abrupt/unwelcome* **change** in her attitude towards work – it was like she was a different person.
   5 The government **have put forward a number of** *economic/legislative/constitutional* **reforms** which will be debated next week.
   6 During his first season as manager he **made some** *unexpected/rapid/unforeseen* **changes** – the captain was dropped from the first team.

3 We can use many different verbs to talk about change. For **a–c**, complete each gap with the correct form of the words in blue. One of the words in each group is not needed. Use the words in **bold** to help you.
   a *shape   adjust   reform*
   The new minister wants to **radically** _____ **education across the country**. I don't think he understands how long it would take for teachers and students to _____ **to the new system**.
   b *vary   distort   modify*
   Attitudes towards technology seem to _____ **considerably between** generations. Some older people think it is _____ normal human communication **to a dangerous degree**.
   c *remodel   convert   amend*
   Sandra and Tim want to _____ the old library **into** a restaurant. They've spoken to several builders about how much it would cost to _____ **the structure** to allow more light in.

4 💬 What do you think will be the biggest changes to the following in the next ten years? Use the language from exercises 2 and 3 to help you.
   • your life
   • your hometown
   • your country

Unit 6 Changing times

Listening Part 3
Multiple choice 🔊 2.01

1 💬 **Discuss these questions with a partner.**
   1 What do you like to do in your free time? How has this changed since you were younger?
   2 Do you ever take part in gaming during your free time? If so, how often and what kind of games do you play? If not, have you ever played any video games in the past?

2 🔊 **You will hear part of an interview with two gaming enthusiasts, called Lisa Jones and Andy Mitchell, talking about the future of gaming and changes to the way people play computer games. For questions 1–6, choose the answer (A, B, C or D) which fits best according to what you hear.**

1 Lisa thinks that gaming is going through a big period of change mainly
   A thanks to games being more affordable.
   B because of increased availability and access.
   C as a consequence of first-generation users ageing.
   D in response to the demands of end users.

2 Andy thinks that game-playing will grow
   A as a result of people having increased leisure time.
   B as a way of enhancing personal bonds.
   C as a means of coping with stressful lives.
   D as a reaction to fundamental changes in society.

3 According to Lisa, the industry is exploring trends in games which involve
   A using enhanced design to improve the experience.
   B providing people with a place to talk about their jobs.
   C existing ways of communicating.
   D allowing players to build societies.

4 Andy thinks that in the future it is likely that
   A people will be able to decide their own price for games.
   B gamers will pay to watch games being created.
   C big studios will pay for users' ideas.
   D gamers will be able to interact with characters in games.

5 Lisa predicts a time when games are
   A made by the people who play them.
   B only played online.
   C allowed to be copied without charge.
   D the result of gamers selling their ideas to companies.

6 Andy and Lisa agree that at the moment, virtual reality
   A is too expensive for many customers.
   B improves the gaming experience.
   C is relatively simple to create.
   D needs to attract more investment.

3 💬 **Work in pairs.** What changes have you seen to popular culture in your country? Do you think these things will continue to change at the same rate?

Unit 6 Changing times

Language focus 1
Passives

1a Use the words in the box to complete each of the passive structures in these extracts from the listening.

| are   be   get   have |

1 … it's so easy to _____ lost amongst all the newly developed products.
2 We might not see a time when individuals _____ games created for them specifically …
3 … but developers _____ expected to involve gamers in content creation …
4 This process will probably _____ replicated in the console sector by developers.

1b Check your answers in the listening script on pages 146–147.

Read more about passives in the Grammar Reference pages 124–125.

2 For questions **1–8**, complete the second sentence so that it has a similar meaning to the first sentence using the word given.

1 We decided to try again tomorrow.
   WOULD
   It _____ try again the next day.

2 Most of the board members believed it was not a practical strategy.
   NOT
   It _____ a practical strategy by most of the board members.

3 Experts have estimated that the painting is worth at least $10,000.
   ESTIMATED
   The painting _____ at least $10,000.

4 There is a rumour that the couple are going to get married next month.
   THOUGHT
   The couple _____ getting married next month.

5 Apparently the door was opened from the inside.
   APPEARS
   The door _____ from the inside.

6 Your car needs washing.
   NEED
   You _____ washed.

7 We have agreed to meet again next week.
   WILL
   It has _____ meet again next week.

8 The manager should have informed them about the decision last week.
   BEEN
   They _____ about the decision last week.

3 Work in pairs. Tell your partner about
- something you've had done recently
- something you're hoping to get done
- something which happened to you last week
- a time you got completely lost

Speaking Part 3
Collaborative task

1a Work in pairs. Here are some issues that are important today and a question for you to discuss. Talk to each other about why these issues are important.

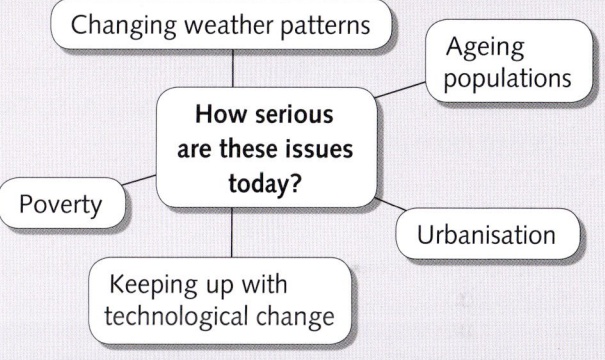

1b Now discuss and decide which two issues you think are the most urgent to address.

Useful language

Giving opinions:
*It seems pretty obvious that …   The way I see it …
I'm of the opinion that …*

Giving examples and explanations:
*Let me give you an example …   A case in point is …
… which is why …*

Agreeing/Disagreeing:
*I couldn't agree more.   But you can't deny that …
Precisely.   I'm afraid I don't agree with you there.*

Qualifying agreement:
That may be true, but …   That's a good point, but …

Concluding the discussion:
*So, as far as I'm concerned, the most urgent issue is …
Would you agree that … is an issue that needs to be addressed urgently?*

2 Now do the Speaking Part 4 task on page 107.

Unit 6 Changing times

Reading and Use of English Part 6
Cross-text multiple matching

1a Work in pairs. Discuss three stories which are currently in the news. Rank them in order of importance, giving reasons.

1b How did you initially hear about the news stories?
- on TV
- in the newspapers
- online/social media
- word of mouth/through friends or family
- on the radio

1c Read the following dictionary entry and discuss the questions with your partner.

> *citizen journalism* NOUN
> the recording, reporting and discussion of news events by members of the public using mobile technology and new media

1 Can you think of any recent examples of citizen journalism?
2 If you found yourself in the middle of a newsworthy event would you like to be a citizen journalist? Why/Why not?

2 You are going to read four extracts on the subject of citizen journalism. For questions 1–4, choose from extracts A–D. The extracts may be chosen more than once.

Which writer	
has a similar opinion to writer A about the limitations of conventional news organisations?	1
shares writer C's opinion regarding the need for validity in citizen journalism?	2
expresses an opposing view to writer B about the extent of influence of citizen journalism?	3
takes a similar view to writer D on the immediacy of citizen journalism?	4

3 Do you think that online news has the same value as print/broadcast news? Why/Why not?

Remember
- Read the rubric, title and subtitle carefully. Then decide on the general theme.
- For each question, identify and underline the key information to look for.
- Read the four extracts quickly for gist.
- Identify each writer's opinion and compare it to that of the other writers.

Four writers comment on the rise of a new kind of journalist and the impact of this on the way we get our news.

A

When people read the news in a paper, or watch a report on TV, they are generally given a single angle to a story. This tends to occur because only one camera or reporter is assigned to a news scene. Citizen journalism adds a new dimension to the presentation of events as we now see the same event from a range of perspectives, all created by members of the public. In addition, the news of up-to-the-minute events can be reported quickly and directly from smaller communities, with a more local angle. In the past this wouldn't have been considered for budget reasons. The technology available to citizen journalists is changing the processes and economics of reportage. Citizen journalism is expected to take emergent technology and use it to push the boundaries of modern reporting.

Citizen journalism

B

These days who gets to report and, crucially, how a story is reported has irrevocably changed. Anyone with a mobile device and access to the internet can be driven to capture and post an event that they feel needs to be shared with the wider world. The press, even in states that claim to uphold the right of free speech, are often tied up in big business and politics. The editors and owners decide which stories are important and the presentation is often skewed by their own agendas. Citizen journalism allows activists to bypass this and publish their content on social media. Through 'likes' and 'shares' these posts can often go viral and can bolster support for a cause, or at the very least get people talking about the event or issue. The ripple effect of influence on bystanders should not be underestimated. It can and has been a catalyst for real change in many regions. The opinions of citizen journalists are always valid, no matter what they are or what differences there are between them, since they celebrate freedom of expression and form a true picture of what real people believe.

C

In the past few years, it has become increasingly easy for people, whether individuals, groups or organisations, to share their views and promote their agenda via platforms such as blogs, social media or video-sharing sites. This has many benefits but not everyone is doing it with what most of us would consider to be good intentions. With so much information, and in some cases, misinformation, flooding our screens, feeds and inboxes, it's increasingly difficult to know what's real and what's not. In a news landscape where third party content is becoming increasingly commonplace, impartiality is more important than ever. If I'm going to read something, I need to know it can be trusted and I know a lot of people feel the same. So how much of a role does citizen journalism really play in forming our opinions of events?

D

It is said that citizen journalism will reinvent media like no other cultural development. However, when it comes down to it, citizen journalists have not put the hard work and study into being a journalist in the more conventional sense. As such, when I've browsed their work on citizen journalism sites, they essentially appear to be parodying channel news reporters and columnists in the press. Sometimes this is quite successful, often not so much. My main issue is that the basic fundamentals of reporting are missing. Little thought is given to the process of information gathering. Critically, citizen journalists do not seem to understand how essential it is to validate claims made by interviewees – no matter how difficult that can sometimes be. Conducting verifications always pays off – an original quote is invaluable. Instead what we frequently see are quotes from mainstream news sources – and frankly what's the point in that? I'm not saying that I'm anti this style of journalism – far from it. It has proven time and again how powerful it can be. People feeling compelled to share stories they are experiencing in the here and now is a wonderful thing. It's my belief that if citizen journalists ensure they adhere to sound journalistic principles, the medium could win much more professional acceptance.

Unit 6 Changing times

Language focus 2
Passives of reporting verbs

1a Reporting verbs are often used with passive constructions to introduce generalised opinions and facts.

It + passive + that clause
It is said that citizen journalism will reinvent media like no other cultural development.

subject + passive + infinitive
A powerful story is understood to be a catalyst of change.

<u>Underline</u> the infinitive in sentences **1–3** below. Identify which form it is – simple, continuous or perfect.
1 The internet is thought to be doubling in size every five years.
2 Hunter S. Thompson is known to have written some of the most provocative journalism in modern America.
3 Listening to music is said to help the brain to concentrate on tasks.

1b Match the reason (**a–c**) why each form was used in sentences **1–3**.
a to refer to something in the present
b to emphasise something that is still in progress
c to refer to something in the past

1c Rewrite sentences **1–3** using the *It* + passive + *that* clause structure.

Read more about passives of reporting verbs in the Grammar Reference page 125.

2a Rewrite these sentences using the passive structures from exercise **1a**.
0 Industry analysts predict that virtual reality technology will change the way we work and play.
It is predicted that virtual reality technology will change the way we work and play.
Virtual reality is predicted to change the way we work and play.
1 Scientists expect that climate change will become an unstoppable phenomenon.
2 Record companies claim that illegal downloading is destroying the music industry.
3 Many music journalists think Jimi Hendrix was the greatest guitarist of all time.
4 People say that life is changing faster than ever before.
5 The media say crime levels are in decline.

2b Work in pairs. Do you agree with the statements in **2a**? Give reasons and examples.

3a Work in small groups to write a news story based on one of the headlines below or using your own idea. Use the passive structures covered in this unit.

NEW LIFE FORM DISCOVERED

CROWN JEWELS STOLEN

POLITICAL SCANDAL

3b Present your news story to the rest of the class.

Reading and Use of English Part 2
Open cloze

1 Discuss these questions with your partner.
1 How do you access and listen to music? What influences you?
2 Are releases of new films or albums an important event for you? Why/Why not?
3 Do you think that people are really interested in events in popular culture or that the events become important because of media attention? Give reasons for your answer.

Unit 6 Changing times

2 For questions **1–8**, read the text below and think of the word which best fits each gap. Use only **one** word in each gap. There is an example at the beginning (**0**).

Don't believe the hype?

Outside Madison Square Gardens the air was buzzing (**0**) ...... WITH ...... excitement. Was it the launch of a new album, a fashion show, a celebrity circus? As the crowds grew ever larger, there was the wail of a siren and the obligatory cop barking instructions.

We took to (**1**) .... seats as the speakers groaned and began to shudder. A hype man, standing next to me and my cousin, told (**2**) .... we were free to dance. Suddenly, figures swarmed over the stage, revealing expressionless models staring out into the crowd who roared its appreciation, and boom, (**3**) .... more step in the evolution of a cultural icon was complete.

But (**4**) .... this kind of fanfare, are music fans actually interested in (**5**) .... is going on with every new release? Does the concept of an album actually mean anything anymore? Last year CD and digital album sales dropped by around 6%. Of course, such statistics don't (**6**) .... into account streaming equivalents – which are set (**7**) .... rise year-on-year. But it is worth noting that, while artists might be keen to promote a new creative masterpiece, listeners only seem to want to hear it (**8**) .... their own terms.

3 💬 Work in pairs. Which recent events involving public figures have interested you the most? Why?

Remember
- Fill in each gap with one word only. Contracted words, e.g. *isn't*, count as two words so will not be an answer in this part of the exam.
- Think about what type of word the answer is likely to be, e.g. a preposition, a linking word, etc.
- If you are uncertain, guess. Marks are not deducted for incorrect answers.

Vocabulary
Figurative language

1 Read the dictionary definition below, then underline examples of figurative language in the Reading and Use of English Part 2 text.

figurative language: words not used in their normal, literal meaning, but in a way that makes description more interesting or impressive
the lion roared (literal); *the crowd roared its appreciation* (figurative)

2 Match each word in the box to its literal meaning.

bark   buzz   clap   groan   shudder   swarm   roar   wail

1 _____: when your body shakes because you are cold or frightened
2 _____: a loud sound made by hitting your hands together
3 _____: to shout or cry with a long high sound to show you are in pain or very sad
4 _____: the short loud sound a dog makes
5 _____: the loud deep sound made by a lion
6 _____: the continuous sound made by a bee or fly
7 _____: a long low sound a person makes, especially when they are in pain or unhappy
8 _____: a large group of insects flying or moving together

3 Now complete the figurative sentences **1–8** with the correct form of a word from exercise **2**.

1 At the final whistle the crowd _____ on to the pitch – they had won the World Cup.
2 We could hear an ambulance _____ in the distance. There must have been a crash.
3 The rest of the audience _____ with laughter, but I couldn't see the funny side.
4 I turned the key and the engine, starting up with difficulty, slowly _____ into life.
5 I can't stand my gym class, the instructor's always _____ instructions at me.
6 The kids were _____ with excitement as we headed towards the cinema.
7 The bench _____ under the weight of so many people.
8 There was a huge _____ of thunder and the whole sky was lit up.

4 💬 Work in pairs. Discuss a concert or a festival you have been to, using words from exercise **3**.

Unit 6 Changing times

Writing Part 1
Essay

1 💬 Read the following Part 1 task and tell your partner:
- where you get your news from.
- whether you agree with the opinions expressed in the debate and why.
- what your opinon is on the factors affecting print media.

Your class recently attended a debate about the factors causing the decline in print media in the modern age. You have made the notes below.

> **Factors affecting print media**
> - 24-hour news on TV
> - online sources
> - cost

> **Some opinions expressed in the debate:**
> 'I can turn on my TV at any time and get up-to-date analysis of current events.'
> 'It's quicker to check what's going on in the world using social media.'
> 'There's just too much celebrity interest and gossip in the papers these days. I'm not going to spend money on that.'

Write an essay for your tutor discussing **two** of the factors in your notes. You should **explain which factor has contributed the most** to the decline of print media, **giving reasons** to support your opinion.

You may, if you wish, make use of the opinions expressed in the debate, but you should use your own words as far as possible.

2 Read the model answer and note down any similarities with the ideas you discussed in exercise **1**.

> As people become more used to living online, many traditional areas of news and entertainment are undergoing radical change. The role of the traditional media has long been in decline in most countries and, as a result, we have seen numerous newspapers and magazines moving from print to digital platforms.
>
> However, perhaps the most important factor in their decline has been the unprecedented growth of 24-hour news broadcasting. Most television companies now provide news on a rolling basis. This means that they are constantly updating content and can rapidly respond to any new developments in current affairs. Print media cannot offer such immediate analysis.
>
> Another key factor is the emergence of the internet as a source of news. According to recent statistics, nearly 75% of young people in the UK get their news online. Many people think that online news will soon completely dominate the way we learn about important events. Supporters of this view believe that as social media sites can be updated so quickly, they will soon overtake other channels of information. While the speed of these formats is undeniable, it is worth considering the role of balance and accuracy in journalism. Stories in traditional media are checked editorially before they are published. This is not the case with the so-called 'new' media, where standards are not as high.
>
> To conclude, while it is true that the growth of online newspapers and social media have affected print journalism, we need to accept that the biggest threat has come from television. 24-hour news TV offers the same high-quality reporting and analysis, but can bring this analysis to us faster.

3 👥 Work in pairs. Read the model answer again and discuss the following questions. Give examples from the essay to justify your answers.

Content	Have two factors been discussed? Has a decision been made about the factor with the most impact?
Communicative achievement	Does the writer use clear topic sentences to introduce ideas?
Organisation	Is there a variety of appropriate linkers? Has the writer used appropriate paragraphs?
Language	Is the language formal? Is there a good range of grammatical structures and vocabulary?

4 When you write a formal essay, you should begin with an opening statement before expressing opinions and reasons which support these. You can also refer to other people's opinions, reports and statistics. You should finish your essay with an appropriate conclusion. Complete the table with expressions from the model answer.

1	Expressing an opinion	*perhaps the most important factor has been ...*
2	Referring to others' opinions	
3	Referring to sources	
4	Concluding with a decision	

5 Match phrases **a–j** to the appropriate function **1–4** in exercise **4**.

a There can be no doubt …
b There are those who argue …
c According to a report from …
d … is undoubtedly … because …
e Opponents/Supporters of … argue/claim …
f All the evidence suggests …
g It is often claimed …
h It is probably true to say …
i Studies show …
j It can be concluded …

6 Now write an answer to the following Part 1 task. You should write **220–260** words.

Your class has listened to a radio discussion programme about declining sales in the music industry. You have made the notes below.

> **Factors affecting music sales**
> - streaming sites like Spotify
> - people copying and sharing music files
> - competition from other forms of entertainment

> **Some opinions expressed in the programme:**
> 'I can just stream new music on my laptop or smartphone – I don't need to buy it anymore.'
>
> 'People send links to new tunes, then I pass them on. It's a better way to hear new music without having to buy it.'
>
> 'Most young people spend their money on technology or gaming these days – music isn't really of as much interest.'

Write an essay for your tutor discussing **two** of the factors in your notes. You should **explain which factor has contributed the most** to the decline of sales in the music industry, **giving reasons** to support your opinion.

You may, if you wish, make use of the opinions expressed in the programme, but you should use your own words as far as possible.

Help

- Read the whole task carefully. Decide which two points you want to respond to in your answer. Your decision should be based on whether you can expand and develop the points by providing relevant examples and support.
- To make sure that your reader is fully informed, decide which of the two points is most important and note down one or two clear reasons for this choice. This can be stated in the final paragraph.
- Organise your main points into separate sections. Think about appropriate linking words to show the relationships between them.
- Paraphrase the given opinions to demonstrate a broad range of vocabulary and structures.

More information in the Writing Bank pages 130–131.

Review | Units 5 and 6

Reading and Use of English Part 4
Key word transformation

For questions **1–6**, complete the second sentence so that it has a similar meaning to the first sentence, using the word given. **Do not change the word given.** You must use between **three** and **six** words, including the word given.

1 If they get enough votes from the judges, which isn't likely, they'd win the competition.

   EVENT

   In the .... for them, they'd win the competition.

2 Arno missed the job opportunity because he arrived late for the interview.

   TIME

   If only .... for the interview, he wouldn't have missed the job opportunity.

3 If only I had applied for a job in finance after I graduated.

   NOT

   I .... into finance after I graduated.

4 The mayor promised to get someone to remove the litter in the town centre.

   HAVE

   The mayor promised he .... up the litter in the town centre.

5 I'm sure you'll get a pay rise soon.

   LONG

   I'm sure it .... you get a pay rise.

6 Interest rates rose steadily as the economy began to recover.

   RISE

   There .... interest rates as the economy began to recover.

Reading and Use of English Part 3
Word formation

For questions **1–8**, read the text below. Use the word given in capitals at the end of some of the lines to form a word that fits in the gap **in the same line**. There is an example at the beginning **(0)**.

Interning	
Over the last decade unpaid internships have been becoming **(0)** ..*INCREASINGLY*.. popular with both employers and employees alike. As graduates strive to stand out from the crowd, an internship is now a must-have on the CV of every **(1)**	INCREASE APPLY
Internships ensure a sense of engagement with the working world and help build a bank of transferable skills. There are of course **(2)** .... perks too, as interns often establish potentially beneficial networks. In certain disciplines, learning within the workplace under the **(3)** .... of qualified and experienced colleagues can prove to be **(4)**	 DENY SUPERVISE VALUE
Despite these **(5)** .... , research has shown that graduates who do internships often move from one to the next without securing full-time employment. **(6)** .... , less intensive internships, which often form part of university or college degrees, result in better employment outcomes.	ASSUME SEEM
Perhaps one solution to the current situation would be to make internships an **(7)** .... part of all degree courses. Alternatively, university students could work one or two days a week alongside their **(8)** .... field of study.	 OBLIGE CHOOSE

Vocabulary

1 Complete each gap with one word.

1 If you're not cut _____ to be a lawyer, perhaps you should consider changing your career? You could line _____ a new job in no time.
2 Our team have put _____ a few suggestions on how the business could be restructured. It will mean staff members taking _____ more responsibilities.
3 It took me such a long time to get _____ to speed with all the reforms that have been made _____ company policy.
4 I feel so sorry for her. She's feeling really run-_____ but can't rest as she's completely snowed _____ with assignments.
5 He didn't go _____ politics just to make minor changes. He's looking to shape the way this country works and change attitudes _____ education.
6 The manager's tactics varied _____ matches, which paid off. Now he's _____ the running for an international position.

2 Underline the correct alternative in *italics*.

1 The boxer's medical team *shuddered/swarmed* into the ring and started binding his *fractured/sprained* ribs.
2 Despite the *dislocated/pulled* muscles and *bruised/torn* bodies, the team were *buzzing/barking* – they had beaten their rivals at last.
3 The medic put an ice pack against my *dislocated/twisted* shoulder as in the distance I heard the *groaning/wailing* of an ambulance.
4 She *barked/roared* with laughter, then began coughing violently. She's OK but has a bit of a *bruised/sore* throat.
5 The train *shuddered/roared* to a halt and I jumped off onto the platform. Unfortunately I landed badly, resulting in a *sprained/pulled* ankle.
6 There was another enormous *clap/wail* of thunder and it began to pour. Wearily, I put one *groaning/blistered* foot in front of the other. This was going to be a long hike home.

Language focus

1 Complete each gap with one or two words.

1 If you _____ follow me madam, I _____ show you to your rooms.
2 Sandra, you _____ put some music on if it _____ help you let off some steam.
3 If it _____ for the rain, I _____ suggested going for a picnic.
4 If you _____ been so stubborn and apologised, we _____ gone to the party.

2 Rewrite the sentences using the passive. Do not use the underlined words.

1 <u>Nobody</u> knows exactly when <u>someone</u> designed the first open-plan office.
It _____ .
2 <u>We</u> are dealing with your complaint.
Your _____ .
3 <u>The authorities</u> initially thought that high summer temperatures caused the fires.
It _____ .
4 It is possible that <u>we</u> may extend his contract for another few months.
His _____ .
5 <u>Someone</u> will service my car soon. <u>Someone</u> does it every six months.
I'm _____ .
6 <u>Somebody</u> smashed Peter's car window with a brick.
Peter's _____ .
7 <u>Another business</u> has taken over our main accounts.
Our _____ .
8 <u>They</u> think that this change has affected a lot of people.
A lot _____ .

7 Brave new worlds

Speaking
The future

1 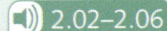 Read the quotations about the future and discuss these questions with your partner. Give reasons for your opinions.
   1 What is each quotation trying to say?
   2 Which is your favourite? Why?

2 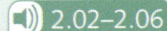 Work in pairs. How optimistic are you about the future?

In this bright future you can't forget your past.

Bob Marley

Listening Part 4
Multiple matching 2.02–2.06

1 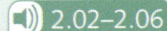 What do you think will be the most important technological development in the next twenty years? What impact do you expect it to have on your life?

2 You will hear five short extracts in which people are talking about technology.

While you listen you must complete both tasks.

TASK ONE

For questions **1–5**, choose from the list (**A–H**) what impact a piece of technology has had on each speakers' life.

A It has enabled them to watch films and shows on demand.
B It has made it easier to be in contact with friends.
C It has led them to spend less time with friends.
D It has caused an unexpected problem.
E It has encouraged them to lead a healthier lifestyle.
F It has made their job easier to do.
G It has helped them to keep their household organised.
H It has had a negative effect on their fitness.

Speaker 1 [1]
Speaker 2 [2]
Speaker 3 [3]
Speaker 4 [4]
Speaker 5 [5]

TASK TWO

For questions **6–10**, choose from the list (**A–H**) how each speaker feels about the technology.

A dissatisfied with the flexibility it allows
B concerned about its overuse
C impressed by its many uses
D unconvinced about how useful it is
E interested in learning more about it
F pleased about having more free time
G thrilled with the changes it has led to
H appreciative of its shape and size

Speaker 1 [6]
Speaker 2 [7]
Speaker 3 [8]
Speaker 4 [9]
Speaker 5 [10]

3 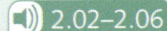 Discuss these questions with your partner.
   1 What type of person do you think each speaker is?
   2 Is their outlook generally positive or negative?
   3 Which person do you most/least identify with? Why?

Unit 7 Brave new worlds

"The past is always tense, the future perfect."
Zadie Smith

"Real generosity towards the future lies in giving all to the present."
Albert Camus

Language focus 1
Future forms (review)

1a Read the message below. <u>Underline</u> the examples of future forms being used.

'I'm going to watch *Modern Family* round Tania's house tonight – it's on at 9 pm. Matthew is coming too. I think it'll be fun – do you want to join us?'

1b All the forms are used to talk about the future but for what specific purpose have they been used?

'going to' is used to talk about plans and arrangements based on intentions

2 Look at sentences **1–3** below and match them to explanations **a–c**.
1 My friends and I *will be running* the Berlin marathon this time next week.
2 I'm hoping that by the end of the year, I*'ll have lost* 5 kg.
3 Next February, I*'ll have been living* in the countryside for a year.
a an activity which has started now or in the past and will continue up until a particular point in the future
b an event which will be finished before a certain point in the future
c an activity which will be in progress at a certain point in the future

⚙ Check your answers to exercises **1a and 1b** and **2** and read more about future forms in the Grammar Reference page 125.

Other ways of expressing the future

3a Match the expression in **bold** to the expression which has a similar meaning, **a** or **b**.
1 As a profession, *it* is **on the verge of** disappearing completely – I'm one of the few people left.
 a very near to the moment of
 b beyond the point of
2 *It* **is bound to** have a significant impact on resources and famine may become commonplace as a result.
 a has an obligation to
 b will almost certainly
3 *It* **is due to** be completed next week, but I wouldn't start cleaning out your desk just yet.
 a is expected to
 b is unlikely to
4 *It* **is set to** be opened in time for the peak season.
 a is ready to
 b has already (been)
5 **It's high time** the council knocked *it* down. It really is an eyesore.
 a It's now too late for
 b (The council) should already have
6 Glasgow **is to** host *it* next year.
 a has been chosen to
 b has expressed its intention to
7 Rachel **is on the point of** losing her temper. I hope *it* arrives soon.
 a has already (lost)
 b is just about to (lose)
8 *It* **is about to** start so please be quiet.
 a is going to (start) in a minute
 b is possibly going to
9 *It* **is unlikely to** be ready by one o'clock – I haven't even iced *it* yet.
 a probably will
 b probably won't

3b 💬 Work in pairs. What do you the think the *it* in *italics* in each sentence refers to?

⚙ Read more about other ways of expressing the future in the Grammar Reference page 126.

4a Write six statements about your own future. Use three of the future forms from exercises **1a** and **2**, and three of the expressions from exercise **3a**.

4b 💬 Compare your ideas with a partner. How likely do you think your statements are to come true? Give reasons for your answers.

67

Unit 7 Brave new worlds

Speaking Part 3
Collaborative task

1a 💬 Work in pairs. Some ideas suggested by a recent campaign to find solutions to environmental issues are given in **2a** below. Match each idea to a photo.

1b 💬 Brainstorm some alternative ideas of your own.

2a 💬 Work in pairs. Here are some solutions to various environmental concerns and a question for you to discuss. Talk to each other about what global issues each solution might help us resolve.

- Renewable energy
- Recycling
- Irrigation
- Ecofuels
- Reforestation

How effective do you think these solutions will be in resolving global issues?

2b 💬 Now discuss and decide which solution might have the greatest positive impact in the coming decades.

Useful language

Use a variety of phrases when considering different key points.
… will be useful in solving/reducing …
… will have a major impact on …
… would be extremely beneficial in (solving) …
… is of paramount importance/absolutely essential/ particularly vital/fundamentally important.

3 💬 Now do the Speaking Part 4 task on page 109.

Reading and Use of English Part 1
Multiple-choice cloze

For questions 1–8, read the text below and decide which answer (**A, B, C** or **D**) best fits each gap. There is an example at the beginning (**0**).

WASH

Two United Nations agencies, WHO and UNICEF, have (**0**) ..**B**.. up to oversee the international WASH programme. WASH (**1**) ..... for Water, Sanitation and Hygiene, and it has undertaken to resolve public health issues around the globe. (**2**) ..... to recent studies, more than a third of the world's population live without basic sanitation facilities and around 750 million lack (**3**) ..... to safe, clean drinking water. By addressing the interconnected issues of water (**4**) ....., upgrading sanitation facilities and education in hygiene, WASH partner agencies hope to improve life expectancy and living standards as well as economic productivity. Their education projects have already produced significant (**5**) ..... in the reduction of hygiene-related illnesses. One (**6**) ..... difficulty for WASH is the increasing concentration of populations in urban areas, where facilities were not originally (**7**) ..... for so many people living together. The gravity of the task (**8**) ..... should not be underestimated, as the UN's target is to halve the number of people without clean water by the end of the decade.

0	A grouped	B <u>teamed</u>	C formed	D united
1	A means	B represents	C stands	D translates
2	A Due	B Related	C Associated	D According
3	A access	B supply	C provision	D source
4	A supply	B resource	C store	D delivery
5	A increase	B progress	C advance	D effect
6	A certain	B peculiar	C firm	D particular
7	A devised	B designed	C derived	D directed
8	A forward	B upfront	C ahead	D opposite

Vocabulary 1
Verbs with *up-*, *down-*, *over-* and *under-*

1a Find verbs 1–4 in the text above. Use the context to help you match them to four of the definitions a–h.

1 oversee   3 upgrade
2 undertake 4 underestimate

a fail to consider or to recognise
b treat something in a way that shows that you think it is now less important than it was
c promise to do something
d check that something works or happens in the way that it should
e improve the quality of something
f think or guess that something is smaller or less important than it really is
g consider something to be better than it really is
h become better than something/body else

1b Now match verbs 5–8 to the unused definitions above.

5 overlook   7 downgrade
6 overtake   8 overestimate

2 Complete the sentences. Use the correct form of the verb in brackets and add *up-*, *down-*, *over-* or *under-*.

1 Dr Taylor recommended investing in a new project, but his proposal was _____ (rule).
2 Immediately after the company announced plans _____ (size) their staff. Many of the older employees started applying for jobs.
3 The president took a vow _____ (hold) the democratic principles upon which the country's constitution is based.
4 We haven't yet identified the reasons why the team is _____ (perform) at the moment. If things don't improve, we'll be relegated.
5 The software you're using is obsolete. I think you should _____ (date) it.
6 I'm confident we'll be able _____ (come) all the obstacles.

3 💬 Work in pairs. Tell your partner about:
- a problem whose importance you once **underestimated**.
- a TV series or film you recently **downloaded**.

Unit 7 Brave new worlds

Listening Part 1
Multiple choice 2.07–2.09

1 You will hear three different extracts. For questions 1–6, choose the answer (A, B or C) which fits best according to what you hear. There are two questions for each extract.

Extract One
You overhear a conversation between two people about recycling.

1 How do Fiona and John both feel about the recent developments?
  A They don't really believe the explanations given by the city council.
  B They are worried that the investment in the scheme has been wasted.
  C They are disappointed about the council reversing their decision.

2 What does Fiona propose?
  A collecting signatures to protest against the decision
  B starting a media campaign to support the scheme
  C meeting their local council member to find out his views

Extract Two
You hear two researchers talking about their work.

3 What reason does Sally give for not going to the conference?
  A She will be too busy in the near future to attend.
  B A delay on a research project means she has to stay in the office.
  C She has appointed someone else to take her place.

4 How does Mark feel about Sally's promotion?
  A disappointed that Sally is not travelling with him
  B pleased about Sally's progress in the company
  C concerned for Sally because of her new responsibilities

Extract Three
You overhear a conversation between a customer and a shop assistant in a technology store.

5 Why does the shop assistant mention the cost of tablets?
  A to persuade the customer to buy one instead of a laptop
  B to give an example of their advantages compared to laptops
  C to explain why people prefer them to laptops

6 How does the shop assistant suggest the customer should make his decision?
  A by comparing the technical features of both devices
  B by getting advice from other people who do similar work
  C by identifying what he will be using the device for

Remember
- The questions and options give you an idea about the context for each extract.
- If you are not sure of an answer, it is a good idea to put a pencil mark next to the option you think is correct on the first listening. Then check again on the second listening.
- Think about how the options might be expressed in the script, e.g. in **2A** 'collecting signatures to protest against the decision' – *gather signatures, oppose the decision, start a petition*, etc.

2 Work in small groups. Think of a cause you would like to support and how you could organise a successful petition. Discuss:
- what/who you are campaigning for/against.
- how you would encourage people to sign.

A cause that's really close to my heart is …

For me, … is a really worthy cause because …

Language focus 2
Future in the past

1 Look at these examples of the sentences from the listening script that talk about the future from a past perspective. In each case, was the intention carried out successfully? Why/Why not?
  1 I **was going to** buy a new laptop but now I'm looking at these tablets you've got.
  2 You **were supposed to** be going too, weren't you?
  3 It **was due to have been** completed by September.

2 We use a range of different expressions to describe the future from a point of view in the past for various reasons. Complete the explanations with a word from the box.

> intentions   interrupted   happen (x2)
> perspective   predictions

  1 Actions or events that were _____:
    She **was about to** board the train when she realised she'd left her ticket at home.
    He **was on the point of/on the verge of** quitting his job when they offered him a promotion.
  2 Unfulfilled _____:
    Peter **was going/hoping/meant to** move to Atlanta but he didn't get the job he wanted.
  3 Future events that did actually _____:
    Warren **would/was to** become one of the most successful businessmen of his generation.
  4 To talk about the future from a past _____:
    Michael **was coming/due** home in 10 minutes so I had to tidy up quickly.
    When I saw him, he **was about/going/due to** have an operation.
  5 Future events that did not actually _____:
    The shop **was to have** opened in December.
    The motorway **was due/supposed/meant to** be completed/have been completed by now.
  6 To make _____ about the future from a past perspective:
    I just knew it **would be** absolutely packed – after all, it is a public holiday today.
    Everyone thought we **would be driving** flying cars by now.
    The game **was always going to be** difficult to win.

⚙ Check your answers and read more about future in the past in the Grammar Reference page 126.

3 💬 For **1–8**, underline the correct expression in *italics*.

When Apollo 11 landed on the moon in 1969, everyone thought humanity **1** *would be exploring/would have explored* the solar system first-hand for many years to come. It was announced that in the following decades they **2** *were about to/were going to* send manned missions to Mars and, possibly, to Venus. A permanent base **3** *was to be/was* built on the moon by the 1970s. But it all just **4** *wasn't/weren't* to be. Within merely two years of the first moon landing, it was decided there **5** *were going/were meant* to be no more manned missions there. The plans for people to visit Mars and Venus **6** *were to be/were on the point of being* shelved for a while. Imagine my disappointment! I **7** *supposed to/was supposed to* spend my holidays in space. Or so I imagined as a kid. But just as I **8** *was about to/was bound to* give up hope, the announcement came that NASA might launch a manned mission to the Red Planet as soon as the 2030s.

4 💬 Work in pairs. Do you feel disappointed about any similar hopes or predictions for the future that haven't yet happened? Consider the following themes or your own ideas.

- education
- transport
- fashion
- careers
- entertainment
- environment

Unit 7 Brave new worlds

Reading and Use of English Part 5
Multiple choice

1 💬 Do you recognise the film in the photo? What do you think happens in the film?

2 You are going to read a magazine article about a film. For questions 1–6, choose the answer (**A**, **B**, **C** or **D**) which you think fits best according to the text.

Stranded on another planet

Based on a 2011 novel by Andy Weir, *The Martian*, Ridley Scott's latest sci-fi drama garnered glowing reviews and an enthusiastic response from audiences around the globe. Although the nominal star of the film is Matt Damon, playing astronaut Mark Watney, perhaps the real star of the show is science. Many might consider a film about science tedious and difficult, but this could not be further from the truth. So, as exhilarating as the ride is, just how accurate is the science? Well, the answer is: for a Hollywood spectacular, very.

The film sets up Watney as a near-future Robinson Crusoe, stranded on an alien planet, struggling to survive with bleak prospects and dwindling supplies. After an emergency evacuation of their research base on Mars, the astronauts of *Ares III* leave him behind, mistakenly presuming he is dead. In order to stay alive until any rescue mission can be mounted to bring him home, Watney is forced to improvise one ingenious scheme after another. He converts the astronauts' abandoned habitat – a pod-like building – into a greenhouse, where he grows potatoes in Martian soil. He fixes up a contraption to extract water from hydrazene – fuel from the rocket engines of the *Ares* landing craft – almost blowing himself and his home up in the process. He even digs up a radioactive fuel cell to warm his rover, the mission's surface transport, with plutonium. He then drives his vehicle across the endless Martian plains to retrieve and repair NASA's real-life Martian probe, Pathfinder, to use its radio for communicating with Earth.

Obviously, *The Martian* is a piece of fiction, which means Weir and Scott take several liberties with science to tell a gripping story – but not necessarily with those elements that many viewers may find the most far-fetched. Both the processes of painstakingly fertilising nutrient-deficient Martian soil for cultivation and of using catalysis to produce water from oxygen and hydrogen are well within the realms of possibility. Having said that, a real-life Watney may have an easier time extracting water from the ice trapped beneath the surface all over Mars. To be fair, though, that is according to fairly recent NASA findings, which Weir would not have known about back in 2011.

What is more hard to believe is Watney's unwarranted anxiety about radiation damage from the shielded storage capsule of plutonium he carries around in his rover. Mars has a thin atmosphere and a negligible magnetic field, which means astronauts walking around outside would have no protection whatsoever from cosmic radiation. Watney would receive a much more harmful dose from just being on Mars than he would from his makeshift heating device. And Weir himself has openly admitted that the event that sets the whole plot in motion: the Martian windstorm – was his greatest conscious break from scientific fact. 'I needed a way to force the astronauts off the planet,' he said in a press statement. 'Plus, I thought the storm would be pretty cool.' The atmospheric pressure on Mars is a mere 0.6% of that of Earth. Although a storm raging at a speed of 190 kilometres an hour would be an awesome destructive force on our planet, it would barely stir up dust on Mars – let alone threaten to topple a massive rocketship.

The film is supposed to take place in late 2035. The technology depicted in the film is possible for the timeframe and consistent with NASA projects in their current stages of development. The way artificial gravity is generated in the interplanetary spaceship, *Hermes*, is the solution currently being pursued by NASA engineers. It is hoped it will protect human crews from the physical damage that can occur in extended stays in zero gravity. Additionally, the slingshot manoeuvre proposed by a young engineer in the film to divert the spacecraft back to Mars is one that has been used by NASA since the 1960s. In fact, it is a departure from reality when the fictional engineer has to explain the basics of the technique to the NASA director played by Jeff Daniels. A space administrator who was oblivious of the slingshot manoeuvre ought to resign his post immediately.

So, will humanity have gone to Mars by the 2030s? There are many open questions about this. The presence of water hints at the intriguing possibility of life on Mars, but it also brings up the issue of astronauts accidentally infecting any microscopic life forms with germs from Earth. With our less-than-perfect procedures for spacecraft sterilisation, the concern is not without foundation. So perhaps the question is not whether we could send people to Mars, but whether we really should. The best thing for now is to sit back and enjoy *The Martian* for a sense of what that adventure might be like.

1 How does the author summarise people's expectations of films focusing on science?
   A Reviewers and audiences usually respond very positively to intelligent films.
   B Audiences sometimes find such films dull and challenging to watch.
   C The audience's opinions usually depend on how accurately science is depicted.
   D Cinema-goers do not expect films to be too connected to science.

2 Watney in the film gets in touch with people on Earth by
   A fixing the radio on board the abandoned spaceship.
   B using atomic radiation for his signals.
   C converting the astronauts' habitat's communication facilities.
   D locating and restarting old NASA equipment.

3 Which of Watney's challenges was depicted accurately in the film?
   A Rocket fuel can provide the means to make drinking water.
   B Dust storms on the planet often cause enormous damage.
   C Dangerous radiation from plutonium threatened Mark's survival.
   D There is a way to produce water from ice in the Martian soil.

4 In what way is space exploration different from how it is shown in the film?
   A The suggested technology to provide gravity on board the spacecraft is impractical.
   B The flight procedure proposed in the film has not been used since the Apollo missions in the 1960s.
   C Space agency administrators normally have knowledge of common spacecraft manoeuvres.
   D Zero gravity does not usually have a negative impact on astronauts' health and fitness.

5 According to the writer, a potential threat to future Mars missions is
   A the risk of infection for the human crews.
   B the difficulty involved in building the spacecraft.
   C the possibility of Earth bacteria affecting any Martian life forms.
   D securing funding for missions with uncertain objectives.

6 How could the writer's personal opinion about the film be best summarised?
   A The focus on technological accuracy negatively affected the plot.
   B Despite some scientific errors, the film is a great experience.
   C Many ideas about living in space were too far-fetched to believe.
   D It was enjoyable except for its central concept of a stranded astronaut.

Remember
- Underline the part of the text that relates to each question.
- Compare the four options carefully to the part you underlined.
- Make sure your answer is true according to the text, not because of what else you personally know about the subject or what your opinions are.

3 **Discuss these questions with a partner.**
   1 What's the best science fiction film you've seen?
   2 How accurately do you think science was represented in the film?
   3 Do science fiction films need to be accurate about science? Why/Why not?

Vocabulary 2
Science and research

1a Underline the correct word in *italics*.
   1 Watney is forced to *propose/investigate/improvise* one ingenious scheme after another to stay alive.
   2 He *converts/dissolves/determines* the astronauts' abandoned habitat into a greenhouse.
   3 The technology is consistent with NASA projects in their current stages of *validation/development/relevance*.
   4 With our less-than-perfect *principles/criteria/procedures* for spacecraft sterilisation ....

1b Check your answers in the article.

2 Use a dictionary to look up the meaning of the words you didn't use in exercise 1a.

3 Complete the sentences with the correct form of a suitable word from exercise 1a.
   1 Task completion and accuracy are the main evaluation _____ in the grammar test.
   2 Genes from both parents _____ the colour of their children's hair and eyes.
   3 Sugar easily _____ in water, which makes it possible for us to sweeten our drinks.
   4 Experts have _____ several solutions to the problem but these have all been rejected.
   5 Landline telephone technology has little _____ in today's world of communications.
   6 The scientific _____ on which the project was based were later found to be flawed.

4 In small groups, imagine you are planning a visit to Mars. Discuss your ideas for:
   - preparations you'll need to make.
   - experiments you would like to do.

Unit 7 Brave new worlds

Writing Part 2
Review

1 💬 **Discuss these questions with a partner.**
1 How do you usually decide what films or TV programmes you want to watch, or what books you want to read?
2 What information can you normally find in a film, TV or book review?
3 Do you usually agree with critics' reviews of books and films?

2 **Read the following Part 2 question and model answer. Which book would you choose to write about? Why?**

> A popular magazine invited people to send in their reviews of their favourite science fiction or fantasy books. Write a review of a science fiction or fantasy book you particularly enjoyed. Highlight its strong points and explain what readers might like most about reading it. Also include why you would recommend it to others.

Write your **review**.

3 **What is the purpose of each of the four paragraphs in the model answer?**

Paragraph 1: background information about the book and its author, the setting and timeframe

---

The Bone Clocks

'The Bone Clocks' is a masterpiece of a fantasy novel by David Mitchell, the bestselling author of 'Cloud Atlas'. Though it is mostly set in the modern day, the events described in the novel take place between 1984 and 2043.

What makes this such a fascinating read is the vivid depiction of the central character – Holly Sykes. Other intriguing characters come into contact with her at various points in the eventful story of her life. Readers will want to keep on reading long into the night when Holly becomes entangled in a battle between immortal beings – which is previously only hinted at in the segments set in the real world. The whole 'universe' of the novel is incredibly well-thought-out.

The book employs different first-person narrators covering six connected stories, describing the same or related events from a range of viewpoints. Each narrator has a distinct style of their own, but the writing always remains elegant and effortless. Mitchell expertly balances the realistic and fantastic elements. With just enough allusions to the latter to keep readers intrigued, he avoids distracting from the human drama unfolding in the lives of the believable characters. What makes his writing particularly enjoyable is the way he recycles themes, imagery and ideas in different contexts – subtly changing their meaning and significance each time.

Not all the plot twists are wholly convincing, but that's beside the point. As long as you are willing to go where Mitchell leads you, you are guaranteed to have fun. It is his complete unpredictability that makes his books such a joy to read.

4 **Look through the model answer and find words and phrases that:**
1 describe the plot
2 describe characters in the book
3 express the reader's opinion about the qualities of the book
4 give recommendations

5 **Either write your answer to the question in exercise 2, or write an answer to the following question.**

> Your school's English club has asked people to post reviews of films or TV dramas students have recently seen and enjoyed on their website. Write a review of a film or TV drama, describing its main strengths and suggesting who you think it would appeal to. You should include just enough information to convince people to see it, without giving away too much detail about the plot.

Write your **review**. You should write **220–260** words in an appropriate style.

Remember

- Prepare a plan. Include all the points from the question.
- Use expressive adjectives and adverbs to make your writing more engaging.
- Check your writing for errors.

More information in the Writing Bank page 136.

8 Getting through

Vocabulary 1
Expressing feelings

1. 💬 Work in pairs. How do you think learning to read body language and facial expressions could benefit people?

2. Complete each gap with a word from the box that has the same meaning as the word(s) in brackets.

astounded indifferent devastated wary petrified elated troubled lost livid disgusted smug frustrated

1. A: I was _____ by her reaction. I hadn't expected her to get so angry. (*very surprised*)
   B: I know! She was absolutely _____ when she heard that you'd broken her tablet. (*angry*)
2. I could tell you were getting _____ by the task. You kept frowning and sighing. (*annoyed and impatient*)
3. A: Did you see how they reacted when they heard the result? They were _____ . (*very happy*)
   B: I thought they seemed a bit too _____ . They didn't handle it that well. (*self-satisfied*)
4. Sandra was really engaged in the lesson, but Ricardo was totally _____ . He kept fidgeting and staring off into space. (*lacking interest*)
5. A: She's a bit _____ around dogs – see how wide her eyes have got. (*nervous*)
   B: I was like that when I was young. I was _____ of them – I'd panic if they came near me. (*very frightened*)
6. She was _____ by the bad news – her face crumpled and soon she began to cry. (*very upset*)
7. A: When he entered the room, he folded his arms and knitted his eyebrows in a _____ frown. (*worried*)
   B: Do you think he felt a bit _____ in a room full of strangers? (*not confident*)
8. I couldn't help being _____ by his table manners. He kept opening his mouth when there was still food in it. (*feeling extreme dislike or disapproval of something*)

3. 💬 Work in pairs. Look at photographs 1–4 and discuss these questions.
   1. What kind of body language/facial expression is being shown in each photograph?
   2. How does the body language/facial expression in each photograph make you feel?

75

Unit 8 Getting through

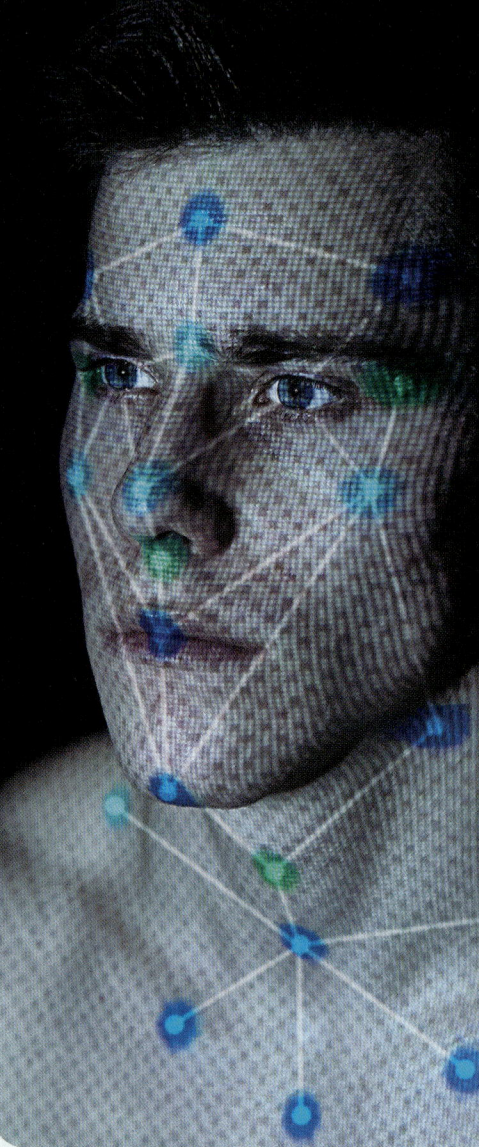

Listening Part 2
Sentence completion 🔊 2.10

1 💬 **Discuss these questions with a partner.**
   1 How do you prefer to communicate with people? Why?
   2 Does this change depending upon who you are communicating with?

2a Read the extract from a magazine article about 'affective computing'.

> The emergence of Artificial Intelligence (AI) as a future for human–computer interaction has raised many questions, not least of which is: *How will machines, which deal in hard-data, relate to us with all our emotional uncertainties?* One way of addressing this is through 'affective computing' – the study and development of systems and devices that can recognise, interpret, process, and eventually simulate human emotions.

2b 💬 Do you have any devices or computer systems that you regularly interact with? How? Is it important for machines to be able to understand human emotion? Why/Why not?

3 🔊 You will hear a science journalist called Ben Frost talking about the development and role of affective computing. For questions **1–8**, complete the sentences with a word or short phrase.

TALKING TO TECHNOLOGY THAT KNOWS WHAT WE FEEL

Ben states that banks are currently using AI to carry out trade and (1) .... assessments.

Recently, programs have been created which use the information they process to come to (2) ....

Ben states that emotional understanding can help direct people's (3) ....

The first attempts at affective computing focused on information like a person's (4) .... to understand emotion.

One finding of the research into emotions is that everyone displays their own (5) .... of behaviour.

Computers can use statistics to track (6) .... of the face that match recognised emotions.

Affective computing has been used to check (7) .... to various forms of entertainment.

Ben predicts a situation where affective computing will be used by people working in (8) .... and advertising.

Remember
- Write down the exact word or phrase that you hear.
- Watch out for distractors. Always use the context surrounding an item to help select the most appropriate answer.

4 💬 **Discuss these questions with your partner.**
   1 Can you think of any other practical uses for computer programs that read emotions? Who could they help?
   2 What do you think the future of communication will be like? How will it change the way we live/work/study?

Language focus 1
Conjunctions

1 We use conjunctions to link ideas within a sentence. They can be used at the beginning or middle of a sentence to improve a text's cohesion and to make sentences more complex.

Read sentences **1–3**, taken from the listening, and match each of the underlined conjunctions with a function **a–c**.

1 Globally, scientists in different fields of research have joined forces with engineers to establish <u>whether</u> this can be made a reality.
2 <u>Although</u> AI has started to make inroads on 'reason', understanding emotion is a greater challenge.
3 <u>Provided</u> they are displayed consistently, wearable computers can be taught to recognise those patterns.

a making a contrast/concession
b giving a condition
c reason and result

⚙ Read more about conjunctions in the Grammar Reference pages 126–127.

2a In **1–7**, join the sentences together using the conjunctions given in brackets. Make any other changes you think necessary to improve the cohesion of the sentence. Look at the example (**0**).

0 My salary has increased every year. My colleague's salary has decreased. (whereas)
My salary has increased every year whereas my colleague's has decreased.

1 I'll lend you the money. You must pay me back by next month. (provided)
2 Marko and Amy's original plan might not work out. They should have a back-up plan. (in case)
3 We have to get this computer fixed. We can't do any work. (otherwise)
4 They had been in the area a long time. They still didn't know the quickest way to the hospital. (even though)
5 He wasn't a fan of social media. He had to admit it was sometimes very useful. (although)
6 I'll finish work at 5. I'll pick the kids up from their swimming lessons. (after)
7 Joe was messaging Danilo. The lecturer was talking. (whilst)

2b What is the function of each of the conjunctions in **2a**?

Vocabulary 2
Onomatopoeic words

1 Onomatopoeic words sound like the noise they refer to. Read the dialogue. <u>Underline</u> the sounds and say them aloud. What else do you usually associate them with?

> Do you think that there are any drawbacks to using a smartphone to communicate?

> Not really. The constant ping of notifications or the buzz of texts coming in can be annoying, but aside from that I couldn't be without it.

2 💬 Work in pairs. Decide which category (**a** or **b**) each word in *italics* belongs to. Say the words aloud to help you.

1 a sound of rain   b sound of river
  roar   patter   drip   gush
2 a sound of animal   b sound of objects breaking
  croak   shatter   growl   hiss
3 a sound of voices   b sound of movement
  whisper   whoosh   chatter   hum
4 a quiet sounds   b loud sounds
  crackle   pop   bang   rustle
5 a sound of wind   b sound of leaves
  swoosh   whistle   howl   sigh
6 a sound of anger   b sound of sorrow
  screech   sigh   shriek   snarl

3 <u>Underline</u> the correct word in *italics*.

1 The rain steadily *pattered/shattered* against the window pane.
2 There was a storm outside, the wind *whistled/growled* through the trees and the windows shook.
3 Standing on the stage, I could hear the faint *hum/growl* of conversation from the audience.
4 If you listen carefully, you can hear the *crackling/rustling* of small animals among the leaves.
5 With a sudden *whooshing/howling* sound the plane took off.
6 As we walked through the rainforest, we heard the *shriek/roar* of the river up ahead.

4 💬 Work in pairs. Discuss whether there are any particular sounds you like or dislike. Give reasons. Are there any specific sounds that you associate with where you live/work/study?

Reading and Use of English Part 7
Gapped text

1 💬 Discuss these questions with a partner.
1 What are some of the benefits of speaking a second language? Are there any drawbacks?
2 Do you think that there is too much emphasis on language learning in your country?

2 Read the title and first paragraph of the article. Predict which general points the article will mention.

3 You are going to read an extract from a magazine article. Six paragraphs have been removed from the extract. Choose from the paragraphs **A–G** the one which fits each gap (**1–6**). There is one extra paragraph which you do not need to use.

Remember
- After skim reading the main text, read all the missing paragraphs and try to identify the purpose of each one. Are they explaining a point, illustrating an example or showing contrast?
- Focus on the information before and after the gaps.
- Check your answers by reading the whole article.

The more the better?

The more we endeavour to communicate, the more we realise the world is a decidedly multilingual place. It is estimated that at least half of the world's population, over 3 billion people, use more than one language in everyday life. According to the European Commission, 54% of European citizens are bilingual. Britain has long been considered to be one of the most monolingual countries – even so, 39% of the UK population speak more than one language. Owing to a rise in those figures, academic interest in the field has grown.

1

Among child psychologists there is **general consensus** that being able to communicate in more than one language has positive effects on our children's brain development. Similarly, studies of older people show that it is never too late to learn a second one: using two languages may protect the brain from cognitive* decline in older age. This is borne out in many research papers where it has been proven that speaking a second language provides some form of benefit – be it social, communicative or supporting better mental health.

2

Having an objective understanding of how well you can do something – one that **tallies with** your actual successes or failures – is fundamental to decision-making processes, and ensuring clear communication of ideas. But problems can occur when there is a **slight mismatch** between what you achieved and your assessment of it.

3

The study found that bilingual participants were, on average, 10% less accurate than monolinguals in evaluating their own performance. Monolingual speakers were therefore more aware of **identifying errors** and distinguishing accuracy. Given the increasing frequency of bilingualism in the world, some analysts suggest this line of research has **practical implications**.

4

As regards concentration, studies led by the same group of researchers found that children who speak two languages outperform their monolingual peers in the classroom because they are more likely to filter out disruptive noises. This is because a bilingual student develops a more **acute** sense for words, helping them to stay on task in noisy environments.

5

Being able to focus on the key content of communication when there is a large volume of background information present is an extremely valuable skill set to have at your disposal. During the research, it emerged that, on the whole, bilingual pupils outperformed monolingual pupils by almost 10% in comprehension tasks where subjects were asked to process information while listening to simulated classroom sounds.

6

Accordingly, these studies show that bilingualism has a range of cognitive effects that sometimes can be interpreted as 'advantages' and sometimes as 'disadvantages.' But what is without doubt is that the ability to speak more than one language gives people different perspectives on life, and a better understanding of others. And perhaps that is a message well worth communicating.

*cognitive = in psychology, a cognitive science or process is one that is connected with recognising and understanding things

A Researchers asked groups of bilingual and monolingual speakers to make rapid decisions during a computer task. Two circles were shown on a screen, each containing a number of dots. Participants were asked to decide which circles contained more dots and rate how confident they were in their decision.

B Furthermore, the tests showed that the ability to overcome verbal interference also improved with age, but again only with bilingual speakers. This effect on cognitive development would seem to indicate the importance of learning a second language early within formal educational systems.

C Despite such beliefs, the research team stress that perceived disadvantages are minimal. They have stated that more research is required to study the relationship between our ability to monitor our own performance and other aspects of cognition that have previously been found to be enhanced by bilingualism, such as attention span and memory.

D Scientists have only recently started to study humans' ability to acquire multiple languages. One of the most fascinating questions addressed in this research is how our brain deals with having two or more languages, and what the implications are for cognitive development and society.

E Studies show certain types of mental decline can be slowed by bilingualism. Compartmentalising languages, plus switching between them at the right time, exercises the brain and has a protective function.

F According to researchers, the ability to block out background sounds has benefits in early-learning environments. Primary schools are important sites for the development of formal education and social interaction. However, small children can be remarkably noisy.

G However, one recent piece of work, carried out by Cambridge University, has provided results contrary to expectations. They discovered a bilingual disadvantage in a very specific area called 'metacognitive processing' – our ability to monitor our own performance.

4 Match the phrases in **bold** in the article to the appropriate definition 1–6.

1 a difference between reality and expectation
2 possible uses
3 matches
4 quick and accurate
5 agreement among all people involved
6 noticing mistakes

5 💬 Discuss these questions with your partner.

1 How important is it for people joining a community to speak the language?
2 Do you think that the teaching of foreign languages should be compulsory? Why/Why not?

Unit 8 Getting through

Word formation
Nouns 2

1 Complete sentences **1–5**, taken from the article on pages 78–79, using the correct form of the words in brackets.

1 Among child _____ there is general consensus that being able to communicate in more than one language has positive effects on our children's brain _____ . (*psychology/develop*)

2 The study found that bilingual _____ were, on average, 10% less accurate than monolinguals in evaluating their own _____ . (*participate/perform*)

3 But problems can occur when there is a slight _____ between what you achieved and your _____ of it. (*match/assess*)

4 Being able to focus on the key _____ of communication, when there is a large volume of background information present, is an extremely valuable skill set to have at your _____ . (*contain/dispose*)

5 One of the most fascinating questions addressed in this research is how our brain deals with having two or more languages, and what the implications are for cognitive _____ and _____ . (*develop/social*)

2 Complete sentence **b** so that it has a similar meaning to sentence **a**. Use a suffix from exercise **1** and a negative prefix if necessary.

1 a He last <u>appeared</u> in public in the early 90s.
  b His _____ from public life occurred during the early 90s.

2 a I was surprised that Antonia <u>refused</u> to admit that she'd made a mistake.
  b I was surprised by Antonia's _____ to admit she'd made a mistake.

3 a I hope they are going to <u>acknowledge</u> where the ideas came from.
  b I hope there's some _____ of where the ideas came from.

4 a The styles of fashion worn by young people here <u>vary</u> a great deal.
  b There's a great deal of _____ in the fashions worn here by young people.

5 a I am a person who believes we should protect our <u>environment</u>.
  b I'd describe myself as an _____ .

6 a All the people who are taking part in the <u>contest</u> should come up onto the stage.
  b All _____ should come up onto the stage.

Speaking Part 2
Long turn

1 💬 Work in pairs. Look at the photographs. What ways of communicating do they show? Have you ever used them? Why/Why not?

2 💬 Look at the three photographs again. They show **different ways of communicating**.

Student A: Compare **two** of the pictures, and say **why people might choose to communicate in this way**, and **what might have motivated them to get in touch with the other person/people**.

Student B: When your partner has finished, answer the following question.

In which situation do you think people can communicate the most effectively?

- Why might people choose to communicate in this way?
- What might have motivated them to get in touch with the other person/people?

3 💬 Now change roles. Look at the photographs on page 111 and follow the instructions.

Useful language

Comparing and contrasting:

This kind of communication is more widespread than …

People tend to … less frequently than … because …

… offers immediate communication. In contrast …

… is fairly similar to …

… is considerably different from …

Speculating:

It's possible that …

It's unlikely that …

Although it seems that …
(+ contrastive statement)

Reading and Use of English Part 3
Word formation

1 For questions **1–8**, read the text below. Use the words given in capitals at the end of some of the lines to form a word that fits in the gap **in the same line**. There is an example at the beginning (**0**).

It's the way we talk

Like any brave new world, the internet has millions of (**0**) _INHABITANTS_ who are looking to meet and share information and experiences. Since their popular (**1**) .... in the first decade of the new millennium, social networking sites have become a key cultural phenomenon.   **INHABIT**   **EMERGE**

There is an acceptance that while the features of these sites share some (**2**) .... , the cultures that form around them may differ greatly. However, adherents of the social media revolution would all agree on one thing – real-time (**3**) .... is king.   **SIMILAR**   **COMMUNICATE**

We now live in an age where each digital pronouncement is instantly assessed and evaluated. Perhaps in (**4**) .... our status, or commenting 'below the line' we are seeking (**5**) .... from our wider community. Only an idealist would suggest that this pressure to communicate is always a positive thing. The (**6**) .... of some users to overshare and the accompanying embarrassment this can cause will remain a source of (**7**) .... for the media.   **DATE**   **APPROVE**   **TEND**   **FASCINATE**

As a result there has been some (**8**) .... criticism about falling moral standards.   **AVOID**

Help

- Quickly read the text to get an overview of the topic.
- Getting an overview helps you establish the context, the direction of the argument and the writer's viewpoint.
- Use the context to decide whether to use singular or plural forms, as well as positives or negatives.

2 💬 Work in pairs. Which forms of communication do you think are the most trustworthy? Why? Do you feel that people share too much about their lives on social media or do you think it is a good way of recording experiences/memories?

Unit 8 Getting through

Language focus 2
Discourse markers

1 Read sentences 1–5, taken from the reading text on pages 78–79. Match the words in **bold** to their use a–d.

1 **However**, one recent piece of work, carried out by Cambridge University, has provided results contrary to expectations.
2 **Furthermore**, the tests showed that the ability to overcome verbal interference also improved with age.
3 **Accordingly**, these studies show that bilingualism has a range of cognitive effects that sometimes can be interpreted as 'advantages'.
4 During the research, it emerged that, **on the whole**, bilingual pupils outperformed monolingual pupils by almost 10%.
5 **Owing to** a rise in those figures, academic interest in the field has grown.

a Adding information/Developing a point
b Contrast
c Cause and result
d Generalising

2 Now decide on the use (a–d) of the following words and phrases. Some discourse markers may be matched to more than one use.

> in addition to   consequently   besides
> by and large   what's more   having said that
> nevertheless   moreover   conversely   in fact
> on the contrary   not only … but also

⚙ Read more about discourse markers in the Grammar Reference page 127.

3 <u>Underline</u> the appropriate discourse marker in *italics*.

Smartphones have now surpassed laptops as the most popular way of accessing the internet. 1 *By and large/Conversely* this growth has been stimulated by the extension of 4G networks globally. There is a tendency for 4G users to make more face-to-face calls. 2 *Essentially/Likewise* they send more photos and videos over the phone. 3 *Consequently/Specifically* instant messaging services have increased in profile. While some critics may not approve of the ongoing shift towards online existence, 64% of online adults agree that being online is invaluable for keeping informed about current affairs. 4 *What's more/However* 60% state that it plays an increasingly important role in maintaining relationships with close family and friends.

Most young people now watch on-demand and catch-up programmes on phones rather than TV. 5 *Furthermore/Therefore* a growing number prefer to access short videos from video-sharing websites. 6 *Incidentally/Having said that*, smartphones still linger behind television as the electronic device we interact with most regularly as a whole society.

4  Work in pairs. Read the following statements and write at least three sentences for each using a range of appropriate linking devices.

- Smartphone usage is irreversibly changing the way we live.
- Online video content will end traditional TV broadcasting.
- Social media communication is more important than any other medium.

Writing Part 2
Letter/email

1 Read the following Part 2 task, and tell your partner:
- what action people can take to improve their communication skills.
- what benefits these actions can bring to an individual.
- what some of the possible drawbacks might be.

> You recently studied abroad on an intensive three-month language course. A friend, who is planning to study abroad, has written to ask you about your experience.

> I'm not sure about where to live when I go abroad to study. Should I live with local people, or other students? What would be best? Did you feel that the whole experience of living and studying in another country was actually worthwhile?

Write a **letter** telling your friend about some of the positive and negative aspects of your experience, giving reasons for your opinions and saying whether you would recommend the experience.

2 Read the model answer and note down any similarities between it and the ideas you discussed in exercise **1**.

> Dear Sophie,
>
> Thanks for your email – it's been too long. I've been meaning to get in touch about my experience abroad for ages. It's great to hear that you're considering taking up a similar opportunity – I can't recommend it highly enough. You'd get so much out of it.
>
> On the whole, I really feel like my language has improved enormously, so much so that I'm considering taking some advanced exams. I think studying abroad would be a marvellous opportunity for you, too. Not only do you build on what you've learnt at college, but you also meet up with so many diverse people from around the world. I've added so many more people to my social network as a result of my trip.
>
> Whatever you do, make sure that you choose to live with a local family. Being part of a household where there was constant (sometimes very loud) interaction really helped me to build on my listening skills. Also, I had to become more fluent, as clear pronunciation was important for talking with family members who were not really used to communicating with foreigners. There's not much point living with a group of students from your own country. In general people end up just using their native tongue, and that doesn't really lead to much improvement in their language skills.
>
> Apart from the costs, which can be quite high, I'd say that there's no better way of developing your language skills. When you compare it with going to classes week in week out, the financial side of things probably balances out. Anyway, I know you'd love to see a bit more of the world.
>
> Let me know what you decide.
>
> All the best,
>
> Tobi

3 Informal letters should outline the reasons for writing and provide a relevant opening and closing. You may also be required to persuade or advise somebody to do something. Complete the table with expressions from the model answer.

Reasons for writing	Thanks for your email I've been meaning to get in touch about … for ages
Persuading	
Advising	

4 Add the following phrases to the table in exercise **3**.

> Just think of …
> You'd be much better off …
> I wouldn't … if I were you.
> Remember that … I told you about?
> I'm convinced that you'd …
> I'm getting in touch to let you know about …
> Just imagine how it would …, not to mention …

5 The writer of the letter has developed the points in the task by using their imagination. Underline examples of this.

<u>my language has improved enormously …</u>

6 Write your own answer to the task in exercise **1** in 220–260 words.

Help

Plan what you are going to write. Note down your ideas then organise the best ones into logical paragraphs. When you write your letter
- make sure you have covered all the points in the task to avoid losing marks.
- include some negative comments, but balance these with positives where possible.
- link ideas using appropriate adverbials and conjunctions.

More information in the Writing Bank page 134.

Review | Units 7 and 8

Reading and Use of English Part 4
Key word transformation

For questions **1–6**, complete the second sentence so that it has a similar meaning to the first sentence, using the word given. **Do not change the word given.** You must use between **three** and **six** words, including the word given.

1 She's well-known for her expertise in medical research.

   FIELD

   She's a renowned .... medical research.

2 I really don't mind whether we stay at home or go out tonight.

   DIFFERENCE

   It really .... whether we stay at home or go out tonight.

3 They were supposed to publish the report today, but it's been delayed.

   DUE

   Although the report .... today, it's been delayed.

4 He told me that he doesn't intend to stop working.

   INTENTION

   He told me that he .... up his job.

5 His views on transport have been criticised over the last few weeks.

   COME

   His views on transport have .... weeks.

6 I can always tell when Simon is about to lose his temper.

   VERGE

   I can always tell when Simon is .... his temper.

Remember

- Do not change the word given.
- Think about what area of grammar, phrasal verb or expression the given word could relate to.
- Re-read the whole sentence to make sure you haven't left out or added any information.

Reading and Use of English Part 2
Open cloze

For questions **1–8**, read the text below and think of the word that best fits each gap. Use only **one** word in each gap. There is an example at the beginning **(0)**.

Renewing interest in energy

As climate change becomes more apparent, there is an increasing interest **(0)** ....*IN*.... renewables satisfying our energy needs. It is a well-known fact **(1)** ...., if exploited to its full potential, enough sunlight falls on the earth's surface every hour to meet world energy demands for an entire year. But **(2)** .... people often fail to realise is how big an employer the 'clean' energy industry is.

Three times more jobs stem **(3)** .... the renewable sector than are created by fossil fuel industries. The significance **(4)** .... this is considerable but it is scientific research and development, by **(5)** .... accounts, which will see the largest percentage of future spending on energy.

Interestingly enough, **(6)** .... governments have been slow to implement energy initiatives, many private companies have caught **(7)** .... to the benefits of renewables. Though **(8)** .... interest is often derived from a desire to save money, it too has a positive impact on the future of spending on the sciences.

Vocabulary

1 Match the adjectives **1–12** with an adjective with a similar meaning **a–l**.

1 astounded		a	worried
2 smug		b	delighted
3 indifferent		c	cautious
4 livid		d	shocked
5 disgusted		e	uninterested
6 petrified		f	terrified
7 elated		g	not confident
8 troubled		h	self-satisfied
9 lost		i	furious
10 frustrated		j	very upset
11 devastated		k	extreme dislike
12 wary		l	annoyed

2 For sentences **1–8**, complete the first gap using the correct form of the verb in brackets with an *up-*, *down-*, *over-* or *under-* prefix. Complete the second gap with the correct form of a word from the box below.

| development   improvise   relevance   convert |
| determine   criteria   propose   investigate |

1 It's very important that governments don't _____ (value) the importance of scientific research. It can help to boost a country's economy and has a lot of _____ for future employment opportunities.
2 We cannot _____ (emphasise) how vital it is to stick to the _____ set out in the handbook.
3 The company has had to _____ (size) considerably in the past couple of years, and now it has been _____ by some members of the board that the company should be sold off completely.
4 Dr Williams will _____ (see) the experiment, which is designed to _____ the theoretical existence of dark matter in the outer reaches of space.
5 The chef had seriously _____ (estimate) the number of guests, so he had to _____ to make the ingredients go further.
6 For a small country, with limited resources, they tend to _____ (perform) academically. It's a phenomenon which is worth _____ in more detail.
7 Jennifer said that she would _____ (load) her photos of the event to the university's social networking site. She just needs to _____ them into a suitable format first.
8 The university has promised to _____ (grade) the research lab, which means _____ of the product should be completed much sooner than expected.

3 Complete each gap with the correct form of a word from the box.

| sigh   crackle   growl   chatter   drip   screech |

1 My dog always _____ at people he doesn't know but he would never bite them.
2 Stacey _____ in despair – there was no way she was going to finish the essay by tomorrow.
3 He was _____ at the waiter that he'd got his order wrong. There just isn't any need to talk to people like that.
4 The theatre was full of excited _____ as the audience waited for the show to begin.
5 The log cabin was completely silent except for the _____ of the wood burning in the fireplace.
6 The tap had been _____ all night but Simon was too tired to get up to turn it off.

Language focus

1 <u>Underline</u> the correct alternative in *italics*.
1 The graphics in his latest game are quite good. *Even so/Even though*, I soon got bored of playing it.
2 *Provided/Because* you follow all the different stages in the experiment, it should have consistent results.
3 I don't mind where we go, as *yet/long* as we have decent WiFi so *as/that* I can watch NetFlix.
4 You need to get in touch with her soon, *otherwise/moreover* she'll unfriend you.
5 I understand why she's angry, *although/whereas* I still don't agree with her views.
6 They've changed their broadband provider *so as to/as a result of* get a better deal.
7 He's one of the friendliest people I know. *Specifically/Having said that*, he's a bit irritating.
8 There seems to be a lot of interest in physics these days. *By and large/Consequently*, this is due to projects like CERN.

2 Complete sentences **1–6** with a phrase from the box.

| bound to   on the point of   not to be   to be |
| the verge of   always going to be |

1 The final was _____ a wonderful occasion but it exceeded everyone's expectations.
2 Sadly, studies have shown that the species is on _____ extinction.
3 The government is _____ increase its investment into green energy.
4 The announcement is _____ made by the head of the research team, Dr Shaw.
5 Kate was _____ leaving when the phone rang.
6 This medicine is _____ taken by anyone under 16. It could make them very ill.

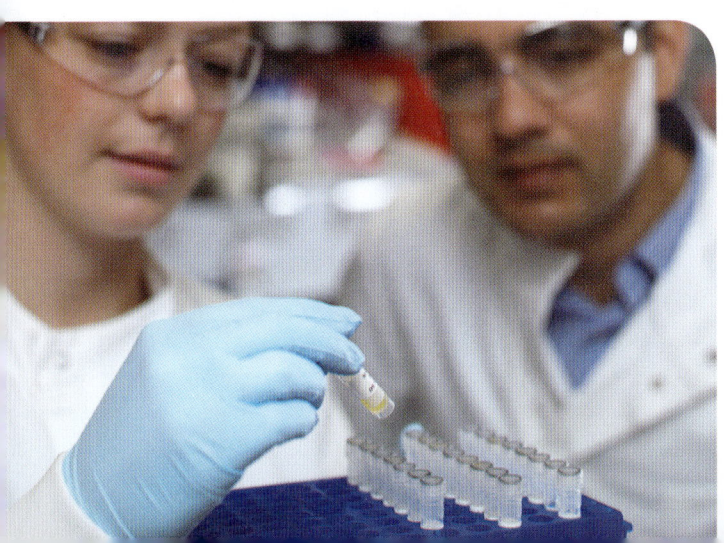

85

9 To the market

Speaking Part 3
Collaborative task

1. 💬 Work in pairs. Look at the products and advertisements in pictures **1–4**. Discuss what is being sold and how the advertising method works.

2a. 💬 Here are some methods of promoting products and a question for you to discuss. Talk to each other about how effective these methods are in promoting products.

- Sponsoring events
- Using celebrity endorsements
- Using influential bloggers/vloggers
- Advertising on TV
- Advertising on social media

How effective are these methods of promoting products?

2b. 💬 Now decide which two methods are the most effective.

Useful language

- Use a range of structures to evaluate ideas.
  Evaluating effectiveness:
  This will/might have a meaningful impact/influence on …
  This would certainly/probably be influential/successful in (helping to …)
  … might have a significant/considerable effect on …
  … doesn't have the same effect as it once did.

- You can extend each other's ideas to show that you are collaborating.
  Extending ideas:
  And another thing …
  As well as that …
  Not only that, but …
  That's an interesting point. It reminds me of …
  Agree/disagree with your partner:
  I couldn't agree with you more.
  That's a really good point … but …
  I'm not sure I agree with you there …

3. 💬 Now do the Speaking Part 4 task on page 112.

Unit 9 To the market

Listening Part 3
Multiple choice 🔊 2.11

1 💬 **Discuss these questions with your partner.**
  1 What was the last product you bought that you really wanted? What influenced you to buy it?
  2 Do you have any favourite advertisements? If so, why do they appeal to you?

2 🔊 **You will hear part of an interview with two industry experts called Simon Ryder and Lucy Francis talking about changes in advertising. For questions 1–6, choose the answer (A, B, C or D) which fits best according to what you hear.**

1 Lucy states that advertising nowadays
  A is much more persuasive than in the past.
  B relies solely upon research.
  C has adopted different techniques to those used in the past.
  D often makes exaggerated claims about products.

2 Simon believes the principal challenge facing advertising is that people
  A are not fooled by the methods being used.
  B no longer have any trust in it.
  C place too much emphasis on each other's opinions.
  D have changed the way they make decisions.

3 Lucy says that in order to appeal to families, advertisers need to
  A have a clearer message.
  B promote healthy living.
  C take into account a range of opinions.
  D be more realistic in their expectations.

4 In Simon's view, future advertising will be
  A based online.
  B affected by privacy laws.
  C much more influential.
  D tailored to individuals.

5 Lucy says that large, well-known companies need to
  A use well-known people to promote their products.
  B reflect their customers more closely.
  C offer the public a luxurious lifestyle.
  D respond to criticism more quickly.

6 Simon believes that brands can win back public support by
  A advertising on social media.
  B consulting with customers.
  C reducing costs to consumers.
  D honestly expressing their purpose.

3 **Look at the listening script on pages 149–150. For questions 1–6 <u>underline</u> the part of the script that gives you the answer and explain why the other options are wrong.**

4 💬 **Work in pairs. Do you trust companies when they are trying to sell you something? Do you think that the future of advertising described by the speakers is a positive or negative one?**

Unit 9 To the market

Language focus 1
Determiners and pronouns 🔊 2.12

1 🔊 Complete these sentences from the listening on page 87 with a word from the box. Then listen and check.

this   another   both   few   lots of   many   one

1. So, what kind of impact does _____ have on big, established brands?
2. Well, the implication for _____ brands is huge.
3. Consumers may respond to _____ but they also want to be talked with, not talked at.
4. Over the last _____ decades, consumer trust has been gradually worn away. In _____ respect, this is a problem for advertisers, but it presents opportunities in _____ .
5. There's _____ attention being paid to the power of brands.

2 Read the information below and decide if the words in exercise **1** are used as determiners or as pronouns.
- Determiners can be used before nouns to talk about amounts:
  too much emphasis   ***some*** strange ideas
- Some determiners can also be used as pronouns:
  That paella looks delicious.
  Do you mind if I have ***some***?

⚙ Read more about determiners and pronouns in the Grammar Reference pages 127–128.

3a Underline the correct pronoun or determiner in *italics*.

1. According to the latest reports, in virtually *some/every* country there are *few/another* job opportunities for older people. However not *plenty/all* the news is bad. *Much/Most* is being done by employers to rectify the situation.
2. Countries should help *one/each* another if they get into financial difficulties. If *much/several* countries, for example within the EU, work collectively to solve economic problems, then in the long term *none/all* of them will benefit.
3. *Every/Most* people believe that *such/more* things as bank cards and cash will not be replaced by *other/another* forms of payment *any/some* time soon.

3b 💬 Work in pairs. Do you agree with the ideas in exercise **3a**? Why/Why not?

4 Decide whether the determiners in sentences 1–4 are correct or incorrect. Correct any errors.
1. Very little people have shown an interest in their latest product.
2. It rains every days during the winter here.
3. Every of the two teams could have won the tournament.
4. It took some two days before the news of the event reached us.

5 Complete the expressions in **bold** with a word from the box. Sometimes more than one answer is possible.

all   every   few   little   many   most   much   none   plenty

1. If businesses spent **a _____ time** improving their staff's skills, they would become more productive.
2. There was a public outcry when the tax details of many major companies were published. **_____ of them** had been paying enough.
3. **_____ remains** to be done in improving people's perception of the banking sector.
4. It's important to **make the _____ of** your savings, as there's **_____ chance** you'll need more money in the future.
5. **Far too _____** companies seem to pay their employees a decent salary. **A good _____** are paying below the market rate.
6. **_____ too often**, disruptive students ruin the class for well-behaved children.
7. In the current business environment **there is _____ of room** for small start-ups with strong ideas.

6 💬 Work in pairs or small groups. Discuss one of the topics below, using a range of expressions from exercise **5**.
- successful businesses in your country
- people's attitudes towards saving
- people's attitudes towards spending

> A good many up-and-coming companies are making the most of the 90s nostalgia trend.

> Banks need to spend a little time rebuilding trust. No one wants to put their money in a savings account at the moment.

> Far too many people are using credit cards to pay for things they can't afford.

Unit 9 To the market

Vocabulary and Speaking
Money

1 💬 Look at photographs **1–4**. Discuss these questions with a partner.
   1 What could each photo represent?
   2 Which do you think is worth spending a lot of money on? Why?
   3 Which do you think is a waste of money? Why?
   4 Do you think there is anything that people in your country tend to spend too much or too little on?

2 Complete each gap with the correct form of one of the words in blue. One of the words in each group is not needed. Use the words in **bold** to help you.

   1 *go   be   shop*
   Sometimes you just have to _____ **on a shopping** spree – buying things can make you feel good. But try _____ **around** for the best price. It's usually online these days.
   2 *drop   fall   stick*
   _____ **to a budget** is very important when you are a student. It's easy to _____ **into debt**.
   3 *extortionate   prosperous   run*
   The last thing you want to do on holiday is _____ **out of cash**, so remember to take plenty. Some of the prices in resorts can be **really** _____ .
   4 *get   break   go*
   Most new companies find it hard to _____ **even** when they start up, but this shouldn't stop people trying. Although I did read that a record number are _____ **bankrupt** in their first five years of business.
   5 *make   put   thin   tight*
   A lot of families are struggling to _____ **ends meet**. The government should be doing more to help them when **money is** _____ . With a bit of financial education, they could be _____ **something away** each month.
   6 *affluent   impoverished   stingy*
   An area of the town which was previously quite **run down and** _____ is now very fashionable. Lots of trendy shops and restaurants have opened branches there. I can't believe how _____ **and expensive** it has become.

3 💬 Work in pairs. Discuss at least four of the situations in exercise **2** based on your own experiences and ideas. Use a range of the phrases in **bold**.

Unit 9 To the market

Reading and Use of English Part 8
Multiple matching

1. Work in pairs. How do you usually pay for the things you buy?

2. Work in pairs. Look at the photograph and discuss the advantages and disadvantages of handling money in this way. Then skim read the texts to see if any of your ideas are mentioned.

3. You are going to read a magazine article in which an expert talks about cash alternatives. For questions 1–10, choose from the sections (A–E). The sections may be chosen more than once.

Remember

- Read the questions first and highlight any key words. If you start by reading the texts first you may waste time trying to understand part of the text or some vocabulary that is not being tested.
- Beware of choosing an answer just because you notice a word in the question that is a synonym for a word in the text. There are often distractors in the text.

In which section is the following mentioned?

the implication that the money has a positive emotional significance	1
the warning that the status of the currency may change in the near future	2
the writer's approval of the flexibility that the currency offers	3
an admission of a previous lack of knowledge on the writer's part	4
a way in which the currency reduces the threat of theft	5
an emphasis on how internationally widespread a certain type of currency is	6
a potential problem with time that is avoided by using the currency	7
the significant role the currency plays in keeping an economy moving	8
a lack of economic infrastructure behind a currency's creation	9
a challenge to a pre-determined notion of the reader	10

4. Work in pairs. Which of the cash alternatives did you find the most interesting/surprising? Can you think of any other objects that could be a suitable alternative to cash?

$how me the money

The rise of digital money has led to us becoming less dependent on cold, hard cash. But many other forms of currencies exist. Sophie Glass takes us into the weird and wonderful world of cash alternatives.

A It's 1990 and my mother hands me some chocolate coins and thus unwittingly sparks within me a lifelong passion … not for chocolate … but for money. Now let me state that I am not a materialistic person or a miser zealously counting every cent. I'm talking about currency in all its forms. Despite what you may think, equating chocolate with money is not as ridiculous as it may sound. The cocoa bean was the currency of choice in Central America in days gone by. In fact, cultures from all over the world have seen the value in edible currency. Up until the 1930s, tea bricks, made from compressed tea leaves, were widespread in Central and Eastern Asia. Traditionally used to treat illnesses and eaten as a source of nourishment when food was scarce, they were also repurposed to purchase livestock and pay taxes.

B This isn't just all in the dim and distant past. A bank in the Emilia Romagna region of Italy accepts wheels of Parmesan cheese from dairy farmers as collateral on loans. This is due to Parmesan taking two years to mature, sometimes leaving farmers with little or no cash flow. The bank's vault has at times contained up to $187 million worth of the prized dairy product and has even been targeted by 'cheese thieves'. Banks have played a part in the development of more technologically-minded currency too. As a matter of fact, banking was very much at the forefront of my mind during a recent two-month work assignment in Kenya.

C I had spent one too many days looking for somewhere to wire money* and had ended up venting my frustration to the hotel concierge. He informed me about M-Pesa (*m* for *mobile*, *pesa* the Swahili word for *money*), a system where airtime minutes can be utilised to pay for goods and services, which had risen up in response to the lack of accessible banks. Launched in 2007, it has also meant that individuals can control their own finances without recourse to banks and their fees and has helped to safeguard people's finances against hyperinflation. That's certainly a compelling case for mobile payment. I deposited some money at one of the shops involved in the scheme and just like that my problem was solved! What makes this truly beneficial is that not only does it eliminate the usual risks associated with carrying cash, but city workers can easily send their salaries to family members in rural communities without delays. The implications of this are huge and I anticipate that it will become prevalent in many areas before long.

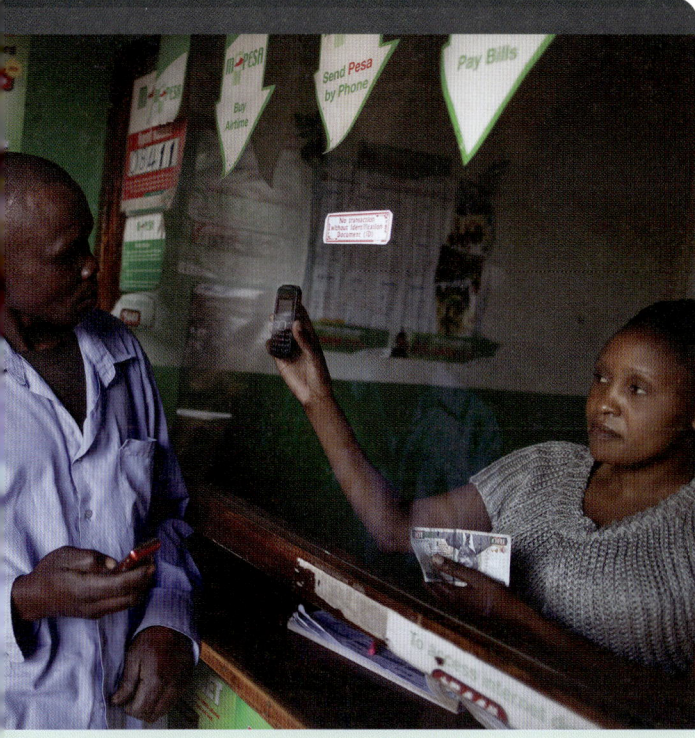

D Many people I know would be incredulous that I find paying for taxis more troublesome in my native Vancouver, where most drivers insist on cash only, than I did in Kenya. But in all honesty, do Canadians have any right to question non-conventional forms of payment? My fellow citizens do, after all, have a dogged fondness for the monopoly-style Canadian Tire Money (CTM) notes – a customer loyalty reward system created by a chain of gas stations and convenience stores. Almost everyone has a story about them. As a child I would ritualistically save them up to buy an especially craved-for toy. Whilst CTM's monetary value has rapidly declined in the past few decades, people's affection for it has not. Perhaps what makes a currency special isn't always something solid. Although the opposite is true of rai stones, the ancient currency still in use on the Micronesian island of Yap.

E The first time I saw one of the limestone discs, which measure up to 3.6 metres across and weigh 4 tonnes, I was struck by its solemnity. For many years I had presumed that the size of these remarkable carvings was what determined their value, but this is not the case. The deciding factor is the physical cost that humans have paid in the making and moving of them. The precarious nature of transferring the discs has also led to an oral history of ownership being used as opposed to the traditional method of exchange. A Yap local related the story of how one of the rai stones fell overboard whilst being transported by canoe; it was agreed by all parties involved that whilst it now lay at the bottom of the sea, its worth was not diminished. By and large the changing of hands of the rai stones – usually to mark social transactions such as marriage and inheritance – is cemented by a ceremony. Despite this rich history, one has to wonder with the ongoing march of the digital age, whether the people of Yap will resolve to ensure their survival.

*to wire money – to send money directly from one bank to another using an electronic system

Unit 9 To the market

Language focus 2
Reference, substitution and ellipsis
Reference

1 Find the following sentences in the article and decide what the word in **bold** refers to.
1 **This** isn't just all in the dim and distant past. (B)
2 Launched in 2007, **it** has also meant that individuals can control their own finances. (C)
3 **That's** certainly a compelling case for mobile payment. (C)
4 Almost everyone has a story about **them**. (D)
5 … whether the people of Yap will resolve to ensure **their** survival. (E)

Substitution

We use substitution to avoid too much repetition and to help our writing flow well.
Is it going to be with us in another fifty years?
I think so.

2 Underline the correct substitute word.
1 He did not have dinner that night, *nor/neither/so/not* the night after.
2 Could I borrow your scissors? This *one/pair/lot/it* is broken.
3 A: Do you think that many people will buy these?
   B: Yes, I hope *that/not/so/will*.
4 They have very strict rules about their new products. All *these/them/this/those* that fail quality control tests are immediately destroyed.
5 Have you downloaded any new tunes lately? I'm tired of these old *some/many/ones/all*.
6 Could you lend me a bit of cash? If *yes/no/not/so*, don't worry, Karim will.

3 Complete the sentences with the correct form of the auxiliaries *have* or *do* or modals *will* or *shall*. Make the verb form negative where required.
1 A: Have you read the headlines today?
   B: No, I _____ yet, but I _____ .
2 I'm glad you told him exactly what you thought, because if you _____, I certainly _____ have.
3 A: Joel got a bit annoyed in the meeting and started shouting at everyone.
   B: He _____, did he? That's unlikely to win him many friends.
4 Analysts predict that the price of silver might drop. If it _____, I'd advise buying some.
5 A: I think I might buy this pair – they look pretty good on me.
   B: You _____ – you look great in that shade.

91

Unit 9 To the market

Ellipsis

Ellipsis means omitting words to avoid repetition.
A Are you coming tonight?
B Yes I am ~~coming tonight~~.

4 In sentences 1–3 decide which words to omit.
1 They asked me to send a covering letter with my CV, but I already had sent a covering letter.
2 There was a sudden increase in the sales of hats. I have no idea why there was a sudden increase in the sales of hats.
3 He always comes to meetings in the afternoon, but he hardly ever comes to meetings in the morning.

 Read more about reference, substitution and ellipsis in the Grammar Reference pages 128–129.

5 Use reference, substitution or ellipsis to reduce the repetition in the text below.

> **Shop 'til you drop**
>
> As most people find shopping a stressful experience, as a result more people are choosing to do their shopping online. In the period of seven years, from 2008–2015, official statistics showed that there was a 20% increase in online shopping among men. In the period from 2008–2015, official statistics showed that there was a 26% increase in online shopping among women. Although most people buy goods and services online, buying goods and services online only accounts for about 15% of all retailing.

As most people find shopping a stressful experience, more are ...

Reading and Use of English Part 1
Multiple-choice cloze

1 Work in pairs. What factor do you think is the most important to making a difference in peoples' lives – access to electricity, education or healthcare? Why?

2 For questions 1–8, read the text below and decide which answer (**A**, **B**, **C** or **D**) best fits each gap. There is an example at the beginning (**0**).

Crowdfunding change

Sudha Kheterpal, percussionist for the band *Faithless*, often looked out over crowds during concerts and wondered (**0**) ..C.. the energy she saw could be used somehow. This (**1**) ..... helped her to design a simple shaker, known as SPARK. The device, containing a magnet, wire coil and rechargeable battery, can be shaken to generate and (**2**) ..... energy. That energy can then be (**3**) ..... to power reading lights or charge mobile phones. The (**4**) ..... of this for areas of the developing world, where resources are often difficult to access, are considerable. Not only does it mean children will have (**5**) ..... light to use for doing homework, but also (**6**) ..... the need for kerosene lamps – making living environments safer.

After testing prototypes with a number of different communities in Kenya, Kheterpal (**7**) ..... a Kickstarter project to raise money for the development, production and distribution of the devices. After posting videos online, there was an enormous surge of interest. Backers from across Europe and the United States have committed (**8**) ..... to the project and Kheterpal's presentations at TED conferences have significantly boosted further investment.

0	A when	B where	C <u>whether</u>	D why
1	A belief	B notion	C concern	D plan
2	A store	B keep	C load	D stack
3	A recharged	B reduced	C reused	D released
4	A implications	B associations	C valuations	D suggestions
5	A numerous	B extensive	C sufficient	D widespread
6	A eliminates	B dismisses	C terminates	D fulfils
7	A activated	B launched	C motivated	D generated
8	A proceeds	B incomes	C funds	D shares

3 Do you think crowdfunding is a good idea? Why/Why not?

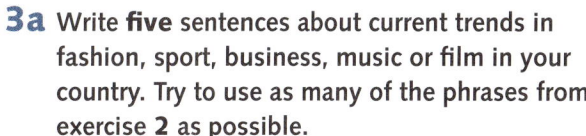

Vocabulary
Describing trends

1 Read these sentences from the text on page 92. What kind of change are they describing? Underline the phrases which show this.

  a After posting videos online, there was an enormous surge of interest.

  b Kheterpal's presentations at TED conferences have significantly boosted further investment.

2 When you discuss trends it is often important to talk about scale and speed. Underline the correct word in *italics* to complete the sentences.

  1 Initially there was *enormous/rapid* **interest** in the website, and the servers could barely cope. However, after a few months there was a *disastrous/steady* **decline** in visits, but nothing to worry about too much.

  2 Following a *significant/slight* **drop** in sales, the CEO resigned and a lot of people lost their jobs. Under new management, there have been *substantial/moderate* **signs of growth**, so the shareholders are feeling a bit more positive.

  3 Organisers of the event decided to cancel after news of *spectacular/disappointing* ticket **sales** was reported in the media.

  4 Despite its *rapid/moderate* **growth**, there have been *slight/substantial* **investments** made in his business throughout the year.

  5 Her *enormous/spectacular* **rise** to stardom coincided with a high-profile court case. News of this meant she experienced a(n) *slight/encouraging* **drop** in the number of roles she was offered, although she remains popular.

  6 We saw a *disappointing/substantial* **increase** in the number of digital album sales earlier this year. It surprised most analysts who thought there would be a downturn in the industry.

3a Write **five** sentences about current trends in fashion, sport, business, music or film in your country. Try to use as many of the phrases from exercise **2** as possible.

3b 💬 Work in pairs. Compare and discuss your sentences.

4a Underline the correct word in *italics* to complete the phrases in **bold**.

  1 According to some reports, crowdfunding films is set to **catch** *on/up* as a serious venture.

  2 Sales of smartphones **peaked** *at/in* a billion, before dropping away.

  3 Despite a poor first quarter, we're hoping that sales in clothing **pick** *on/up* soon.

  4 Over the last few weeks we've seen a **dip** *on/in* the average daytime temperature.

  5 House prices were extremely high around here. Fortunately they've started to **level** *off/up* now.

  6 Current sales are low, but we predict that they'll **catch** *up/out* **with** our competitors soon.

  7 Industry analysts had predicted that oil prices would suddenly **shoot** *out/up* after such a long downturn.

  8 The population of the city **remained stable** *between/among* 2008 and 2012.

4b Match the phrases in bold in exercise **4a** to a definition a–h.

  a to stop becoming more or less, and remain the same
  b to increase quickly by a large amount
  c a reduction in the amount or level of something
  d to become popular or fashionable
  e to stay more or less the same
  f to improve in order to reach the same standard or rate as someone or something
  g to reach the highest amount or level, before becoming lower
  h to improve

5 💬 Work in small groups. Use a range of words and phrases from this section to discuss the following topics.

- the number of people studying at university
- the way the internet has changed life
- the number of people who use smartphones

Unit 9 To the market

Writing Part 2
Proposal

1a Read the following Part 2 task and the model answer.

> Your city has been nominated to host a fundraising R'n'B concert for an international charity this summer. You have been asked to write a proposal for the concert organisers, stating why your city would be the best place to hold the event. Your proposal should provide information on transport, accommodation, possible venues and anything else you feel your city could offer.

Write your **proposal** in 220–260 words in an appropriate style.

> *Children's Foundation Fundraising Concert: Bari, Italy*
>
> *Introduction*
> Bari is a bustling city on the Adriatic coast and is used to dealing with streams of people from its busy port.
>
> *Transport*
> With its conveniently located port, train station and airport, the city is ideal for visitors arriving domestically and from overseas. The airport on the outskirts of the city has frequent shuttle buses and trains linking it to the city centre. The city is well-served by an extensive bus network and several taxi companies, which ¹*most of the time* are reasonably priced.
>
> *Accommodation*
> ²*It's evident that*, as a popular tourist destination, Bari has a wide selection of places to stay to suit every need. The winding streets of the scenic old town are home to more than 20 guesthouses. In the modern and sleek Poggiofranco district, there are several four- and five-star hotels complete with gyms and swimming pools.
>
> *Venues*
> The recently restored Petruzzelli Theatre, perfectly situated on the seafront, would, ³*I'm absolutely certain*, be a spectacular venue and would definitely provide the singers with amazing acoustics. Another option is the magnificently designed San Nicola stadium, which can seat over 55,000 people.
>
> *Food*
> ⁴*To be honest*, the food of southern Italy is second to none. Visitors can enjoy the freshly-caught seafood and world-famous pizzas in a variety of restaurants and cafés throughout the city.
>
> ⁵*In my opinion*, I do not think you could hope to find a more suitable and hospitable city to host your concert.

1b Replace the underlined phrases with an adverb/adverbial phrase with the same meaning from the box below. You will not need to use two of the words.

> apparently   undoubtedly   generally speaking
> frankly   obviously   personally   fortunately

2 Which of the features below are important to include in a proposal?
1. The subject of the proposal is clearly established.
2. The writing style is clear and concise.
3. Arguments for and against the proposal should be included.
4. Headings should be used to lead the reader.
5. Personal opinions should be clearly stated.
6. Recommendations should be given based on surveys the reader has carried out.
7. It should finish with a statement summarising the writer's position.
8. Recommendations and suggestions should be made based on facts.
9. Bullet points should be used to give examples of facilities, transport, etc.

3 Write your own answer to the task in exercise **1a**. The city you choose does not necessarily have to be your home town.

4 When you have finished your proposal, check that it includes the features you identified in exercise **2**.

Remember
- Plan what you are going to write.
- Write in a suitably formal or neutral style.
- Make polite recommendations and suggestions supported by facts.
- Use a range of persuasive language.

10 School of thought

Speaking
Learning

💬 Work in pairs. Read the following 'facts' about learning. Which do you think are true and which are false?

1 Multi-tasking makes you less productive. When you try to do lots of things at once, your brain jumps rapidly between tasks, resulting in decreased attention span.
2 Albert Einstein holds the record for the highest ever recorded IQ.
3 The youngest ever member of MENSA was ten years old.
4 The University of Oxford is the oldest in Europe.
5 The Japanese have the highest average IQ: 111.

Check your answers on page 112.

Listening Part 4
Multiple matching 🔊 2.13–2.17

1 💬 Discuss these questions with your partner.
   1 What are the most important things you have ever learnt?
   2 How did you learn these?
   3 Who, if anyone, taught you?
   4 What do you wish you had been taught when you were younger? Why?

2 🔊 You will hear five short extracts in which people are talking about different learning experiences.

3 💬 Work in pairs. Identify the learning experiences or methods presented in the listening. Discuss which you would benefit the most from.

4 💬 Discuss these questions with your partner. Give reasons.
   1 Would you ever consider teaching other people?
   2 What skills or support could you offer?
   3 Who would you like to teach?

While you listen you must complete both tasks.

TASK ONE
For questions **1–5**, choose from the list (**A–H**) what made the speaker want to learn.

A a need to earn more money
B a need for professional development
C the need for a challenge
D a requirement for study purposes
E a requirement for a visa application
F a sense of personal enjoyment
G the need to understand a culture
H a change in circumstances

Speaker 1 [1]
Speaker 2 [2]
Speaker 3 [3]
Speaker 4 [4]
Speaker 5 [5]

TASK TWO
For questions **6–10**, choose from the list (**A–H**) what the speaker mainly gained from the experience.

A They became more positive.
B They felt more in control.
C They grew closer to their community.
D They developed computing skills.
E They increased their earnings potential.
F They discovered a new ability.
G They became more interested in academic study.
H They achieved all their goals.

Speaker 1 [6]
Speaker 2 [7]
Speaker 3 [8]
Speaker 4 [9]
Speaker 5 [10]

Unit 10 School of thought

Vocabulary
Academic language

1 💬 Work in pairs. Do most young people in your country want to go to university? Why/Why not? Do you think that university education should be free or paid for by students?

2 Match the academic terms in **bold** to the correct definition a–g below.

1 She studied for a **degree** in the arts at the University of Bologna. Her *major* was European literature and her *minor* course was English language.
2 At the beginning of each *semester* a reading list and a **syllabus** will be posted on the department's web page. Use this to plan your research and identify which *lectures* to attend.
3 In the months before **graduation**, most *undergraduates* are sitting exams. For *postgraduates*, this is the time for writing up and correcting their thesis.
4 If you have any questions regarding a particular area of your course, speak to your **tutor**. Every *term* you'll have the opportunity to discuss other issues with a Director of Studies.
5 At the end of the **module** on new materials, we had a quick test to make sure we could identify the qualities of each. We discussed the results in the following *seminar*.
6 She did a **diploma** in engineering at the local college. While she enjoyed the practical work, she wasn't too impressed with the quality of the *lecturers*.
7 You need to send your application letter and original examination certificates to the **Faculty** of Engineering. They'll let you know if you have the grades to enrol on a *Bachelor's* or *Master's* course.

a the act of receiving your qualification after finishing your studies
b a department or group of departments at a university
c one of the separate units of a course of study
d a course of study, often in a vocational subject
e a teacher in a college or university
f the qualification that you get after completing the course
g a list of the main subjects in a course of study

3 💬 Work in pairs. Take turns explaining the difference between the pairs of terms below.

- Bachelor's/Master's
- undergraduate/postgraduate
- lecturer/tutor
- major/minor
- lecture/seminar
- semester/term

Speaking Part 2
Long turn

1 💬 Look at the photographs. They show **different ways of learning**.

Student A: Compare **two** of the pictures, and say **why the people might enjoy learning in this way**, and **what difficulties they may face**.
Student B: When your partner has finished, answer the following question.
Which way of learning do you think would be the most stressful?

- Why might the people enjoy learning in this way?
- What difficulties might they face?

2 💬 Now change roles. Look at the photographs on page 113 and follow the instructions.

Writing Part 2
Report

1 💬 Read the following Part 2 task and identify the examples that the writer uses for each bullet point in the sample answer.

> An international research group is carrying out a study on educational opportunities for young people aged 5–16 around the world. You have been asked by the group to write a report about your local area, including the following points:
> - current types of educational opportunities available to young people in your area
> - some of the challenges faced by young people seeking educational opportunities
> - possible future developments in education for young people in your area.
>
> Write your **report**.

Introduction

This is my report about educational opportunities for young people around the world. Here, the focus is on my country. I will talk about current opportunities, some challenges facing young people and possible future developments.

Current opportunities

At the moment, there are many different opportunities for young people. The government pays for every child to be educated from the age of five until they are sixteen years old. This means that they have free access to school. On top of this, there are lots of private schools where they can study other subjects in their own time.

Challenges facing students

A significant issue that causes problems for many students is cost. Although there are private language schools and colleges where students can do many different things, these are increasingly expensive. This means that not everybody can get the education they want. By reducing costs this would be better. Another challenge is that classes are so busy. There are far too many people in each school.

Future developments in education

Because classes are busy and expensive, I would strongly recommend that more is done online. There are many very good learning platforms where students can get the best education. If more people are using this technology for study, then classes will be smaller. Also the students will learn a range of digital skills which can be used in their future working lives.

In conclusion, I want to draw your attention to the fact that with additional fundings provided, there could be greater educational opportunities in this country and others.

---

2 💬 Work in pairs. Read the sample answer again and discuss the following questions. Give examples from the report to justify your answers.
1. Have all the bullet points been covered?
2. Is the information relevant?
3. Does the report use evaluative language?
4. Are the paragraphs and headings clear?
5. Does the introduction use different wording from the task itself?
6. Does the report make clear recommendations?
7. Does the conclusion summarise the writer's viewpoint and make a recommendation?
8. Is the register appropriate?

3 Write your own **report** for the task in exercise **1**. You should write **220–260** words.

Unit 10 School of thought

Vocabulary and Speaking
The mind and brain

1a 💬 Work in pairs. Look at the images below. Answer the questions, then try to explain what you think is happening.

1 Are the circles the same colour?

2 Do you see anything where the white lines meet?

3 Is there a difference in size between the orange circles?

1b Match each image to an explanation on page 112.

2a Complete each phrase in **bold** with the correct form of *think*.

1 **Am I right in _____ that** you studied Philosophy at university?
2 **I've _____ long and hard about it**, and I've decided to apply for the job.
3 **I wasn't _____ straight**, and I said some things I didn't really mean.
4 **I _____ very highly of** Paul – he's worked hard to set up his own business.
5 She's incredibly driven – she'd **_____ nothing of** working through the night to get something done.
6 It might just be **wishful _____** but I reckon that things are going to start getting better round here.
7 I said 'yes' to helping Sandra with the talent show but I heard it goes on for hours so now I'm **having second _____ about** it.
8 I'd **_____ twice about it** if I were you, I've read some pretty bad reviews of that resort.

2b 💬 Write your own sentences using the phrases in **bold** from exercise **2a**. Then discuss them with your partner.

3 <u>Underline</u> the correct word in *italics* to complete sentences 1–6.

1 Although they work as a team, she's definitely **the** *brains/minds* **behind** the operation.
2 I have **half a** *sense/mind* to tell them that I won't be coming back – I can't stand this place.
3 A: If you need **a bit of** *head/thought* **space**, you can always come and stay with us for a while.
   B: Thanks, I'll bear that in *mind/brain*.
4 You've studied this before, haven't you? **Do you** *mind/worry* if I **pick your** *ideas/brains* for a moment and ask you a few questions?
5 It's about time that someone started **talking** some *sense/knowledge* **about** the issue.
6 Although he's **relatively** *mindful/unknown* in this country, he's considered **a leading** *intellect/head* on brain development.

4a 💬 Work in pairs. Discuss the following subjects using phrases from exercises **2** and **3**.
- work
- study
- free-time
- travel

4b 💬 Work with a new partner. You should both share what you discussed with your previous partners in **4a**. You should say whether you agree or disagree with the opinions shared and why.

Reading and Use of English Part 6
Cross-text multiple matching

1 💬 The text is about a talk on the power of visualisation. Do you think that imagining yourself being successful can help you to achieve your ambitions? Why/Why not?

2 You are going to read four commentaries on a talk about the power of visualisation. For questions 1–4, choose from extracts **A–D**. The extracts may be chosen more than once.

IMAGING YOUR WAY TO SUCCESS

Four writers comment on sports psychologist Thomas O'Rourke's talk.

A Thomas O'Rourke brought his usual brand of warmth and humour to the packed-out Alexandria Expo Hall. As he paced around the stage, the key theme of his talk emerged: anyone with a small scrap of talent can be successful, they just have to picture it. It is certainly a compelling thought. O'Rourke described how the day before a match, Wayne Rooney visualises himself scoring goals – the feel of the ball on his foot, the smell of the grass, the roar of the crowd. Using vivid imagery helps Rooney to feel confident and primes his muscles through neural impulses. He was just one of many sportspeople mentioned during the talk and it enthralled the audience. Less engaging was O'Rourke's own melancholy tale, which seemed somewhat insincere, about how he mended a friendship on the rocks. To the audience largely made up of personal trainers, aspiring athletes and journalists, the science seemed sound enough but it all seems rather fanciful – surely no psychologist worth their salt would give any validation to these theories.

B As I watched Thomas O'Rourke hold forth on the power of visualisation, the reason he is such a leading light in the field of psychology became very clear. A natural raconteur, he soon had the audience eating out of the palm of his hand. By the end of the talk, everyone was feeling as passionate about the subject as he evidently is. For those who are quick to dismiss him as a psych-celebrity, they are far off the mark. O'Rourke has certainly compiled a significant amount of research in the field. The work he has personally carried out with tennis players is remarkable – he found that the muscle patterns produced when just imagining that you are hitting a forehand were identical to actually doing it. O'Rourke's research could make real changes when the doubters in the field come round to this alternative way of thinking.

C Weak science and celebrity stories made for a rather confused lecture on what our mothers have been telling us for years – believe and you can achieve. Employing a mixture of charm and the odd smattering of statistics, Thomas O'Rourke tried to convince the audience that he had come up with some revolutionary idea by recycling psychology fundamentals. Frankly, anyone with the vaguest of links with this field of study would have seen straight through it. As far as the value of visualisation goes, I'm not about to go and craft myself a 'vision board' but I can see how 'visually rehearsing' a business meeting could help to improve body language, reduce anxiety and help build self-esteem – I think everyone could get on side with that, but is it really necessary for O'Rourke to point this out to us in an hour-long sermon?

D Thomas O'Rourke has the smug expression of a man who is accustomed to being adored. This, coupled with name-dropping celebrity clients, whose successes he rather arrogantly attributes to himself, would normally have me running for the hills. However, once all the showmanship is wiped away, the essence of what he is saying is incredibly insightful. And despite my initial impressions, I was genuinely moved by his story of how the power of thought helped him to resolve a quarrel with an old school pal. He has clearly spent hours studying the value of visualisation and doesn't claim that if you just imagine having a physique like the latest action-hero, you can have it. Rather he sets out to prove that it can give training and athletes in competitions that extra boost. Judging from the enthusiastic response from the psychologists in the audience, it seems that O'Rourke may have hit upon something that could change the way we think forever.

Which writer

has a contrasting opinion to the others in regard to O'Rourke's style of presenting? ☐ 1

shares writer A's opinion on how much attention other psychologists would pay O'Rourke's findings? ☐ 2

expresses a different opinion to writer D on O'Rourke's use of a personal anecdote? ☐ 3

takes a similar view to writer A on the effect that O'Rourke had on his audience? ☐ 4

3 💬 **Discuss these questions in small groups.**
1 Have you or anyone you know ever used the methods of visualisation or growth mindset mentioned in the texts? If so, did they work?
2 Some people say that intelligence is best measured by academic success. Do you agree? Why/Why not?
3 What do you believe is the main reason behind people becoming very successful? Is it luck, hard work, networking, natural talent, or something else? Give reasons for your answer.

Unit 10 School of thought

Language focus 1
Emphasis with cleft sentences

Look at the following sentence.
I am interested in the effects of visualisation on success.

There are many ways that we could emphasise part of this sentence. The following structures are quite common:

All What The thing Something	*I am interested in is the effects of visualisation on success.*
It's	*the effects of visualisation on success I am interested in.*

1a Find the underlined sentences in the reading texts which are similar to **1–4** below.

1. … what became very clear is the reason he is such a leading light in the field of psychology. (B)
2. … all they need to do is picture it. (A)
3. It was the story of how the power of thought helped him to resolve a quarrel with an old school pal that I was genuinely moved by. (D)
4. It's only when the doubters in the field come round to this alternative way of thinking that O'Rourke's research could make real changes. (B)

1b Work in pairs. Compare each sentence in exercise **1a** to its equivalent in the reading text. Which part of the sentence is emphasised in each case?

1c Complete the explanations **A–C** with one item from the box.

> a certain time   a noun   the only thing that
> a prepositional phrase   an action/actions

A *What* can be used to emphasise _____:
   What I really need is to go home early, have a bath and then go to sleep.
   or _____.
   What I find really irritating is overcooked vegetables.

B *All* can be used instead of *What*, meaning _____:
   All I want for my birthday is a new bike.

C *It* can be used to emphasise _____:
   It was in New York that he made a name for himself.
   or with *when* to emphasise _____:
   It was only when I saw him again that I realised how much I missed him.

⚙ Read more about cleft sentences in the Grammar Reference page 129.

2 Rephrase the sentences making them more emphatic. More than one answer may be possible.
1. A university degree can change the course of your life.
2. Her lectures always confuse me.
3. First you have to decide on your goals in life.
4. You should consider taking an IQ test.
5. Their lack of concentration annoys me the most.
6. The government should help out with the cost of studies.

3 💬 Work in pairs. Complete the following sentences with your own ideas, and then discuss them further.
1. What I can't stand about …
2. All I really want is …
3. The thing that annoys me the most is …
4. It's only when … that …
5. It surprises me that …
6. All I did last weekend was …

Speaking Part 3
Collaborative task

1a 💬 Work in pairs. Here are some factors which influence happiness and a question for you to discuss. Talk to each other about how these factors influence happiness.

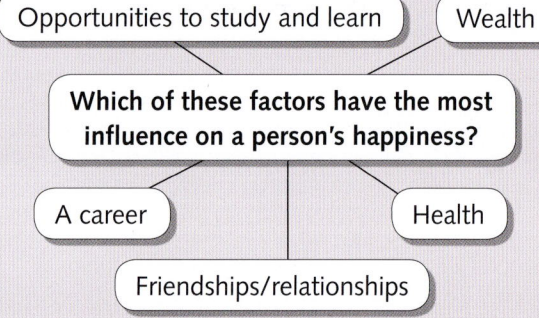

1b 💬 Now discuss and decide which two factors are the most important.

Useful language

Speculate:
It's most likely that …
I think that on the whole people would …

Compare and contrast:
Compared to X, Y has greater significance as …
I'd consider this factor more important than the others because …

Concluding the discussion:
So, the most important factor would seem to be …
What we could say is that …

2 💬 Now do the Speaking Part 4 task on page 114.

Listening Part 2
Sentence completion 🔊 2.18

1 💬 Look at photographs **a** and **b** and discuss the following questions with your partner.
1. Which environment would you have preferred to learn in as a child? Why?
2. Which environment would you prefer to teach in? Why?

2 🔊 You will hear an education correspondent called Lesley Rankin talking about approaches to improve learning environments. For questions **1–8**, complete the sentences with a word or short phrase.

WHERE AND HOW WE LEARN

Lesley notes that many families in cities do not possess the equipment that
(1) .... demands.

Lesley mentions research which points out that
(2) .... can have a negative effect on achievement.

Conventional classroom design enables teachers to survey the class and to
(3) ....

In classrooms with more cooperative layouts, there are increases in engagement and
(4) ....

Lesley describes the ability to reach solutions with others as an **(5)** .... for being successful in life.

Many schools are promoting
(6) .... as role models for their learners.

Lesley highlights how business people can influence students' attitudes towards
(7) .... in the classroom.

Lesley identifies a project called
(8) '..' as an initiative which assists students in preparing for the future.

3 💬 Discuss these questions with your partner.
1. Do you think that it's important for students to meet role models from the working world? Why/Why not?
2. Is there someone you would like to learn from? Who? Why?

4 💬 Work in small groups. Discuss how you would design a perfect learning environment. Think about the following points.
- the setting
- the facilities
- the interior design
- the staff

Present your ideas to the whole class.

> I think I'd have lots of green areas in the campus, as they tend to be relaxing. The less stressed you feel, the more you can achieve.

> True, but you'd want to make sure that there was sufficient space for sports facilities, too.

Unit 10 School of thought

Language focus 2
Participle clauses 🔊 2.19

1a 🔊 **Listen to the following three extracts from the listening and complete the gaps.**
1. _____ teachers are faced with growing class numbers, they have to address this issue.
2. … children _____ are studying in low-sensory environments tend to be able to focus better on tasks.
3. _____ one particular school had made this change to more collaborative designs, they saw an increase in levels of engagement …

Check your ideas in the listening script on page 151.

1b Now look at how the sentences are expressed using participle clauses. What changes have been made?
1. Faced with growing class numbers, teachers have to address this issue.
2. Children studying in low-sensory environments tend to be able to focus better on tasks.
3. Having made this change to more collaborative designs, one particular school saw an increase in levels of engagement.

2 Underline the correct word in *italics* to complete the information about participle clauses. Look back at the sentences in exercise **1b** to help you.

Participle clauses are clauses which *begin/end* with a present or past participle verb. They help a text to become concise and coherent, and are most often used in *spoken/written* English. Participle clauses can be used instead of relative clauses and pronouns, and to replace certain *conjunctions/determiners*.

⚙ **Read more about participle clauses in the Grammar Reference page 129.**

3 Rewrite sentences **1–10** using a participle clause.
1. They realised that there was nobody home, so they left the parcel with a neighbour. _____
2. I opened the cupboard and found that it was empty. _____
3. The children shrieked and screamed as they jumped into the pool. _____
4. She had acquired the business as a young woman, so she was reluctant to sell. _____
5. He was criticised by his boss, then asked to resign. _____
6. We didn't want to wake the children, so we left the house quietly. _____
7. If you look after it carefully, this laptop should last until you leave university. _____
8. I didn't know how I was going to get home because I had no money and no phone. _____
9. The photo, which was taken a long time ago, was of my grandfather and his best friend. _____
10. As Danny drove home, he realised he'd left his wallet at the shop. _____

4 Read the statements, then complete the responses with the correct form of the words from the box.

| consider judge speak take |

1. Based on our current data, at least 75% of students stated a preference for studying science over other subjects.
   Generally _____ , the students seemed to be more interested in sciences than the arts.
2. Well, I know it's getting a lot of press these days, but I find it all a bit tedious.
   _____ **from your response**, I take it that you're not really interested in neurology.
3. Although most people were happy to hand over personal data, many were unsure of how it would be used.
   _____ **a broad view**, I can see where there might be problems for some participants.
4. The research project cost the university €1.5 million, but has encouraged the government to fund a new department for research and development.
   All things _____ , the research has definitely been worth the investment.

5 💬 Write your own sentences about the following topics using the fixed expressions in **bold** from exercise 4. Share your sentence with your partner, and discuss the issues you raise.
- the importance of science to society
- the role natural talent plays in success
- the best ways to learn new skills
- the decision of whether to go to university

Word formation
Affixes review

1 Look at this extract.

... members of the public compete against one another ...

What nouns, verbs and adjectives can be formed from the word *compete*?

2a Read sentences **1–6** and decide which type of word is needed – noun, verb or adjective. Identify whether the missing word is singular or plural.

1. He's an incredibly _____ young man who is always at the library and will probably go on to do well at university.
2. Not only were the results of the experiment proven to be wrong, but the whole research project was considered _____.
3. Perhaps one of the most significant _____ of their time in charge was that pass rates declined so much.
4. Travelling around the world really helped to _____ my mind.
5. The lecturers at the university are known for their _____ and expertise.
6. The coach encourages the players to _____ themselves achieving their goal.

2b Complete each sentence in exercise **2a** with the correct form of a word from the box.

| dedicate fail broad |
| study science visual |

Reading and Use of English Part 2
Open cloze

1 💬 Discuss these questions with a partner.
1. What kind of programmes are currently popular on TV in your country?
2. Why are so many people interested in showing off their abilities on TV/online?

2 Skim read the text, ignoring the gaps. Were any of your ideas from exercise **1** mentioned?

Remember
- Read the text quickly for gist.
- Read each sentence again carefully. Look at the words before and after the gap.
- Think about verbs with dependent prepositions, fixed expressions and collocations.

3 For questions **1–8**, read the text and think of the word which best fits each gap. Write only **one** word in each gap. There is an example at the beginning (0).

Talents shown?

Many people have forecast the end of our interest (0) ..*IN*.. low-cost TV talent shows, yet they doggedly refuse to disappear. While it has been suggested that the format of programmes (1) .... see members of the public compete against one another as they bake, dance, sing or sew are becoming tired, their popularity and viewing figures continually grow. The question is, why are they so popular? (2) .... it be that in times of economic downturn big budget programming is (3) .... appealing to broadcasters, or is there (4) .... reason entirely?

More positive assessments tend to focus upon the inherent human interest of the format. It seems that most of us would (5) .... watch people that we can identify with completing challenges than long dramas. Evidently (6) .... is due to the fact that we subconsciously identify with contestants like us – eliciting a feeling that (7) .... they can do it, so could I. More importantly perhaps, the programmes provide a communal viewing experience. That's all (8) .... rare in our dislocated world of downloads and TV on demand.

4 💬 Work in small groups. Think of your own idea for a TV programme which shows off people's skills and abilities. How would it be organised?

103

Review | Units 9 and 10

Reading and Use of English Part 4
Key word transformation

For questions **1–6**, complete the second sentence so that it has a similar meaning to the first sentence, using the word given. **Do not change the word given.** You must use between **three** and **six** words, including the word given.

1. Christopher has always admired Joanna as an academic.

   HIGHLY

   Joanna has always .... as an academic.

2. I hate it when people don't tell me the truth, so I quit my job.

   STAND

   I .... the truth, so I quit my job.

3. Once I looked carefully at the optical illusion, I managed to work it out.

   ONLY

   It .... looked carefully at the optical illusion that I managed to work it out.

4. 'You should stop your children spending so much time online,' Kate's brother said.

   LET

   Kate's brother advised her .... so much time online.

5. She took the best course of action for her, and applied for university.

   DID

   What she ...., which was the best course of action for her.

6. Hassam could still get the job – I don't know why he's being so pessimistic.

   EVERY

   Hassam still .... the job – I don't know why he's being so pessimistic.

Reading and Use of English Part 3
Word formation

For questions **1–8**, read the text below. Use the word given in capitals at the end of some of the lines to form a word that fits in the gap **in the same line**. There is an example at the beginning (**0**).

Brain training

As we get older, our mental processes decline. This is a fact of life. In recent years, there have been a number of claims of variable **(0)** _ACCURACY_ that brain-training games are the answer to this seemingly **(1)** .... state of affairs. **(2)** .... claim that by doing word and picture puzzles people will see measurable results in their mental ability. Most experts believe that while this isn't **(3)** .... true, training your brain can bring some benefits.

A five-minute-a-day game that holds off the effects of old age seems an **(4)** .... proposition, but the fact is that goal remains elusive. There is, however, some suggestion in recent neurobiological studies that **(5)** .... creative tasks can assist in keeping the mind active. The key seems to be practising **(6)** .... yet meaningful tasks.

Over the last few years, experts have had to **(7)** .... that learning a language or a musical instrument can help us to protect minds affected by age or stress. As evidence for this grows, perhaps taking up a new hobby will become more desirable and the brain games offered by big business less **(8)** .... in keeping our minds more active.

ACCURATE

AVOID
DESIGN

NECESSARY

ATTRACT

TAKE

REPEAT

KNOW

INFLUENCE

Vocabulary

1 Match the sentence beginnings **1–7** with the sentence endings **a–g**.

1 Retailers have been disappointed with recent sales of sandals, but things are set to pick
2 After Angelina was seen wearing one of their dresses, they saw a peak
3 Although there were a number of warning signs, people were caught
4 This time last year, these were a 'must have' item, but we've seen a steady
5 Since the start of the year there has been a slight
6 Sales of smartphones have remained fairly stable
7 The housing market has been extremely volatile, but prices have been levelling

a out over the last few months so now could be a good time to buy.
b decline in sales over the last six months.
c out by the sudden fall in the price of oil.
d in both in-store and online sales.
e up soon as the weather improves.
f between 2015 and the present.
g drop in the amount spent on clothing and technology.

2 Complete each gap with the correct form of a phrase from the box.

| right in thinking   think long and hard |
| think straight   think twice |
| have second thoughts   think nothing of |

1 He didn't _____ about going to study there – it isn't an expensive place to live and the university has a great reputation.
2 I've _____ about your offer, and I've decided that yes, I will sell you my share of the business.
3 Am I _____ that the dress she's wearing was designed by Sally LaPointe? It's fabulous.
4 They've heard so many different opinions on the matter that they can barely _____ .
5 I'm afraid she's _____ about going abroad this summer – she thinks it might be better to stay here and work.
6 He's the type of person, who'd _____ buying a €1000 watch.

Language focus

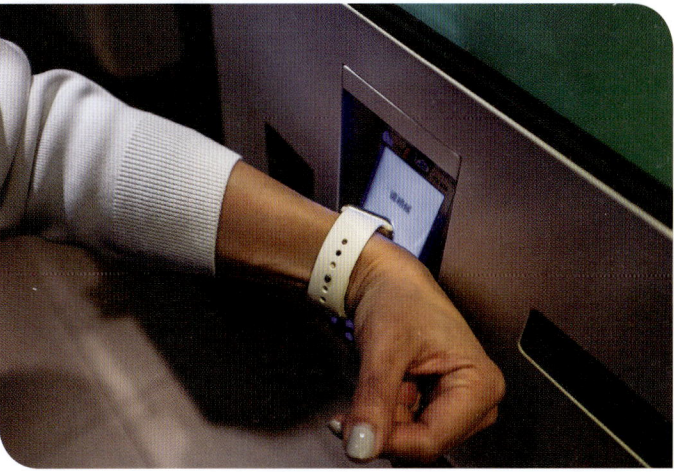

1 Complete each gap with the best option from the box.

| this   that   it   these   those |

1 The Nymi Band is a wearable device which checks the wearer's heartbeat to verify the user's ID. _____ can then be used to make payments or to unlock doors and even devices like smartphones and laptops. _____ is secure because throughout the day _____ tracks the user's unique electrical heart signal. _____ approaches may seem like science fiction, but technology like _____ is set to change the way we do business forever.
2 The Yen is the official currency of Japan. _____ is the third most traded currency in the foreign exchange market. _____ is because _____ tends to keep its value well. The Yen has lost value in the past, but _____ times seem to be over.
3 Guerilla marketing is an advertising concept for businesses to promote their products creatively. Companies often work with artists to make sure _____ process works effectively. While guerrilla marketing is quite a new phenomenon, _____ is becoming increasingly popular as _____ who have used _____ have attracted a lot of media attention.

2 Read the sentences below. Decide which words have been replaced or omitted from each sentence.

0 You might think that this marks a huge change for the way we shop but it doesn't.
    ... but it doesn't <u>mark a huge change for the way we shop</u>.
1 There have been lots of different suggestions for new currencies – too many for me to mention.
2 Will the rise of Bitcoin mean an end to traditional banking? I don't think so.
3 Some people say that the technology can't be trusted but it can.
4 Of all the new ways of paying there aren't many as good as this one.
5 Are these systems any more effective than others we use?

105

Additional Material

Unit 1

Speaking Part 2: Long turn Exercise 2 Page 8

💬 Look at the photographs below. They show **people in challenging situations**.

Student A: Compare **two** of the pictures, and say **why you think the people decided to take up these challenges**, and **what problems they could encounter**.

Student B: When your partner has finished, answer the following question.
Which challenge would you find the most difficult to do?

- Why do you think these people decided to take up these challenges?
- What problems could they encounter?

Unit 1
Speaking Part 1: Interview Exercise 3 Page 10

THE FUTURE
1. What are you most looking forward to doing in the next six months?
2. How do you expect your life will be different in a year? Five years? Ten years?
3. What do you think will be the biggest challenge you will face in the future?
4. Do you usually make plans for holidays or weekends well in advance?
5. What are your ambitions for the years ahead?

ENGLISH
1. How long have you been learning English?
2. What motivated you to begin learning English?
3. What do you find most difficult about learning English?
4. What has been your most rewarding English learning experience so far?
5. What do you enjoy most about learning English?

LEISURE TIME
1. How do you usually relax after a hard day working or studying?
2. What do you most enjoy doing in your free time?
3. Do you prefer to spend your free time alone or with others? Why?
4. How much time on average do you spend doing leisure activities?
5. In your free time, do you prefer physical activities or other ways of relaxing? Why?

HOUSE AND HOME
1. If you could live anywhere in the world, where would you live and why?
2. What is your favourite place in your home? What makes it special?
3. What do you like most about living where you do?
4. What do you do on a typical day in your home?
5. What would your ideal home be like?

TRAVEL AND HOLIDAYS
1. If you could go anywhere in the world, where would you most like to visit? Why?
2. Who do you prefer to go on holiday with? Why?
3. What are your favourite holiday activities? What do you like about them?
4. What advice would you give to someone visiting the place where you live?
5. What is the most memorable travel experience you have ever had?

Unit 6
Speaking Part 4: Discussion Exercise 2 Page 57

💬 Discuss the following questions with your partner.

1. What do you think will be the biggest change you will see in your lifetime?
2. Some people think we should all work together to solve global problems. What do you think?
3. What do you think is the best way to bring world issues to people's attention? Why?
4. Is it important to donate money to international charities? Why/Why not?
5. Do you think that rich people have an obligation to use their money to solve global problems? Why/Why not?
6. Many people think that some of the difficult issues and problems we face today cannot be solved. What do you think?

Additional Material

Unit 3

Speaking Part 2: Long turn Exercise 2 Page 33

💬 Look at the photographs below. They show **people travelling overseas in different ways**.

Student A: Compare **two** of the pictures, and say **what the benefits of travelling in this way could be**, and **how the people might be feeling**.

Student B: When your partner has finished, answer the following question.
Which way of travelling do you think would be the most enjoyable?

- What are the benefits of travelling in this way?
- How might the people be feeling?

108

Unit 4

Speaking Part 4: Discussion Exercise 2 Page 42

💬 **Discuss the following questions with your partner.**

1. Is it important that you know the people who live around you? Why/Why not?
2. Do you think that people have a responsibility to build or live in homes which are environmentally friendly? Why/Why not?
3. What might be the advantages and disadvantages of living alone?
4. How important do you think it is for people to be able to own their own home?
5. Some people say that there is nothing more important in life than a safe, secure home. What do you think?
6. What do you think is the best way to solve the shortage of affordable housing in cities?

Useful language

- In a discussion, you should encourage other people to give their opinions.
  Use expressions like:
  Do you have any thoughts on that?
  What's your reaction to that?
  Where do you stand on …?
  What's your view on this/that?
  What do you reckon?
  Does that make sense to you?
- You can also ask for clarification if you would like something explained in more detail.
  Use expressions like:
  What do you mean by/when you say …?
  Can you explain what you mean by …?
  Could you give me an example?

Unit 7

Speaking Part 4: Discussion Exercise 3 Page 68

💬 **Discuss the following questions with your partner.**

1. Are you optimistic or pessimistic about the future of our planet? Why?
2. How is your own way of life affected by environmental issues?
3. Whose responsibility do you think it is to find ways to address concerns about the environment?
4. Do you think it's a good idea to educate children from an early age about environmental issues? Why/Why not?
5. Some people urge us to give up modern urban lifestyles and return to a simpler way of life. How do you personally feel about this?
6. It is said that every journey begins with the first step. How do you think this idea can be interpreted with regards to the environment?

Unit 5

Speaking Part 2: Long turn Exercise 3 Page 48

💬 Look at the photographs below. They show **people taking part in different sporting activities**.

Student A: Compare **two** of the pictures, and say **what might have attracted the people to this type of activity**, and **what risks they might face whilst doing the activity**.

Student B: When your partner has finished, answer the following question.
Which of the sporting activities in the photographs do you think is the most dangerous?

- What might have attracted the people to this type of activity?
- What risks might they face while doing the activity?

Unit 8

Speaking Part 2: Long turn Exercise 3 Page 81

💬 Look at the photographs below. They show **people communicating in different ways**.

Student A: Compare **two** of the pictures and say **why the people might be communicating in this way**, and **which situation people might find most stressful**.

Student B: When your partner has finished, answer the following question.
In which situation is body language the most important?

- Why might the people be choosing to express themselves in this way?
- Which situation might people find most stressful?

Unit 9

Speaking Part 4: Discussion Exercise 3 Page 86

💬 Discuss the following questions with your partner.

1 In what ways do you think advertising affects people's attitudes and behaviour?
2 Do you think that advertising could ever be considered an art form? Why/Why not?
3 Some people think that increased consumerism can lead to a country having higher standards of living. What's your opinion?
4 Some people think it's important to consider the environment when buying new products. What's your opinion?
5 What kind of products make you happy when you buy them? Why?
6 Do you think people are more materialistic now than they were in the past?

Useful language

Ask for clarification:
What makes you say/think that?
So, what you're saying is (that) [+ rephrase]?
I'm not sure that I understand. Are you saying (that) [+ rephrase]?

Agreeing and Disagreeing:
I couldn't agree with you more.
We clearly have completely different views about this subject.
Whilst I think [partner's name] has a point, I'm of the opinion that …

Fillers to avoid hesitation:
… what do you call it …   *The thing is …*
Well … you know …   *How shall I put it?*
Basically, what I'm trying to say is …   *Let's put it this way …*

Unit 10

Speaking: Learning Page 95

1 Many studies suggest that this is true. Including a study carried out at Stanford University.
2 False. Many people have measured higher than Einstein's IQ of 160. In fact some people's IQs have been recorded at over 200.
3 False. Currently, the youngest member to be accepted was two years old.
4 False. The University of Oxford was established around 1096. The University of Bologna was founded in 1088, making it the oldest in Europe.
5 False. Japan currently comes in third place with an average of 105. Both Singapore and Hong Kong score higher with an average IQ of 108.

Unit 10

Vocabulary and Speaking: The mind and brain Exercise 1b Page 98

a *Hermann grid illusion*
The illusion occurs as people see grey blobs at the intersections of a pale grid on a black background. The grey blobs disappear if you look directly at an intersection. This is caused as light receptors in the eye affect neighbouring ones, making something which isn't there seem to appear.

b *Bezold effect*
This illusion occurs as colours are perceived as being different depending upon the colour next to them. A famous example of this was the internet meme *The Dress*.

c *Ebbinghaus illusion*
This effect is created by a sense of size distortion. The brain is tricked by the size of surrounding objects, or the distance between them.

Unit 10

Speaking Part 2: Long turn Exercise 2 Page 97

💬 Look at the photographs below. They show **people in different learning environments**.

Student A: Compare **two** of the pictures, and say **what some of the challenges might be for teaching and learning in each context**.

Student B: When your partner has finished, answer the following question.
Which of the ways of learning did you prefer as a child? Why?

- What might the challenges be for teaching?
- What might the challenges be for learning?

Unit 10

Speaking Part 4: Discussion Exercise 2 Page 100

💬 Discuss the following questions with your partner.

1 Which subjects do you think are the most important to study at school? Why?
2 What kind of things can younger people learn about life from talking to older people?
3 Some people say that each generation is less intelligent than the one before. Do you agree?
4 Do you think that it is important to learn new skills? Why/Why not?
5 Do you think that university graduates should be paid more than other people at work? Why/Why not?
6 Some people feel that modern technology has had a negative impact on our intelligence and ability to solve problems. What do you think?

Useful language

- In a discussion you should encourage other people to give their opinions.
  Use expressions like:
  What's your view on that?
  Would you tend to agree with that?
  Do you have a different perspective on that?
- You can also ask for clarification or confirmation of ideas. Use expressions like:
  So, in your opinion (+ briefly paraphrase other speaker's view) *is that right?*
  So, let me get this clear, you think (+ briefly paraphrase other speaker's view)
  Basically, what you're saying is (+ briefly paraphrase other speaker's view).
- Sometimes you might need a bit of time to think about what you're going to say.
  Use expressions like the following to help buy you some time:
  That's a really interesting question.
  I've never really thought about that before.
  Well ... let me see ...
  To be honest ...

Grammar Reference

UNIT 1

Present and past perfect – simple and continuous

Present perfect simple

The present perfect simple is used to talk about:

- recent past events with an effect in the present.
  I can't drive you to the airport. I've sold my car.
- events which started in the past and continue in the present.
  My sister's worked in the fashion industry for the past fifteen years.
- unfinished events, which occurred in a time period that is still in progress. We often use time phrases like *this morning/today/this week/this year*.
  The phone has rung at least nine times this morning.
- situations or events that started in the past and continue up to the time of speaking, and may or may not continue in the future. We often use stative verbs with *for* with the time period already elapsed or *since* with the starting point of the time period.
  We've lived in New York since 1994.
  I've known Richard for nearly sixteen years.
- events that happened some time in the past, but the exact time is not important.
  John and Kelly have visited Paris several times.
- the first/second/third, etc. time an event has happened.
  It's the first time I've tried eating with chopsticks.
- experiences with a reference to a superlative.
  Istanbul is the most fascinating city I've ever been to.
- two situations or events, which have existed or happened together.
  I haven't been promoted since I've worked for this company.

Present perfect continuous

The present perfect continuous is used:

- with action verbs, but not stative verbs.
  I've been writing my report all morning.
  NOT *I've been liking spicy foods all my life.*
- to emphasise the duration of an action which started in the past and is continuing in the present. We use *for* to talk about the time period already elapsed or *since* to talk about the starting point of the time period.
  Jake's been doing experiments in his lab for twelve hours.
  He's been working non-stop since he got in.

- to suggest that a situation or activity is temporary.
  My colleague is off sick, so I've been helping her team with their project.
- to focus on a situation or activity that has been repeated. If we say how many times the repeated situation or activity happened, however, we must use the present perfect simple, not the present perfect continuous.
  The phone's been ringing all morning. The phone's rung at least nine times.
  NOT *The phone's been ringing at least nine times.*
- to suggest that an activity is incomplete.
  I've been replying to emails all afternoon.

In contrast, when we emphasise that the activity has been completed, we use the present perfect simple.
  I've replied to about thirty emails this afternoon.

Present perfect simple and continuous

Both the present perfect simple and present perfect continuous can be used to talk about the present effect of a past event.
  I can't play tennis this weekend, I've hurt my shoulder.
  I'm really tired. I've been working all day.

Past perfect simple

The past perfect simple is used:

- to show that a past event or situation occurred before another past event or situation.
  They had driven all night, so when they arrived they were exhausted.
- to talk about situations which started in the past and continued up to a later point in the past.
  Mount Tambora had been dormant for centuries when it unexpectedly erupted in 1815.
- the first/second/third, etc. time an event in the past happened.
  I had my wallet stolen while I was at the market. It was the second time that had happened to me.
- with time linkers such as *when/after/before/by the time/as soon as/until* to emphasise the order of events in the past. However, when the order of events is clear, or when events follow on from one another, we can use the past simple.
  By the time they reached their destination, they had walked fourteen miles.
  As soon as he walked into the living room, everyone jumped up and shouted 'Surprise!'

Past perfect continuous

The past perfect continuous is used to:
- emphasise the duration of an action up to another time in the past. The activity may have finished at that time or continued afterwards. The past perfect continuous cannot be used with stative verbs.
  We**'d been standing** at the bus stop for twenty minutes before a bus finally turned up.
- focus on actions that were repeated in the past.
  Before he was hired, he **had been applying** for jobs for months.
- show the effects of a previous activity in the past.
  He was breathing hard because he**'d been running**.

Describing past experiences: adverbs and time expressions

We use a range of adverbs and time expressions with the perfect tenses to describe past experiences more precisely. These include:

ever, never, already, yet, just, recently, lately, for some time, so far, (a number of) times, all his/her/our lives, (for) long, for ages.

Before we met up again, I hadn't seen Michael **for some time**.

Inversion

We can emphasise particular parts of a sentence by inversion. When we use inversion, certain adverbs or adverbial phrases can be placed at the beginning of the sentence.

1. After inversion, we reverse the order of the subject and the auxiliary verb, where one is used.
   I could never trust him again after what he did.
   = **Never again could I trust** him after what he did.
2. Where there is no auxiliary verb used, we insert do/does or did.
   I rarely ask friends for advice.
   Rarely do I ask friends for advice.
3. We can use inversion:
- after phrases with not: not until, not since, not only.
  Not until we reached the airport **did we discover** we didn't have our tickets with us.
  Not since I first saw Star Wars **have I felt** such excitement at the cinema.
  Not only was he the perfect gentleman, (but) he also turned out to be a great cook.
- after phrases with only: only when, only then, only recently, only later, only (+ period of time), only (+ point in time).
  Only later did we realise that Jenna had told us the truth after all.
- after expressions with no: under no circumstances, on no account, in no way, at no time.
  Under no circumstances are you to disturb me, is that clear?
  On no account should you use someone else's password.
  In no way will the change in plans jeopardise the final deadline.
  At no time did they indicate there was anything wrong with the machine.
- after certain frequency adverbs: never, hardly ever, rarely, seldom.
  Never will I forget their kindness towards me.
- with time phrases: no sooner ... than and hardly/barely/scarcely ... when.
  No sooner had we got to the meeting venue **than** the news of its cancellation reached us.
- with little (in the sense: not at all).
  They didn't suspect at all there was going to be a surprise party.
  = **Little did they suspect** there was going to be a surprise party.
4. We can also use inversion to replace if-clauses in the third conditional. This makes the condition more emphatically the opposite of what happened.
   If I had known about the problem, I would have told you.
   = **Had I known** about the problem, I would have told you.

UNIT 2

Modals

Will

1. will and won't are used to express what we strongly believe to be true about the present. They indicate assumptions based on knowledge of routine, character, and qualities of people and things.
   Is that the phone? It**'ll** be Sara. She said she'd ring tonight.
2. won't expresses refusal, by a person or thing. The past is expressed by wouldn't.
   The car **won't** start.
   The car **wouldn't** start yesterday.
3. will is used to express characteristic behaviour. The past is expressed by would.
   He**'ll** sit for hours talking about his old friends.
   Grandpa **would** always bring sweets when he came to visit.
4. If will is stressed, it suggests irritation or criticism.
   She **will** leave her homework to the last minute.

Must

1. *must* is used to express what we think is the most rational or logical explanation for a situation or event.
   That **must be** her mother, they look so similar.

2. The negative form of this use of *must* is *can't*.
   That **can't be** her mother, they look so different.

3. ***Must* + infinitive without *to* can be used:**
   - to express strong obligation.
     You **must come** here at once.
   - to give strong advice.
     You really **must read** this book.
   - to make polite invitations.
     You **must come** over for dinner sometime.
   - to tell ourselves what we personally feel is necessary.
     I **must remember** to get some milk.

4. *have to* can also be used to express obligation, especially when it is imposed by someone else, or an external circumstance.
   I **have to** wear contact lenses because I'm short-sighted.
   Had + infinitive is used to show obligation and necessity in the past.
   I **had to get** a taxi as I was going to be late.

5. We use *must* + perfect infinitive (*have* + past participle) to express certainty about past situations.
   The house **must have cost** a small fortune – it's absolutely massive.
   We can also use the continuous form of the perfect infinitive.
   She **must have been driving** when I called her.

6. *mustn't* + infinitive without *to* expresses prohibition.
   You **mustn't run** in the school halls.

Should and ought to

1. *should* expresses what may reasonably be expected to happen. It usually expresses the idea that we want whatever is predicted to happen. *Should* also suggests a sense of condition.
   We **should** be moving into the apartment soon (as long as the sale goes through smoothly).

2. *should(n't)* and *ought (not) to* are used to give advice or say what we think is the right thing to do.
   People **shouldn't** kill endangered species, they **ought to** protect them.

3. *had/'d better (not)* + infinitive without *to* is also used to give advice and warnings. It suggests the speaker thinks there will be a negative consequence if the advice is not followed.
   You**'d better speak** to someone in IT support – it looks like the system might crash.

May, might, could and can

1. *may/might/could* + infinitive without *to* express present and future possibility.
   He **might/may remember** you but he was a child when he last saw you.
   We **could** still **win** – the game isn't over yet.

2. *couldn't* is not used to express future possibility. *Might not* or *may not* are used instead.
   He **might not come** this weekend.

3. *couldn't/can't* + perfect infinitive (*have* + past participle) can be used to express disbelief.
   Surely she **couldn't have got** here so quickly.

4. We use *can't/couldn't* + perfect infinitive to express certainty about past situations.
   Laura **couldn't have committed** the crime.
   We can also use the continuous form of the perfect infinitive.
   You **can't have been listening** to what he said – otherwise you'd know what to do.

5. We use *may (not)/might (not)/could* + perfect infinitive to express uncertainty about the past.
   I **might have left** the letter on my desk.
   The continuous form is also possible.
   Gamekeepers think that a lioness **may have been hunting** in the region.

6. We use *can* to express what is generally true, and logically possible.
   Buying a house in the city **can** be expensive.

7. *can* is not used to predict future possibility. We must use *will be possible* or *will be able to*.
   One day it **will be possible** for humans to live on Mars.
   In a few years **we'll be able to** afford a family home.

8. *can/could* is used to express ability in the present/past.
   I **can** swim really well. I **could** swim when I was five.

9. To express a particular ability on one occasion in the past, *could* is not used. Instead, *was able to* or *managed to* is used.
   He **managed to** find a job in Berlin.
   I **was able to** meet the deadline.

10. *can't* + infinitive without *to* is used to express prohibition.
    You **can't pay** by credit card here.

Need

1. *need* + infinitive is used to express necessity.
   I **need to call** my mum.

2. *needn't* + infinitive without *to* and *don't need to* express a lack of necessity. However, *needn't* usually refers to immediate necessity and tends to be used to give permission not to do something. The authority comes from the speaker.
   You **needn't come** in until 10 tomorrow morning.

3 *needn't* + perfect infinitive is used to talk about an action which was performed but which was unnecessary.
   You **needn't have brought** snacks, we've got plenty here.

4 *not need* + infinitive is used to talk about an action which was unnecessary. The context usually makes it clear whether the action was performed or not.
   He **didn't need to keep** in touch, but he felt that he ought to.

5 *There is/was no need (for someone)* + infinitive with *to* can also be used to express a lack of necessity in the past or present.
   There's no need (for you) to get so angry! It was an accident.

Other structures
Obligation
1 *make* + noun/pronoun + infinitive without *to* is used to express obligation.
   My kids **make me play** Katy Perry's album in the car.

2 In the passive, *made* is followed by the infinitive with *to*.
   He **was made to pay** for breaking the window.

3 *don't have to* expresses a lack of obligation.
   You **don't have to** answer all those questions, they are optional.

Prohibition
1 Negative forms of *let* + infinitive without *to* and *allow* + infinitive are used to express prohibition.
   My parents **wouldn't let me watch** that film when I was younger.
   My parents **wouldn't allow me to watch** that film when I was younger.

2 *allow* + infinitive is also commonly used in the passive.
   Residents **are not allowed to make** noise after 11 pm.

Relative clauses
Defining relative clauses
1 Defining relative clauses identify, or define, who or what we are talking about and are essential for our understanding of the whole sentence.
   There are a few sites **where** you can download apps for vocabulary building.
   Commas are not required at the beginning or end of the relative clause. The relative pronoun *that* can be used instead of *who* and *which*.
   I've got a good friend **who/that** I met on social media.

2 The relative pronouns *who*, *which* and *that* can be omitted, but only if they are the object of the verb in the defining relative clause.
   Thank you for the message **(which)** you sent me.

3 The relative adverbs *when* and *why* can also sometimes be omitted in defining relative clauses.
   Do you remember the reason **(why)** they were arguing?
   He talked about the day **(when)** he won the competition.

4 The relative pronoun *what* can be used in defining relative clauses and means 'the thing which'.
   He told me **what** you said.

5 *where* cannot be omitted from defining relative clauses.
   Compare the following:
   That's the café **where** I met Julia.
   That's the café **(which/that)** I met Julia in.

6 The relative pronoun *what* can be used in defining relative clauses and means 'the thing which'.
   He told me **what** you'd said.

7 A second relative clause, introduced by *and* or *but*, usually takes a *wh-* pronoun, not *that*.
   Someone that I greatly admire, **but who** I've never met, is Jeff Mills.

8 Relative clauses beginning with *whatever*, *whoever* and *whichever* are used to talk about things or people that are indefinite or unknown.
   I'll enjoy eating **whatever** you cook.
   Whoever wins is likely to play Italy in the final.
   You can choose **whichever** date is most suitable for you.

Non-defining relative clauses
1 Non-defining relative clauses contain information which is not essential to our understanding of who or what we are writing or talking about. The main clause would make sense even without this information.
   Koh Phi Phi, **where the movie** The Beach **was filmed**, is a beautiful island in Thailand.

2 Commas are used to separate the relative clause from the main clause. *That* cannot be used instead of *who* or *which*, and the relative pronoun cannot be omitted.
   Jesse Eisenberg, **who once suffered from anxiety**, is an award-winning actor.
   They travelled to Nara, **where the capital city once stood**.

3 The relative pronoun *which* can be used to refer to the whole main clause.
   They had a huge argument, **which** means they aren't speaking to each other.

4 We can use the following phrases at the beginning of a non-defining relative clause: *at which point/time*, *by which point/time*, *during which time*, *in which case*.
   We should arrive at 6 pm on Saturday, **at which point** we'll be in contact.
   The next World Cup is in two years, **by which time** he'll be 32.

*Kim lived in China for four years, **during which time** she travelled all over the country.*

*It might rain this weekend, **in which case** we won't have a barbecue.*

Whom

In both defining and non-defining relative clauses *whom* can be used instead of *who* when it is the object of the verb in the relative clause.

*There's someone here **whom** I'd like you to meet.*

Note that many speakers consider *whom* to be too formal, and avoid using it.

Relative clauses and prepositions

1. Prepositions can be placed at the end of both defining and non-defining relative clauses.

   *It was written by Ma Jian, who I have a lot of respect **for**.*

   *It wasn't a topic (which/that) I had an opinion **on**.*

2. In more formal English, the preposition often appears immediately before the relative pronouns *whom* (for people) and *which* (for things).

   *It was written by Ma Jian, **for whom** I have a lot of respect.*

   *It wasn't a topic **on which** I had an opinion.*

   If the verb in the relative clause is a multi-part verb (e.g. *come across*, *fill up*, *go through*, etc.) it is more natural not to use these forms:

   ~~She's one of the few people **to whom** I look up to.~~ X

   *She's one of the few people **(who/that)** I look up to.*

3. In formal written English we often use *of which* rather than *whose* to talk about things.

   Compare:

   *A huge storm occurred, the effects **of which** are still being felt.*

   *A huge storm occurred, **whose** effects are still being felt.*

4. We can also use *that ... of* instead of *of which* in less formal, mainly spoken English.

   Compare:

   *The website **that** he is moderator **of** is growing in popularity.*

   *The website **of which** he is moderator is growing in popularity.*

UNIT 3

Gerunds and infinitives

Gerunds

1. **The gerund is used:**

- as the subject, object or complement of a sentence or clause.

   ***Hiking** always makes me feel better. I love **going** on long walks in the mountains. But what I love most is **sleeping** late in the mornings.*

- after prepositions.

   *Are you afraid **of walking** home after dark?*

- after certain expressions:

   have difficulty/trouble/problems, there's no/little point (in), it's/there's no use/good, it's not worth, spend/waste time

   *I **had trouble reading** the cinema programme because the print was too small.*

   ***There's little point in** cooking him dinner, he's a really fussy eater.*

   ***It's no use** asking me – I don't know the answer.*

   *It's **not worth complaining** about television shows – just turn them off if they annoy you.*

   *I've **spent** a lot of **time looking** for an address that didn't even exist.*

- after the following verbs:

   admit, adore, advise, anticipate, appreciate, avoid, can't help, can't stand, consider, delay, deny, detest, dislike, end up, enjoy, feel like, finish, give up, imagine, involve, keep, (don't) mind, miss, postpone, practise, propose, put off, recommend, resent, resist, risk, suggest, worth

   *We **considered sponsoring** the event, but in the end decided against it.*

   *Lara **suggested taking** a taxi, but everyone else wanted to walk.*

2. Where the subject of the main verb is different from the subject of the gerund, we use an object (pronoun) or a possessive adjective before the gerund.

   *Would you **mind my asking** you a personal question?*

   *I **can't stand John/him singing** in that awful voice.*

3. We place *not* before the gerund to make it negative.

   *Can you **imagine not having** a car?*

4. We use certain verbs with a dependent preposition before the gerund:

   accuse of, adapt to, adjust to, admit to, approve of, be/get used to, concentrate on, confess to, count on, depend on, focus on, get round to, insist on, look forward to, object to, own up to, rely on, resort to

   *He **admitted to lying** about the accident.*

Infinitives

1. **The infinitive with *to* is used:**

- to say why you do something.

   *I'm telling you this **to avoid** any misunderstandings.*

- after the verb *be* to give orders or to express an arrangement.

   *You**'re to phone** me the moment the job's done.*

   *The director of the company **is to open** the ceremony.*

- after certain adjectives:

   difficult, easy, essential, important, lovely, (un)necessary, (im)possible, (un)usual, wonderful, delighted, disappointed, (un)happy, (un)lucky, sad, surprising/surprised

*It was **easy to make** friends, but a lot more **difficult to say** goodbye.*

- after certain nouns:
  ability, attempt, capacity, chance, decision, desire, determination, effort, failure, idea, intention, need, opportunity, permission, plan, proposal, refusal, right, tendency, way, willingness

  *His **tendency to switch** back into his native language didn't help his **attempts to get** his ideas across.*

- after the following verbs:
  afford, agree, appear, arrange, ask, attempt, choose, decide, demand, deserve, expect, help*, hesitate, hope, learn, manage, offer, prepare, pretend, promise, refuse, seem, tend, threaten

  *We **managed to visit** three museums in a single day, but we **decided to take** things more slowly the following day.*

- after the following verbs, followed by an object:
  advise, allow, ask, challenge, enable, encourage, force, get, intend, invite, lead, order, persuade, recommend, remind, teach, tell, urge, warn

  *The weather conditions **forced me to give up** my world record attempt.*

- after *would like/hate/love/prefer, ask, expect, help*, need, want*, with or without an object.

  *What **would** you **like me to do** next?*
  *I don't know why we **need to go** there.*
  *Can you **help us to find** the way?*

* We can use *help* with an infinitive with or without *to*: see below.

2 We place *not* before the infinitive to make it negative.
   *I **warned him not to get** too close to the edge.*

3 We use the infinitive without *to*:

- after modal verbs.
  *You **should bring** an umbrella with you. It **might rain** today.*

- after *help, let, make, would rather/sooner, had better*.
  *I'**d rather be** on time today.*

4 We use *let* and *make* with a direct object.
   *It wasn't my idea – he **made me do** it.*

5 We can use *help* with or without a direct object.
   *Can you **help us find** the way?*
   *The new scheme will **help boost** trade.*

Gerunds or infinitives

1 The following verbs can be followed by a gerund or an infinitive with *to*, with no change in meaning:
   begin, can't bear, continue, hate, intend, like, love, prefer, start

   *The orchestra **began to play/playing**.*

   We do not normally use the gerund after a continuous verb.

   *Look! It's **starting to rain**.* NOT ~~Look! It's starting raining~~.

2 With *can't bear, hate, like, love* and *prefer*, the infinitive with *to* usually refers to specific situations or particular conditions.
   *I **like swimming**. It's my favourite sport.* (in general)
   *I **like to swim** when it's cold outside.* (specifically)

3 We can use certain verbs followed by a gerund or an infinitive with *to*, but the meaning is different:

- with *remember, forget, stop* and *go on*, the gerund refers to actions or situations happening before these verbs, while the infinitive with *to* refers to things happening afterwards.

  *John **remembered visiting** his cousin.* (= he recalled a previous visit)
  *John **remembered to visit** his cousin.* (= he visited her because he had intended to or because he was supposed to do so)
  *I'll never **forget calling** her from Paris.* (= I'll always recall an occasion when I phoned her from Paris)
  *I'll not **forget to call** her from Paris.* (= I am certain I will remember to phone her when I am in Paris)
  *I **stopped eating** ice cream when I ran into Susan.* (= I no longer continued eating it)
  *I **stopped to eat** ice cream when I ran into Susan.* (= I interrupted my journey to have ice cream when I met Susan – presumably together)
  *The manager **went on explaining** the new procedures.* (= he had been explaining them for a while and he continued with further details)
  *The manager **went on to explain** the new procedures.* (= he finished his previous topic, then moved on to explain the procedures)

- with *regret*, the gerund refers to past actions or situations which the speaker feels bad about. We can use *regret* in formal English with the infinitive form of *say, tell* or *inform* to express reluctance about the message that will follow.

  *I sincerely **regret borrowing** your bike without your permission.*
  *We **regret to inform** you that your application has been unsuccessful.*

- with *mean*, the gerund means *involve*; the infinitive with *to* means *intend*.

  *Being a backup **means joining** the team if someone else drops out.* (= involves joining the team)
  *I've always **meant to join** the team if I got selected.* (= always intended to join)

- with *try*, the gerund means *experiment with something*; the infinitive with *to* means *make an attempt/effort*.

  ***Try pushing** one of those buttons at the top – maybe one of those will be the off switch.*
  *I've **tried to push** the buttons at the top, but they won't move.*

- with *need*, the gerund expresses a passive meaning, while the infinitive with *to* has an active meaning.

*The plant **needs watering**.*
*You **need to water** the plant.*

- with *require*, the gerund expresses a passive meaning, similar to *need*, but in a more formal style. We only use *require* with a direct object, followed by the infinitive with *to*. A passive form is also commonly used.

  *The document **requires formatting**.* (= needs to be formatted)

  *They **required us to fill** in a form. / We **were required to fill** in a form.*

Reported speech

Tense changes

1. Present tenses change to past; present perfect and past tenses change to past perfect.

   'I'm planning a round-the-world trip,' Bob said.
   *Bob said he **was planning** a round-the-world trip.*
   'We've never been horse riding,' Jake and Bella told me.
   *Jake and Bella told me they **'d never been** horse riding.*

2. Some modal verbs change to a corresponding past form: *will → would, must* (obligation) *→ had to, may → might, can → could*.

   'We must complete everything by tomorrow,' Ginny reminded us.
   *Ginny reminded us that we **had to** complete everything by the following day.*

   We do not need to change *might, could, should, ought to* or *must* (deduction).

   'You must be hungry after travelling all day,' Andrea noted.
   *Andrea noted that we **must** be hungry after travelling all day.*

3. Pronouns, possessive adjectives and phrases indicating time or place change in reported speech depending on the speaker's viewpoint.

   'This shop in our high street was a greengrocer's ten years ago,' Patrick recalled.
   *Patrick recalled that **that/the** shop in **their** high street had been a greengrocer's **ten years earlier**.*

4. We do not change the tense in reported speech:

- if the reporting verb is in the present simple or present perfect.

   'I love oranges,' Lucy says.
   *Lucy **says** she loves oranges.*

- if the statement is in the past perfect.

   'I'd never heard of such a thing,' Chris admitted.
   *Chris admitted he **'d** never **heard** of such a thing.*

- if the statement being reported is still true.

   'I want to be a pilot when I grow up,' Annie said.
   *Annie said she **wants** to be a pilot when she **grows** up.*

5. **For reported questions:**
- we do not use the auxiliary verbs *do/does* or *did*.
- the word order is the same as for statements.
- we use *if/whether* to report *yes/no* questions.
- we do not use a question mark.

   'Who's coming tomorrow?' Nick inquired.
   *Nick inquired **who was coming** the following day.*
   'Do you like passion fruit?' Anita asked me.
   *Anita asked me **if I liked** passion fruit.*
   NOT *Anita asked me did I like passion fruit?*

6. **For reported requests or order:**
- we use a reporting verb + object (pronoun) + infinitive with *to*.

   'Please leave quietly.'
   *They **asked/told us to leave** quietly.*

Reporting verbs

We use several different verb patterns in reported speech with various reporting verbs. Some verbs may be used with more than one pattern. We use:

- a *that*-clause after the following verbs:
  add, admit, announce, argue, claim, complain, concede, conclude, confirm, emphasise, estimate, explain, mention, point out, predict, remark, repeat, say, state, stress, warn

  We may or may not use an indirect object with most of these verbs.

  *We **complained/explained/said/mentioned (to the waiter) that** the tomato soup was too spicy.*

- a *that*-clause with *assure, reassure, remind* and *tell*, and we must always use a direct object.

  *He **assured/reassured/reminded/told us that** all the ingredients were top quality.*

- a *that*-clause with *should* after the following verbs:
  advise, agree, ask, demand, insist, propose, recommend, request, suggest

  We can omit *that*, and in formal style, *should* may also be omitted.

  *The reviewer **insisted/suggested (that)** people **(should)** avoid the disappointing new restaurant.*

- an infinitive with *to* after the following verbs:
  agree, ask, claim, demand, offer, promise, refuse, threaten

  'We can't let you in,' said the doorman.
  *The doorman **refused to let** us in.*

- an infinitive with *to* with a direct object after the following verbs:
  advise, ask, beg, convince, encourage, forbid, instruct, invite, order, persuade, recommend, remind, tell, urge, warn

  *The campaigner **asked/persuaded/invited/urged us to volunteer** for their charity.*

- a gerund after the following verbs:
  admit, advise, deny, recommend, regret, query, suggest.
  Tom **regretted not telling** them the whole truth.
- a preposition before a gerund after the following verbs:
  advise, argue, protest, warn + **against**
  'Don't take the slow train,' he warned me.
  He **warned me against taking** the slow train.
  apologise, blame, forgive, praise, tell off, thank + **for**
  Susan eventually **forgave Daniel for forgetting** her birthday.
  discourage, dissuade + **from**
  The terrible weather **discouraged a lot of people from coming** to the picnic.
  accuse, speak + **of**
  Are you **accusing me of lying**?
  congratulate, insist + **on**
  Some companies **insist on staff doing** first aid training every year.
  admit, confess, consent, object + **to**.
  I **object to paying** that much for a t-shirt.

UNIT 4

Modifying adverbs

Adverbs of degree

1. We use adverbs of degree to modify verbs, adjectives and adverbs. Common intensifying adverbs of degree are *absolutely*, *very*, *really*, *extremely*, *totally*, *utterly*, *entirely* and *highly*. Of these, *very* and *extremely* can't be used to modify verbs.
   I **totally agree** with this review; her performance was **absolutely** terrible.
2. Common softening adverbs are *quite*, *fairly*, *slightly*.
   It's **quite** annoying that the café closes on a Monday morning.
   He **fairly flew** across the room.
   Joshua was limping **slightly**.
3. We do not use the same adverbs of degree to modify all adjectives. Different adverbs are used with gradable (e.g. *tired*) and ungradable (e.g. *exhausted*) adjectives.

Adverbs used with gradable adjectives
very, extremely, fairly, really, slightly, highly
Adverbs used with ungradable adjectives
absolutely, completely, entirely, really, totally, utterly

   Not all combinations of adverbs and adjectives are possible. The only constructions that are always possible are *very* + gradable adjective and *absolutely* + ungradable adjective. *Really* can be used with most gradable and ungradable adjectives.
   Many adverb–adjective combinations are strong collocations, e.g. *highly intelligent*, *completely different*, *terribly sorry*.

Quite

The adverb *quite* has different meanings according to whether it is used with a gradable or ungradable adjective.
The food at the restaurant was **quite tasty** but they needed to use more salt. (= fairly tasty)
The food at the restaurant was **quite delicious**. (= absolutely delicious)
Stress and intonation are also important in expressing the meaning of *quite* + adjective.

Comparison

Comparison and superlative structures

There are a number of structures and expressions used to talk about similarities and differences.

1. We use *the* + comparative, *the* + comparative to show that two changes happen, or vary together. The second is often the result of the first.
   The more we ate, **the sleepier** we became.
   The more that I read of his novel, **the less** I understood.
   Similarly we repeat comparatives or *more/less* with *and* to emphasise increasing/decreasing amounts over a period of time.
   Timothy is getting **taller and taller** every time I see him.
2. We use the phrase *now … more than ever (before)* to compare the past and the present.
   We **now** stay at home **more than ever before**.
3. *The* + superlative/superlative phrase + *of* + noun can be used to put one thing or action above all others in the same category.
   It was **the hottest day of the year** so far.

Qualifying comparisons

There are a number of words and phrases used to qualify comparative and superlative structures.

1. **To talk about big differences we can use:**
- *much*, *(quite) a lot*, *far*, *significantly*, *considerably*, *a great deal* + comparative.
  I feel **a great deal happier than** I did yesterday.
- *nowhere near*, *not nearly*, *twice* + *as … as*.
  The bill is **not nearly as** much **as** I had expected.
- *by far*, *easily* + superlative.
  It was **by far the hottest** day of the year so far.
2. **To talk about small differences we can use:**
- *almost*, *not quite* + *as … as*.
  It's **not quite as** spicy **as** I had expected.
- *a bit*, *a little*, *slightly* + comparative.
  The class was **slightly more difficult than** I had expected.
3. **When there is no difference we can use:**
- *no*, *not any* + comparative.
  He's **no more intelligent than** Tony is.
- *just*, *easily* + *as … as*.
  Her second novel was **just as bad as** her first one.

Like and *as*

Like is used before a noun, pronoun or gerund to make comparisons.

*The whole experience was **like a nightmare**.*

*He's not really **like me**.*

*It was just **like watching** a bunch of kids.*

As is used before subject + verb structures or prepositional expressions to make comparisons.

*They left **as they came**, without a word.*

*In Greece, **as in many countries** …*

As can be used to describe someone or something's job, role, or function.

*He worked **as a chef** in one of Osaka's finest restaurants.*

*It started raining, so I used my jacket **as an umbrella**.*

As is used with verb phrases to make comparisons in a number of common expressions, e.g. *as I said, as you know, as you seem, as I do*. *Like* can also be used in similar expressions, but this is considered informal.

***As/Like** I said, nothing's going to change.*

UNIT 5

Conditionals

1. We use the zero conditional to talk about situations that are always true. (**Zero conditional** = *if* + present simple, present simple)

   *If you **heat** water beyond 100°C, it **boils**.*

2. We use the first conditional to talk about real, possible future situations and their likely results.
   First conditional = *if* + present simple, *will/going to/might/could*

   *If you **study** hard, you**'ll pass** the exam.*

3. We use the second conditional to talk about hypothetical, unlikely or impossible situations.
   Second conditional = *if* + past simple/past continuous, *would/might/could* + base form

   *We **could get** there without the satnav if we **had** a map.*

4. We use the third conditional to talk about hypothetical past events. It is used to speculate how things might have been different in different circumstances.
   Third conditional = *if* + past perfect, *would have* + past participle

   *If you **had sent** me the email, I **would have remembered** about the deadline.*

5. We can use mixed conditionals to speculate about the likely results in the present of a hypothetical past event.
   Mixed conditional (1): *if* + past perfect, *would* + base form

   *If we **had flown** to Paris, we **would be** there by now.*

6. We can also use mixed conditionals to say how changes to a present situation might have affected the past.

   Mixed conditional (2): *if* + past simple, *would have* + past participle

   *If I **weren't** so busy, I **would have gone** to the football match with you.*

Other uses of conditionals

1. To emphasise that the event is unlikely or only a remote possibility, we use:

   - the first conditional with *should* and/or *happen to*.
   ***Should you encounter** any difficulties, we will do our utmost to rectify the situation.*
   *If you **happen to run** into Jack, **will** you **tell** him about the new venue?*

   - the second conditional with *were to* + base form.
   *If I **were to tell** you that you were fired, how **would** you **react**?*
   In formal style, we can use inversion with *were to*.
   ***Were they to reopen** the talks, the outcome might be completely different.*

2. To describe an event which depends on another event, we use:

   - the second conditional with *were(n't) for* + noun phrase.
   *If it **weren't for** the wind, I'd suggest going to the beach.*

   - the third conditional with *had(n't) been for* + noun phrase.
   *If it **hadn't been for** all the encouragement from my friends, I would never have made it through the auditions.*

3. Alternative to *if*:

   - *suppose/supposing* or *imagine*, especially in informal speech.
   ***Supposing** you won the competition, how would you celebrate?*

   - *providing/provided (that)* or *as long as* to emphasise the condition.
   *You can borrow my motorbike **as long as** you bring it back without a scratch!*

   - *unless* to express 'only if not'. We use an affirmative verb after *unless* to express a negative meaning.
   *We'll go to the playground **unless** it rains.*

4. We can introduce the result clause with *otherwise* or *or*, especially to talk about the negative consequences. We use them to give warnings, threats or advice.
   *You need to work harder, **otherwise/or** you'll fail again.*

5. We don't normally use future forms in the *if*-clause except in some special cases:

   - to talk about the refusal to do something or to behave in a certain way.
   *There's little point in trying to persuade him if he**'ll** just **do** what he wants anyway.*

- to talk about the result of the main clause.
  *Take a break, **if it will help** you get a bit less stressed.*
- in polite requests.
  *If you **will/would take** your seats, we'll begin the presentation.*

Unreal time, wishes

We use the verb *wish* when we would like things to be different. We can also use *if only* to express the same ideas. Using *if only* makes the statement more dramatic.

1 With the past simple, we express that we are unhappy with the present situation and would like it to be different, even though that may not be possible. We normally use it with stative verbs or modal auxiliaries (usually for ability or possibility).
   *I **wish I had** more money to travel.*
   If only I could play an instrument.

   With action verbs, we can use *wish/if only* to talk about regular or habitual actions.
   *I **wish the trains didn't arrive** late all the time.*

2 With the past perfect, we express regret about the past.
   *I **wish I hadn't eaten** so much. Now I feel a bit sick.*
   If only I had applied for the job. They might have hired me.

3 We can use *wish/if only* + subject pronoun/noun + *would*, to talk about:
- something we want to happen now or in the future, even though it is unlikely.
  *I **wish the sun would come out** – I'm fed up with all this rain.*
- something that annoys us and we want it to stop/change.
  If only they/the neighbours would stop listening to music at full volume.

4 We can also use the following structures to express the same ideas as *wish/if only*:
- **Present/future**
  I'd rather/sooner go to the cinema than the theatre./I'd prefer to go to the theatre.
  I'd rather/sooner you didn't speak with your mouth full.
  I'd prefer it if you didn't speak with your mouth full.
- **Past**
  I'd rather not have gone swimming./I'd prefer not to have gone swimming.
  I'd like to have done something different./I regret not doing/having done something different.

We can only use the perfect infinitive or perfect gerund with these expressions if the subject of both clauses is the same. If the subject is different, we must use a clause with *that* or *if*, as appropriate.
   *I **regret that they hadn't informed** me properly.*
   NOT *I regret their/them not having informed me properly.*

UNIT 6

Passives

Form

To form the passive we use the appropriate tense of the verb *to be* and the past participle of the main verb.
   *The company **was started** in the early 1990s.*
   *A prototype of the design **will be produced** next year.*
   *A solution **is** currently **being sought**.*

Passives cannot be used with intransitive verbs.
   NOT *The letter was arrived this morning.*

Use

1 We use the passive to focus attention on the person or thing affected by the action, rather than on the agent (the person or thing who performs the action).
   *The company **was taken over** last summer.*

2 If we want to say who the agent is, we use the preposition *by*.
   *The politicians were interviewed **by the journalist** for several hours.*

   If we want to indicate the instrument used by the agent to do the action, we used *with*.
   *The video was shot **with a mobile phone**.*

Non-use of the agent

The agent is not usually included in passive constructions:
- when we do not know the agent or the agent is unimportant.
  *The offices **were opened** twenty years ago.*
- when the agent is obvious from the context.
  *The suspect **was arrested** some time this morning.*
- when the agent is people in general.
  *Zimbabwe used **to be called** Rhodesia.*
- when we want to avoid mentioning the agent.
  *It **has been decided** to cancel this year's pay increase.*
- in official notices to avoid the use of *you*.
  *Work laptops **must be returned** to the admin department.*

Have/get something done

1. We use *have* + object + past participle to show that the subject arranges for the action to be done by someone else. *Get* is a more informal alternative to *have* in these constructions.
   *I'm going to **have/get this image made** into a poster.*
   The same structure is used to describe events outside the speaker's control.
   *I **had my ID card stolen** last week.*

2. *Get* can be used as an informal alternative to *be* or *become* in passive sentences.
   *We **got** sent out of the class for being noisy.*
   It is commonly used with the following past participles: *burnt, caught, dressed, hurt, involved, left, lost, stuck.*
   *We **got stuck** in traffic for hours.*

Passive of reporting verbs

1. Reporting verbs can be used with passive constructions when we want to introduce a widely held opinion or fact. There are two ways of doing this:
   - *It* + passive + *that* clause.
     ***It is said that** the internet has changed our lives more than any other technological innovation.*
     ***It is believed that** the average global temperature will increase by 2°C.*
     ***It is thought that** people lived in the region more than 8000 years ago.*
   - Subject + passive + *to* + infinitive/continuous infinitive/perfect infinitive without *to*.
     ***The internet is said to have changed** our lives more than any other technological innovation.*
     ***The average global temperature is believed to be increasing** by 2°C.*
     ***People are thought to have lived** in the region more than 8000 years ago.*

2. Verbs commonly used with these constructions are *allege, believe, consider, estimate, expect, know, report, say, think* and *understand*.

3. In spoken forms, using the verbs *seem* and *appear* with emphasised stress and the *It* + passive + *that* clause makes the speculation more tentative. This can be further softened by using *would*.
   ***It would seem that** they are paying him too much.*

4. *There* is also used with this structure to create a sense of distance and formality.
   ***There are said to be** five thousand jobs at risk.*

5. *Tell* can be used in the subject + passive + *to* + infinitive construction, but only when *tell* has the meaning *to order*, not *informed*.
   ***He was told to report** the theft to the authorities.*
   NOT *The incident **was told to** have happened in the early morning.*

UNIT 7

The future

Future forms (review)

We can use:

- *will/going to* + base form to make predictions.
  *Hungary **won't win/isn't going to win** the next World Cup.*
  We use *don't think* or *doubt* + affirmative statement to express negative predictions. We don't normally use *I think* + negative statement.
  *I **don't think/doubt I'll be** able to come to the party.*
  NOT *I think I won't be able to come to the party.*

- *going to* + base form to talk about intentions and plans.
  *This summer I**'m going to spend** my holiday in Mallorca.*

- the present continuous to talk about arrangements.
  *I**'m meeting** Jack for coffee at 2.*

- the present simple to talk about timetabled or scheduled events.
  *The flight **departs** at 3.45 from gate 15.*

Future continuous

We use the future continuous (*will be* + *-ing*):

- to talk about actions or events in progress at a given time in the future.
  *This time next week I**'ll be lying** on a beach somewhere in the Seychelles.*

- to talk about future actions or events that are regular or already decided.
  *I presume we**'ll be meeting** in room 5 as usual.*

- to ask about someone's plans politely.
  ***Will you be joining** us for tomorrow's gala dinner?*

Future perfect

We use the future perfect simple (*will have* + past participle):

- to say that an activity will be completed by a given future time.
  *I**'ll have watched** the entire Agents of S.H.I.E.L.D. series by next week.*

- to express an assumption on the part of the speaker.
  *Kim got an early flight so she **will have arrived** at the hotel by now.*

We use the future perfect continuous (*will have been* + *-ing*):

- to talk about actions which continue up to, and possibly beyond, a certain time in the future – there is usually an emphasis on the duration.
  *By April this year, I**'ll have been learning** English for exactly a whole decade.*

125

Other ways of expressing the future

1. *be* + infinitive is used to talk about arrangements.
   The project **is to be** postponed until the next financial year.

2. *be (just) about* + infinitive with *to* is used to talk about the immediate future.
   I'**m just about to go** to the shop. Do you want me to bring you anything?

3. *be (un)likely* + infinitive with *to* is used to express probability.
   The guests **are unlikely to arrive** before eleven.

4. *be bound* + infinitive with *to* is used to express certainty.
   They're by far the best contestants, so they'**re bound to win**.

5. *be due* + infinitive with *to* is used to refer to scheduled times.
   The gallery **is due to be** opened by the Minister of Culture.

6. *be set* + infinitive with *to* is used to say that something is ready to happen.
   Johnson **is set to take over** the department once Brackett retires.

7. *be on the verge/point of* + gerund or noun phrase is used to talk about something being imminent.
   This rare species **is on the verge/brink/point of becoming** extinct within the next decade. (OR … **on the verge/point of extinction**)

8. *It's (high/about) time* + past simple is used to express that the action should be taken soon.
   It's **high time/about time we decided** who's going to represent us at next year's competition.

Future in the past

We can use a range of structures to talk about future predictions, arrangements and intentions from a past perspective. Usually, we use the future in the past to talk about unfulfilled past events – that is events which were intended to take place but which did not happen.

1. All of the structures from **Other ways of expressing the future** above could be used to talk about future in the past. The verb *be* should be used in the past simple.
   Jane **was just about to leave** the house when the thunderstorm started.
   Their preparations had been so inadequate they **were bound to fail**.

2. We can use a perfect infinitive form instead of the infinitive to emphasise that the event had been unfulfilled by our past viewpoint.
   The metro **was to have been** built by an American firm, but they pulled out after only eighteen months.

3. We can use the past continuous, or *plan/hope* + infinitive with *to* to talk about past arrangements, hopes or intentions. We can also use *had been/was thinking of/planning on* + gerund to express the same ideas.
   I **was going/hoping/planning to call** you, but I ran out of battery.
   I'**d been planning on** working, but Julie asked me to go to the cinema with her.

4. We use *be supposed* + infinitive with *to* to talk about other people's expectations.
   I **was supposed to send** in my application for Monday, but I'd completely forgotten.

5. We use *were to/would* + base form to make predictions for events from a past perspective.
   I knew that from that day onwards, we **were to/would remain** friends forever.

6. We use the expression *it/that wasn't to be* to say that something we had predicted/hoped for didn't happen.
   We had been hoping to win the match, but **it/that wasn't to be**.

7. We use *due to* + infinitive when we talk about the future from a past perspective.
   We were **due to go** into the meeting at 2 pm.

8. We can sometimes use the 'future in the past' also to talk about future events that did actually happen.
   He **was to/would** go on to achieve amazing levels of success.

UNIT 8

Conjunctions

We use conjunctions to link ideas within a sentence. They can be used at the beginning or middle of a sentence to improve a text's cohesion and to make sentences more complex. They have a number of different functions.

Reason, result and purpose

For example: *as, because, in case, in order (not) to, otherwise, so, so as (not) to, so that*.

1. *In case* and *so that* can be followed by the present simple to refer to the future.
   Take down my mobile number **in case we get separated**.
   Wear these **so that you don't get** wet feet.

2. *As* and *since* are often used when the reason is already known to the listener/reader, or when it is the most important part of the sentence.
   A more informal version would be to use *so*.
   As/Since it was getting late we decided it was time to leave.
   It was getting late, **so** we decided it was time to leave.

Contrast and concession

For example: *although, but, however, (even) though, whereas, while, whilst.*

1. As a conjunction, *however* means *no matter how*.
   You can design your blog **however** you want.
2. *In spite of the fact that* and *despite the fact that* can also be used to connect two clauses.
   They continued to fund his research, **despite the fact that** he was making little progress.

Time

For example: *after, as, as soon as, before, by the time, hardly, no sooner, once, since, then, until, when, whenever, while.*

Many of these conjunctions are followed by the present tense or present perfect to refer to the future.
Once it stops loading the software, we'll open the documents.

Discourse markers

Discourse markers are words or phrases that are used to provide connections and patterns of organisation in a text. They include linking adverbials, which connect one sentence with another. These frequently appear at the beginning of a sentence and are followed by a comma. They have the effect of making texts more formal than conjunctions. Due to this, they are frequently used in written English.
The conference hall was being set up. **Meanwhile**, we held a meeting to discuss our ideas.

Discourse markers have a number of different functions.

Adding information/Developing a point

For example: *additionally, besides (this), apart from this, as well as this, in addition to this, furthermore, what's more, moreover.*

1. *Furthermore, in addition* and *moreover* are generally used at the beginning of the sentence which contains the additional point.
   We need to consider the impact on the environment. **Moreover**, it is important to take into account the economic effects.
2. *As well as* can be used before the first point, or the additional point. It is followed by a noun phrase or gerund clause.
   As well as changes to global temperatures, the model predicted increased rainfall.
   Changes to global temperatures, **as well as** increasing rainfall were predicted by the models.

Contrast and concession

For example: *besides, having said that, nevertheless, conversely, on the contrary, in fact.*

1. *On the contrary* is used to introduce a positive statement which confirms a negative one.
   His research area isn't very popular. **On the contrary**, very few students are interested in it.
2. *On the other hand* introduces a point which contrasts with a previous one.
   It's a very cheap city to live in. **On the other hand**, it's a long way from the capital.

Cause and result

For example: *consequently, owing to, therefore, on account of this, as a result.*

Note most people avoid using *owing to* after the verb *be*.
The success of the department is largely due to his hard work.
NOT ~~The success of the department is owing to his hard work.~~

Generalising

For example: *on the whole, by and large, in fact.*

These discourse markers can be used to introduce supporting ideas and evidence by either adding detailed information or an example to what has been said,
Many people support the policy. **In fact** a recent survey suggested …
OR by referring to a general or agreed situation.
By and large, the idea of sharing research across international borders is a welcome one.

UNIT 9

Determiners and pronouns

Determiners

1. Determiners are used before nouns. They provide information about whether the noun is specific or general.

- Specific determiners include the definite article *the*, demonstratives (*this, that*, etc.), possessives (*my, his, their*, etc.), and the interrogative *which*.
  It's **her** pen.
  Which shop did you go to with Irena?
  The new one.
  Did you buy **this** top?

- General determiners include the indefinite article (*a, an*), *any, other, another* and the interrogative *what*.
  I want to watch **another** film.
  Shall we watch **a** film?
  What films do you like?
  I'll watch **any**.

2. Quantifiers are a category of determiners. We use these to give information about the quantities and amounts of things. We use the following quantifiers with both countable and uncountable nouns: *all, any, enough, less, a load of, loads of, a lot of, lots of, more, most, no, none of, plenty of, some.*
   Most psychologists agree with the study, although **some** question the methods used.

127

3   Some quantifiers can only be used with countable nouns: *both, a couple of, each, (a) few, fewer, hundreds of, several.*
    Both books are really interesting.
4   *a little, (not) much, a bit of* can only be used with uncountable nouns.
5   With uncountable abstract nouns such *as time, money* and *trouble*, we often use *a good/great deal of*.
    They spent a **great deal of time** travelling through Asia.
6   *either* and *neither* are used to talk about two things. They are followed by a singular noun.
    Neither team played particularly well.
7   *each* and *every* are followed by a singular noun, and mean *all*.
    Each employee was given an extra day off.
8   *few* means *not many* or *not as many as expected or wanted*.
    Few people turned up to the meeting.
    Very can be used to add emphasis.
    Very few people turned up to the meeting.
9   *a few* means *some* or *more than expected*.
    A few people turned up to the meeting.
    Quite can be used to add emphasis.
    Quite a few people turned up to the meeting.
10 *some* can be used to mean *approximately* or *a large amount*.
    I've been working for the company for **some** time.

Pronouns

Most of the determiners above can be used as pronouns. Pronouns are used instead of nouns. Some determiners cannot be used as pronouns. They are as follows:

Determiner	Pronoun
a lot of	a lot
every	each
no	none
other	others

Pronouns can be used:

- on their own.
  'Have you got any money?' '**Not much**.'
- as objects of verbs (*one another, each other*).
  Those two can't stand **each other**.
- after a determiner.
  Look at this **one**.
- *all* and *both* can also be used after a noun, pronoun, modal or auxiliary verb.
  You can keep the books, I've read them **all**.
  We've **all** done stupid things in the past.

Reference, substitution and ellipsis
Reference

Referencing is used to ensure that texts are more cohesive by reducing the amount of repetition. Reference is the use of determiners, pronouns and noun phrases to refer backwards to previously mentioned people, events, things or ideas.

1   You can refer to previous topics by using *this*, *that*, *these*, *those* and *it*. *This* and *that* can be used before nouns or on their own.
    He left the company last year. **This (decision)** surprised many people.
    He didn't like his boss. **That**'s why he left.
2   In their plural form, the determiners *these* and *those* are used. *These* and *those* are more commonly used before nouns.
    … social media and online shopping. **These developments** have changed the way retailers approach advertising.

Substitution

Substitution means replacing one word or phrase with another.

1   The most common form of substitution is nominal substitution, where we substitute a pronoun for a noun, or use words like *one(s), some, pair*.
    The boss has arrived. **He**'s talking to the secretary.
    This **dress** is much too expensive. I'll get the cheaper **one**.
2   If we want to avoid repeating a verb or verb phrase, we use the auxiliary verb *do*. This is called verbal substitution.
    I need to write my assignment, but I'll **do** it tomorrow.
3   If we want to replace a whole clause, we use *do* with *so, too, nor* or *not*.
    She loves shopping **and so do I/ and I do too/ but I don't**.
    She doesn't like shopping and **nor do I**.
4   We can use *so/not* to replace a *that*-clause after *expect, hope, seem, suppose* and *think*.
    'Is she planning to come out this evening?' 'I **think so**.'
5   *if not/so* is used to replace whole clauses.
    Are they planning to invest in our company? **If so**, how much?

Ellipsis

Ellipsis means omitting words completely to avoid repetition.

1   It is common after the conjunctions *and* and *but*.
    I live **and (I)** work in central London.
2   In verb phrases, the main verb can usually be omitted after an auxiliary.
    I'd drive there myself, if I could **(drive)**.

It can't be omitted if the main verb is *be*.
He isn't famous yet, but he will **be**.

3 Adverbs can be placed before the auxiliary.
'Can you contact him please?' 'I **already** *have.'*

4 *been* can be omitted in the perfect passive, except after a modal verb.
'Has Tony been told to go home?' 'Yes, he has **(been)**.*'
He wasn't blamed for the company doing badly, but he **should have been**.

5 Instead of repeating full infinitive expressions, we can use *to*.
I don't play badminton now but I used **to**.

UNIT 10

Cleft sentences

A cleft sentence splits one clause into two. We use cleft sentences to emphasise parts of sentences. There are two main ways of creating cleft sentences:

1 We use *What … is/was …* to emphasise:
- an action or series of actions.
  What happened was that I lost my phone.
  What you do first is look at the image, then you focus on the box.
- a noun.
  What I really wanted to study at university was Philosophy.

If the verb in the original sentence is in the present or past simple, we can use *do/did* to form the cleft sentence.
We'd like to continue our research. → *What we'd like to do is continue our research.*

All can be used instead of *What* to mean *the only thing that*.
All he does during the weekend is watch football on TV.

2 We use *It … is/was …* to emphasise:
- a period of time, when used with *(only) when, while,* or *not until*.
  It was not until he spoke that I recognised him.
- reasons, when used with *because*.
  It's because you never call to say you're late that she gets so annoyed with you.
- prepositional phrases.
  It was at university that I first met my wife.
- a thing or person (*It is/was* + person/thing + relative clause).
  It was Joe who first told me the news.

3 Modal verbs can be used instead of *is/was*.
It might have been the journey that made him feel tired.

Participle clauses

Participle clauses begin with a present or past participle. They help to express ideas clearly and concisely. They can be used:

- to replace relative clauses.
  The police identified the suspect **shown** *in the pictures.* (= who was shown)
- to replace certain adverbial clauses which begin with a conjunction:
  because/so
  Affected *by years of back pain, he had to quit his job.*
  as/while
  Leaving *the city, I felt a sense of relief.*
  when/once/after
  Having chosen *a subject, he applied for university.*
  and
  Opening *his briefcase, he took out a folder.*
  if
  Taken regularly, *this can improve memory and attention.*

Other structures

1 If the action described in the participle is relatively long compared with the one in the main clause, we use *having* + past participle.
  Having eaten *our meal, we paid and left.*

2 Sometimes we can use either present participle or *having* + past participle with a similar meaning. Using a *having* + past participle clause emphasises that something is completed before the action in the main clause begins.
  Compare:
  Taking off *their shoes, the children walked into the house.*
  Having taken off *their shoes, the children walked into the house.*

3 *-ing* forms of stative verbs (e.g. *be, want, know*) can be used in participle clauses.
  Being nervous, *I don't ask many questions in class.*
  NOT ~~I am being nervous, so I don't ask many questions in class.~~

4 The subject of a participle clause is usually the same as the subject of the main clause.
  Working *as a junior doctor, I meet a lot of people each week.*

5 When we introduce a different subject we can use *with*.
  With *both children being at school, we get a lot done each day.*

Writing Bank

Part 1: Essay

Your class has recently attended a panel discussion on what methods governments should adopt to encourage people to live in the countryside. You have made the notes below.

Which methods should governments use to encourage people to live in the countryside?
- subsidised housing
- improved transport links
- increase awareness of the health benefits

Some opinions expressed in the discussion:
'Cheaper homes would encourage young families to move to the country.'
'High-speed trains would make commuting easy.'
'Getting away from the noise and traffic of the city can reduce stress.'

Write an essay discussing **two** of the methods in your notes. You should explain **which method is more important** for the government to consider, **giving reasons** in support of your answer.

You may, if you wish, make use of the opinions expressed in the discussion, but you should use your own words as far as possible.

Encouraging people to move to the countryside

[opening statement to introduce the topic]

It is generally accepted that cities these days are overcrowded and that housing is unaffordable for many people. The simple fact is that urban areas built one or two hundred years ago were not designed to cope with such a high population. In light of this, it has been suggested that governments should encourage people to move to the countryside. This essay shall explore two of the proposed methods for doing this.

[Introduction clearly stating the purpose of essay]

[linking phrases to help cohesion used throughout essay]

Many young families cannot afford the type of housing to meet their needs in the cities. Therefore, if they were offered two- or three-bedroom homes at a reduced price, it would be a great incentive for them to move out of the city. In theory, this seems an excellent idea. In practice, it is doubtful that young families would move to an area without looking into the quality of nearby schools, the leisure facilities available and employment opportunities close by.

[Discussion of first method (point 1 of Notes)]

[appropriately formal style throughout essay]

This brings us on to the next method to be considered — the improvement of transport links into the city. High-speed railways would enable people to commute comfortably and quickly into work in urban areas. Consequently, any concerns over employment would be eliminated. Improving the roads and building motorways would also make leisure facilities more easily accessible.

[Discussion of second method (point 2 of Notes)]

On balance, it appears that the best course of action would be to improve transport links from the countryside to urban areas. Research shows that many people worry about employment opportunities in less built-up areas — improved transport infrastructure would help to reassure them.

[conclusion, stating opinion]

Model answer
Task

Either write your own answer to the task above *or* write an answer to the following question in 220–260 words.

Your class has recently watched a televised panel discussion on what methods governments should adopt to encourage young people to do more sport. You have made the notes below.

How can governments encourage people to do more sport?
- daily exercise classes at school
- wider range of sports taught
- motivational talks by local sportspeople

Some opinions expressed in the discussion:
'Twenty minutes of stretches before classes begin could be a great way to start the day.'
'Many students would enjoy the chance to take up a more unusual sport like fencing.'
'Successful athletes could provide students with a good role model.'

Write an essay discussing **two** of the methods in your notes. You should explain **which method is more important** for the government to consider, **giving reasons** in support of your answer.

You may, if you wish, make use of the opinions expressed in the discussion, but you should use your own words as far as possible.

Useful language for essays

Saying what you personally think	Expressing typical opinions	Giving/Citing evidence	Coming to a conclusion
My own feeling on the subject is that …	Undoubtedly, …	Recent research suggests …	On balance, it appears/seems …
I am of the opinion that …	It is clear …	As little research has been carried out/done in the field of X, it is …	To conclude, …
It goes without saying …	It seems obvious …	The evidence demonstrates/ shows that …	In conclusion, I would say that …
	It is widely held …	According to X, …	To sum up, …
	Those in favour of/against/ opposed to X, …	As X explains/describes/ puts it, …	Ultimately, …
	It is commonly/generally/widely accepted/believed …		
	A commonly held view is …		
	Many are of the belief …		
	It is thought …		

Part 2: Report

The student welfare department of a university has carried out an investigation into why students take up part-time work and what impact this has on their studies. You have been asked to analyse the findings and say how the situation could be improved.

Write your **report**.

Model answer

> **Effects of part-time work on study**
>
> *Introduction*
> The principal purpose of this report is to present findings on students' part-time employment while studying. In addition, recommendations will be made as to how students can better manage their work-study balance.
>
> *Motives behind working*
> Generally speaking, the most common reason that was cited by the survey participants for taking a part-time job was lack of money. Students' loans cover tuition fees and accommodation costs, but there is little left over for day-to-day expenses. A significant proportion also said that they believed their job provides them with invaluable work experience, which would hopefully impress future employers after graduation.
>
> *Impact on studies*
> In terms of the impact of part-time jobs on their studies, the majority of students claimed that their work had no negative effects whatsoever. The average number of hours worked per week ranged from 10 to 25 and many found that their boss was quite flexible with schedules. A small percentage, however, reported negative effects such as feeling tired in lectures and falling grades. The latter was reported by those who tended to work a higher number of hours.
>
> *Recommendations*
> Based on these findings, it is clear that part-time work is now a common aspect of student life and one that provides clear benefits, both financial and otherwise. However, as demonstrating a poor academic performance clearly defeats the purpose of university study, I feel it would be in students' best interests to keep paid employment to under 15 hours and preferably not take on work which involves keeping late hours.

Annotations:
- suitable heading and sub-headings
- use of discourse markers to improve cohesion
- Summarise the aim of the report without copying the wording of the question.
- consistent style used throughout
- language to indicate personal recommendation

Task

Either write your own answer to the task above *or* write an answer to the following question in 220–260 words.

The director of the study exchange department of your university has carried out an investigation into what attracts students to the programme and what impact it has on their studies. You have been asked to analyse the findings of the study and make recommendations on how the programme could be improved.

Write your **report**.

Useful language for reports

Introducing the report	Evaluation	Generalising	Making recommendations
This report will assess/analyse/examine …	It was felt that the … was/were inadequate/disappointing.	In general, …	I believe, therefore, that it would be in our best interests to …
The principal purpose of this report is to describe/analyse/present …	A particularly unsatisfactory aspect was the …	Generally speaking, … On the whole, …	Taking the above factors into consideration, I feel/propose that …

Part 2: Proposal

Your university is failing to attract significant numbers of overseas students. You have been asked to write a proposal for the Board of Directors, stating how more overseas students could be encouraged to take courses there. You should include ideas on how the profile of the university could be raised and made more appealing to international students.

Write your **proposal**.

Model answer

Proposal for attracting more overseas students to Woodford University

Introduction
The purpose of this proposal is to suggest ways in which more international students can be encouraged to attend Woodford University.

(Brief introduction outlining purpose)

Improving the website
The university website should be updated with images of the state-of-the-art self-study centre and show students being helped by academic supervisors. The wide range of courses on offer is also an obvious strength and should be clearly displayed and explained. We also have some internationally renowned lecturers teaching at the university, therefore having mini-profiles on their work and career could be utilised to attract students.

(a suitable heading for each section of the proposal)
(Expand on the task with your own ideas.)

Social media
The university should improve its presence on social media outlets by organising activities and posting updates with photos of students enjoying themselves. After all, university life is not only about academia but also forming new friendships. I believe presenting ourselves as a friendly and welcoming place to study will undoubtedly encourage people from abroad to attend.

(a range of language to avoid repetition)
(State your opinion clearly.)

Student advisers
Living away from home can be difficult for anyone, let alone being in a foreign country. In my opinion, we should set up a student advisers programme to help people to adapt to the way of life here and answer any questions that they may have. These could be on anything from English language questions to the best place to do their shopping in the local town.

In conclusion, I feel that Woodford University has a great deal to offer students from other countries and we should exploit technology to showcase this to the world. I also believe setting up a programme especially for foreign students will make them feel welcome.

(Conclude with a positive statement.)

Task

Either write your own answer to the task above **or** write an answer to the following question in 220–260 words.

You are part of a fundraising committee for your college. In preparation for a meeting, you have been asked to write a proposal to the college board. You should explain what the money is needed for and suggest ways to encourage donations.

Write your **proposal**.

Useful language for proposals

Introduction	Facilities	Making suggestions	Final comments
This proposal examines the …	The venue/college/hotel boasts a range of facilities which …	A programme should be established to …	I have no doubts whatsoever about the suitability of X for …
The purpose of this proposal is to …	The amenities on offer are first-class/second-to-none and include a …	I strongly recommend …	I have every confidence that if X were to be selected/chosen, X would not be disappointed.
		I urge you to consider …	

133

Part 2: Informal letter/email

You recently received an email from a friend telling you that they've just been offered a job in California and will be moving to the USA. Write an email to your friend giving your opinion on their news and offering some advice regarding their move.

Write your **email**.

Model answer

Hi Satoshi

I'm sorry I didn't get back to you right away. First of all, huge congratulations on getting the job. I always knew you'd be head and shoulders above all the other applicants!

Wow! So, you'll be moving to California to work for one of the most innovative IT companies on the planet. What a fantastic opportunity! I'm sure you're well aware of that already, though. I hope you managed to negotiate a good deal for yourself. One thing's for sure is you'll be working with the very best IT professionals out there, so you'll really learn a lot. One of my sister's friends moved over there some years ago for work and she's never looked back.

It will all take a bit of getting used to I guess, as the lifestyle's so different from what you're used to. You'll need time to settle in, but just take it one day at a time. I've heard that people are really friendly and go the extra mile to accommodate those who are new to it all. When do you think you'll start? And will the company help you to relocate from Japan to California? There's bound to be a lot to plan. If I were you, I'd start getting sorted out as soon as possible. It'll help minimise the stress of the move.

I know you've got a busy time coming up but write whenever you can to let me know how you're getting on.

All the best

Irina

Annotations:
- appropriate greeting
- Use idiomatic language.
- Use positive language to offer encouragement.
- Include questions to show interest.
- language for giving advice
- appropriate ending

Task

Either write your own answer to the task above *or* write an answer to the following question in 220–260 words.

You recently received an email from a friend in another country who is hoping to go abroad to attend university. She has asked you for your opinion on her plan and any advice you can give her. Write an email to her commenting on whether or not you think it is a good idea and suggesting possible solutions to problems you think she may encounter.

Write your **email**.

Useful language for informal letters/emails

Opening/Starting off the letter/email	Asking for news	Giving advice	Ending the letter/email
Sorry I haven't been in touch for ages.	So what have you been up to recently?	If it were me, I'd do/use/plan …	Let me know what you decide …
I was so pleased to hear from you after all this time!	What's new with you nowadays/these days?	If you needed to, you could always …	Write back when you get a chance.

Part 2: Formal letter/email

You recently organised a celebration for one of your colleagues at a local hotel. You and your colleagues were not satisfied with the venue or the service you received there. You decide to send an email to the manager of the hotel. Your email should:

- explain your reason for writing
- outline the problem(s) you experienced while at the venue
- include a closing comment to the reader

Write your **email**.

Model answer

Dear Sir/Madam

I am contacting you to express my dissatisfaction with the service a group of us recently received at your hotel. As this was a colleague's engagement party, I wanted to ensure that everything would run smoothly on the evening in question. As it happens, the evening did not live up to expectations and I was put in a very difficult position.

To begin with, the manager, when I made the booking last month, assured me that the hotel had disabled access to the restaurant where the party was being held. Imagine our disappointment when we found that the restaurant was on the top floor and the lift was out of order, leaving it extremely difficult for the disabled members of our party to access. To make matters worse, the staff were not remotely interested when I pointed out how inconvenient this was.

I would also like to point out that the number of vegetarian options on the menu was very limited. Yet again, this was one of the requirements I had discussed, explaining that many of those who would be attending do not eat meat. We were amazed to find only one suitable meal on the entire menu, even though your website advertises 'extensive choice' for non-meat eaters and the restaurant manager had assured me that you would be able to cater for our requirements.

In light of the above, I would sincerely hope that you have the lift repaired and add some vegetarian dishes to your menu as soon as possible.

Yours faithfully,

Prashant Kahlon

Annotations:
- use of less common lexis (run smoothly)
- use of cohesive devices
- brief, relevant opening paragraph
- first reason why the evening did not meet expectations
- second reason why the evening was not a success
- appropriate ending explaining desired outcome

Task

Either write your own answer to the task above *or* write an answer to the following question in 220–260 words.

You recently used an online travel company to book a weekend away to celebrate a family member's birthday. You were not provided with what was included in your deal, and you were disappointed with your experience. You decide to send an email to Mr Layton, the manager of the travel company. Your email should:

- explain your reason for writing
- outline what happened during the weekend
- include a request for action

Write your **email**.

Useful language for formal letters/emails

Reason for writing	Introducing points	Request for action	Ending the letter
I'm contacting you to express (my dissatisfaction with …) I'm writing concerning … I would like to bring to your attention a matter …	To begin with … I would also like to point out … Not only … but …	I would sincerely hope … I strongly recommend …	I look forward to receivng your response. Kind regards Yours sincerely

135

Part 2: Review

An international theatre website has invited people to send in their reviews of plays they have recently watched. Write a review of a play you have seen recently, commenting on its weaknesses as well as its strengths. Support your view with examples, and say whether you consider the play to be worth seeing.

Write your **review**.

Model answer

Matilda the Musical

The recent stage production of Roald Dahl's novel, Matilda, offers us jokes, villains, songs and a touching message. The story centres around a gifted five-year-old girl who loves reading and has the power of telekinesis. She encounters many obstacles from her family and school, and helps her favourite teacher Miss Honey. As we are taken on her journey, the play leaves us in no doubt about the value of believing in yourself and never giving up on your dreams. *(opening statement and summary of what the play is about)*

The lyrics to the musical were written by Tim Minchin, an Australian comedian, so it is not surprising that the songs are hilarious and reflect the narrative of the story brilliantly. The entire cast was superb, including the child actors, who were thoroughly convincing as the students of Crunchem Hall – Matilda's school which is is run by the frightening Miss Trunchbull. For me, though, Cleo Demetriou, in the star role, stole the show with her lovely singing voice. For someone so young she gave a wonderful performance, bringing to life the character of an introverted girl who is intelligent and mischievous, and quietly helps everyone around her. *(use of language to critically evaluate / commenting on the play's strengths)*

However, whilst the director used some highly effective lighting production methods to convey the magic of the story, the set was otherwise somewhat inauthentic with piles of books and alphabet tiles crowding the stage. And to be honest this distracted from the story and gave the actors less space to move around. *(commenting on the play's weakness)*

Overall though, the engaging plot captivated the audience and it was a thoroughly pleasant evening – a definite must-see play for anyone who enjoyed the original novel. *(Include a personal recommendation.)*

Task

Either write your own answer to the task above *or* write an answer to the following question in 220–260 words.

A film website has invited people to send in their reviews of films they have recently watched. Write a review of a film you have recently seen, commenting on its weaknesses as well as its strengths. Support your view with examples, and say whether you consider the film to be worth seeing.

Write your **review**.

Useful language for reviews

Discussing the plot
The plot is (un)predictable/gripping.
The plot fails to impress/lacks impact/keeps you on the edge of your seat.

Commenting critically
The acting was excellent/ever so impressive/unconvincing.
The set was a real highlight of the show.
X gave a particularly powerful/engaging/dazzling/effortless/disappointing/lifeless/wooden performance.
X, playing the role of X, was the undisputed star of the show.
A highlight/feature of the book/play/film/exhibition worth mentioning is the …
The special effects are second to none/fail to impress.

Making recommendations
This play/film will have you crying your eyes out/laughing out loud.
I can/can't think of a better way to spend an evening than watching this film/play.
X is a/an play/film/exhibition not to be missed.

Wordlist

This wordlist contains key vocabulary that is highlighted in Units 1–10. The wordlist is also available on the Student's Resource Centre, where the phonetic script, definitions and example sentences are provided.

adj = adjective   adv = adverb   n = noun   v = verb   sbdy = somebody   sthg = something

Unit 1 Aspire and inspire
Inspiration and success

achieve your goals
encounter obstacles
face your fears
follow in sbdy's footsteps
get up and go
keep driven and focused
keep pushing yourself
make it
reach the pinnacle of sbdy's career
set targets

Unit 2 Working together
Relationships

close (relationship/friend/family) adj
close-knit (family) adj
committed (relationship) adj
complicated (relationship) adj
conventional (upbringing) adj
differ v
dispute n
extended (family) adj
fair-weather (friend) adj
immediate (family) adj
lifelong (friend) adj
mutual (friend) adj
nuclear (family) adj
quarrel v
sheltered (upbringing) adj
stable (relationship) adj
strained (relationship) adj
strict (upbringing) adj
unusual (upbringing) adj

Phrases

drift apart from sbdy
fall out with sbdy
get back together with sbdy
grow up
hit it off with sbdy
keep at arm's length
keep in touch with sbdy
move in the same circles
on the same wavelength
put up with sbdy/sthg
rub shoulders with sbdy
see eye to eye with sbdy
set sbdy up
take after sbdy
take sbdy in
take to sbdy/sthg

Unit 3 A sense of wonder
Travel

economy n
luxuriously adv

Phrases

be on the road
drive a hard bargain
follow an itinerary
get an upgrade
get taken for a ride
go off the beaten track
go with the flow
hit the road
hustle and bustle
laid-back atmosphere
on a shoestring
peace and tranquillity
take in the sights

The senses

appetising adj
aromatic adj
bland adj
breathtaking adj
delicate adj
delicious adj
disgusting adj
dreadful adj
dry adj
faint adj
flavourless adj
foul adj

137

fragrant *adj*
mouth-watering *adj*
overpowering *adj*
pungent *adj*
revolting *adj*
rich *adj*
salty *adj*
smelly *adj*
spectacular *adj*
subtle *adj*
tasty *adj*
vile *adj*

Unit 4 Living in the past
Memory

bring back *v*
haunted by sthg/sbdy *v*
memorable (performance) *adj*
reminisce *v*
share (memories) *v*

Phrases

dim and distant past
distinct impression
faint recollection
foggiest idea
have a memory like a sieve
jog sbdy's memory
spark a memory
stick in sbdy's mind

Rooms and spaces

airy *adj*
brightly (lit) *adv*
conveniently (located) *adv*
cosy *adj*
dark *adj*
dimly (lit) *adv*
dingy *adj*
elegant *adj*
gaudy *adj*
lavishly (decorated) *adv*
light *adj*
messy *adj*
minimally (furnished) *adv*
modestly (decorated) *adv*
old-fashioned *adj*
pleasingly *adv*
retro *adj*
shabby *adj*
simply (furnished) *adv*
smart *adj*
softly (lit) *adv*
solidly (built) *adv*
spacious *adj*
tasteless *adj*
tasteful *adj*

Phrases

bright and cheerful
cramped and cluttered
neat and tidy
sparsely decorated
warm and cosy

Unit 5 Pushing the limits
Work

company car *n*
fill (a position) *v*
hire *v*
internship *n*
low-paid (job) *adj*
pension *n*
perk *n*
position *n*
promotion *n*
unpaid *adj*

Phrases

be in the running for sthg
get up to speed
go into sthg
cut out to be sthg
(30 days') paid holiday
snowed under
take on sthg

Health

ankle *n*
blistered *adj*
blocked *adj*
broken *adj*
bruised *adj*
catch (the flu) *v*
dislocated *adj*
fractured *adj*
muscle *n*
pulled *adj*
rib *n*
run-down *adj*
shoulder *n*
sore *adj*
sprained *adj*
swollen *adj*
throat *n*
torn *adj*
twisted *adj*
worn out *adj*

Phrases

on the mend

under the weather

Unit 6 Changing times
Change

abrupt *adj*

adjust *v*

amend *v*

constitutional *adj*

convert *v*

cosmetic *adj*

distort *v*

economic *adj*

far-reaching *adj*

legislative *adj*

minor *adj*

modify *v*

pleasant *adj*

radical *adj*

rapid *adj*

reform *v*

refreshing *adj*

remodel *v*

shape *v*

significant *adj*

subtle *adj*

sudden *adj*

sweeping *adj*

unexpected *adj*

unforeseen *adj*

unwelcome *adj*

vary *v*

Figurative language

bark *v/n*

buzz *v/n*

clap *v/n*

groan *v/n*

roar *v/n*

shudder *v/n*

swarm *v/n*

wail *v/n*

Unit 7 Brave new worlds
Verbs with *up-*, *down-*, *over-* and *under-*

downgrade *v*

download *v*

downsize *v*

overcome *v*

overestimate *v*

overhear *v*

overlook *v*

overrule *v*

oversee *v*

overtake *v*

underestimate *v*

undertake *v*

underperform *v*

update *v*

upgrade *v*

uphold *v*

Science and research

convert *v*

criteria *n*

determine *v*

development *n*

dissolve *v*

improvise *v*

investigate *v*

principle *n*

procedure *n*

propose *v*

relevance *n*

validation *n*

Unit 8 Getting through
Expressing feelings

astounded *adj*

devastated *adj*

disgusted *adj*

elated *adj*

frustrated *adj*

indifferent *adj*

livid *adj*

lost *adj*

petrified *adj*

smug *adj*

troubled *adj*

wary *adj*

Onomatopoeic words

bang *v/n*

buzz *v/n*

chatter *v/n*

crackle *v/n*

croak *v/n*

drip *v/n*

growl *v/n*

gush *v/n*

hiss *v/n*

howl *v/n*

hum *v/n*

patter *v/n*

ping *v/n*

pop *v/n*

roar *v/n*
rustle *v/n*
screech *v/n*
shatter *v/n*
shriek *v/n*
sigh *v/n*
snarl *v/n*
swoosh *v/n*
whisper *v/n*
whistle *v/n*
whoosh *v/n*

Unit 9 To the market
Money

affluent *adj*
extortionate *adj*
impoverished *adj*
prosperous *adj*
stingy *adj*
tight *adj*

Phrases

break even
fall into debt
go bankrupt
go on a shopping spree
make ends meet
put sthg away
run out of sthg
shop around
stick to a budget

Describing trends

boost *v*
decline *n*
dip *n*
disappointing (sales) *adj*

disastrous *adj*
encouraging *adj*
enormous (interest) *adj*
moderate *adj*
peak *v*
rapid (growth) *adj*
significant (drop) *adj*
slight *adj*
spectacular *adj*
substantial *adj*
surge *v/n*

Phrases

catch on
catch up with sbdy/sthg
level off
pick up
remain stable
shoot up

Unit 10 School of thought
Academic language

Bachelor's (degree) *n*
degree *n*
diploma *n*
faculty *n*
graduation *n*
lecture *n*
lecturer *n*
major *n*
Master's (degree) *n*
minor *n*
module *n*
postgraduate *n*
semester *n*

seminar *n*
syllabus *n*
term *n*
tutor *n*
undergraduate *n*

The mind and brain

head *n*
intellect *n*
leading *adj*
mind *v*
mindful *adj*
unknown *adj*

Phrases

bear in mind
be right in thinking
brains behind sthg
half a mind
have second thoughts about sthg
head space
pick sbdy's brains about sthg
talk sense
think long and hard about sthg
think nothing of
think straight
think twice about sthg
think very highly of sbdy
wishful thinking

Listening scripts

Unit 1 Aspire and inspire

Listening Part 1: Multiple choice

🔊 1.01–1.03

Extract One

You hear two friends talking about role models.

Emily: That was an interesting discussion, wasn't it? So, who would you say your role model was, Gareth? Let me guess, some footballer, no doubt! Cristiano Ronaldo?

Gareth: Very funny! I'm a tech person myself, so, logically, I'd always thought it was Steve Jobs. I've always found his rags-to-riches story of adopted child becomes self-made entrepreneur, then one of the most successful people on the planet really inspiring. I didn't know anything about the other aspects of his life until I saw the film. And to be honest, now I'm not so sure. He wasn't exactly a great family man and there were other aspects of his character that could be called into question, too.

Emily: Sure, but that's what's always bothered me. We expect our role models to be all-round perfect human beings, when it is clearly just a limited part of who they are that inspires us. So I think it's fine to consider him your role model when it concerns your career aspirations, but not necessarily in every area of life.

Gareth: Yeah, true. So, tell me Emily, in what way are you inspired by professional footballers, then?

Emily: You're having a laugh aren't you? I would never choose a footballer as my role model! No, mine's my grandmother – she's such a strong person.

Extract Two

You overhear two students discussing their impressions after a class.

Nick: What did you think of that lecture, Alice? It really wasn't what I'd expected.

Alice: You can say that again! Advertising it as 'Turning points of history', then talking for two whole hours about a bunch of insignificant people … I mean, there are obviously so many different aspects of history he could have talked about. I was going to leave halfway through, but then decided it would be too embarrassing.

Nick: Really? For me, it was time well spent. I don't often come close to tears, but I'll readily admit that I found some of those stories absolutely heartbreaking.

Alice: Yeah, but what did they have to do with historical turning points, Nick? Believing what a baker saw at the battle of Waterloo is relevant, is just preposterous. There's a reason these personal journals haven't been explored before, even if the speaker felt so strongly about them.

Nick: Well, I'm not sure I entirely agree with you. I think we can learn more from how people like ourselves experienced history in the making than we can from official records.

Extract Three

You hear part of an interview on a television programme.

Presenter: How far back can you trace your ancestry, Alex?

Alex: Well, my family's moved around the UK quite a bit in the past few decades, losing a lot of our old papers in the process. And both my parents passed away when I was very young. As a result, I only really knew my grandparents. So beyond that, I'm on less familiar ground.

Presenter: Have you tried looking up records on the internet?

Alex: I'm not quite sure how to do that but I did write a letter to the registry office in the town where my parents used to live and requested some information. According to them, my grandmother's parents came to England from Poland and their family name was Kowalski.

Presenter: Have you found out anything further about them?

Alex: Frustratingly, Kowalski turns out to be a very common name among Poles, so my research ran into a dead end there – I simply didn't know where to go next. Which is why I'm so keen on getting your help in rediscovering my lost family roots.

Language focus 2: Inversion: Exercise 1a

🔊 1.04

1 I didn't know anything about the other aspects of his life until I saw the film.
2 I would never choose a footballer as my role model!
3 I don't often come close to tears …

Unit 2 Working together

Listening Part 2: Sentence completion

🔊 1.05

Anthony Conrad

Networking is something that most people have to do at some point to make contacts and create opportunities in the world of work. However, many of us find it stressful or a cause of social discomfort. Recent Harvard Business School research found that study subjects felt psychologically 'dirty' when asked to participate in networking designed to further their business success. Obviously, when networking is an essential part of getting ahead, such emotions create a negative impact on our ability to communicate and relate as professionals. But, it doesn't have to be like this. Networking can be a positive experience that empowers individuals.

Network ties are essential to advancement in organisations: they open up opportunities, provide insight into processes, office politics and technical knowledge. In the working environment we are involved in two varieties of networking behaviour – personal networking and instrumental networking. Now, personal networking comes naturally to most people. This describes the friendships that you develop with peers and colleagues as you chat, socialise over coffee, and this develops through constant interaction. On the whole these are easy to maintain as the office environment gives you a commonality and a collective identity.

The other form of networking – instrumental networking – has the specific goal of advancement. It's the type people find the most challenging. Interestingly, the Harvard research I mentioned revealed that people in powerful positions tend not to feel the negative psychological effects of networking – it's just part of what they should do. This would suggest that organisations need to create more opportunities for networking so that staff at every level have confidence in engaging in the practice.

So, assuming that those opportunities are provided, what can a person do to improve their networking experience? Build an immediate connection. According to eminent psychologists and business guru Dr Roberta Cialdini, hitting it off with the person you wish to make a connection with is of key importance. With a pre-planned networking meeting, online research can prove to be an invaluable tool. Shared interests quickly establish you as a peer.

Having done this, how will the connection benefit you over time? Again, preparation is key. Perhaps you can introduce your new contact to a different client base. Consider how you can assist them to build their own business role. Show that you are aware of their objectives. In return, they will be more inclined to assist you in your advancement. Even simple gestures like sharing a social media post are likely to strengthen the bond between you.

Once you have established a connection, you can begin to make use of your network. But don't think that your new connections will help you straight away. Allow the relationship to develop and you will reap huge rewards. Although it may be tempting to ask for favours, this often results in losing the contact you've worked hard to find.

Listening Part 4: Multiple matching
🔊 1.06–1.10

Speaker 1
It's true that the isolation can have an incredible effect on you, psychologically. There were times when being so far from anyone and anywhere could make you feel profoundly miserable. But these feelings were often fleeting, and they were overcome after a while. What I hadn't necessarily appreciated from the outset were the inherent risks involved in the work. Mountain gorillas are big, powerful beasts, but sadly they are endangered due to poaching. Sometimes they are killed for bush meat, but more often people want to use body parts in traditional medicines. Nearly every month there were incursions into the national park by hunters seeking trophies. They could be extremely hostile and were often heavily armed. As the risk grew, I couldn't cope with it. In the end, I made a request for a transfer out. Sometimes I regret it, but you have to take these things seriously.

Speaker 2
We'd moved to the city the year before, not long after we'd got married. My husband's job had taken us there. I felt so far from my parents and sisters. It would have been good to have that level of family support around. I wasn't always as self-assured as I am now and back then I was absolutely petrified of going out on my own. Not being able to express myself clearly was the fundamental issue. When I did go out I never really got much from it because I couldn't say what I wanted to. Then one day I met up with a neighbour about the same age as me. We started with the basics, and after that, we were chatting away in no time. Through Zhung Li I met more and more people, and soon we had a close-knit group. We used to meet up and cook together – sharing stories and recipes.

Speaker 3
When I told my family and friends about my plans to head into the rainforest, they thought I was insane. I'd always been fascinated by nature, so the chance to join a research team there seemed too good to miss. All that stuff you see on nature documentaries – the beautiful birds, the dangerous animals – they make you feel so alive. There are some drawbacks though. After a week of solitude, I used to wish I could talk to someone. One time I was standing on the edge of a lake and all the stars were out above me, but they were also below me because of their reflection on the water. I thought 'I really want to share this with someone'. That sense of isolation provided the spark I needed. It inspired me to reflect on the important things in this world and how our actions can impact on it. It certainly helped me to focus on my conservation goals.

Speaker 4
When I first arrived there, the locals were a bit suspicious. I think that they questioned my motives. You often get that as a research scientist. Perhaps they thought we were intending to mine under their village. Despite their reservations, they were extremely helpful – giving invaluable advice on the best way to cope with the day-to-day difficulties. But it was relentless. Any exposed skin got frost bitten immediately, and trying to keep our basic equipment from freezing was a real struggle. Basic actions took forever. We tried to wrap up warm and stay inside as much as possible, but then I felt a bit enclosed and it started to get me down pretty quickly. I kept in regular contact with my family … I couldn't wait till my contract was up and I could see them again.

Speaker 5
Although I'd spent several months in advance learning the local dialect, there were times when even getting something remotely edible for dinner proved a challenge. And coming

from a sprawling city, it was a bit disconcerting to have these vast expanses all around the village. It really was in the middle of nowhere. But I wouldn't have changed things one bit. The steepest part of my learning curve was coming to terms with the local flora and fauna. Gathering samples could be problematic due to the high incidence of toxic plant varieties. And it was necessary to keep a lookout for predators while we conducted field work. Actually, while I was there, I became quite interested in animal behaviour. I used to spend a good deal of my spare time observing them. I'm thinking of using my notes as the basis for an article in a scientific journal.

Unit 3 A sense of wonder

Listening Part 3: Multiple choice

🔊 1.11

(I = Interviewer; S = Dr Susan Cullnean)

I: Our guest tonight is Dr Susan Cullnean from Camford University. Dr Cullnean, as I understand it, you have recently published a book on cross-cultural communication. What do you think makes it a 'hot topic' these days?

S: In today's multicultural societies, and with the increasing opportunities for international travel, more and more often we find ourselves in situations where we have to interact with people from other cultures. These encounters give us an exciting opportunity to learn new things or expand our knowledge about the world. At the same time, it's also a challenge, which can often lead to conflicts.

I: What causes these conflicts?

S: We all follow our own patterns for communication and behaviour, based on our cultural values and assumptions. The problem is that we're not always aware of these, or that they may be different from other people's. **People tend to view their own beliefs and attitudes as** the only logical way to think and act. So when we face an interaction that we don't understand, we often interpret others' behaviour as 'strange' or 'wrong'. If you want to succeed in communicating with people from other cultures, you first need to learn to question and re-evaluate your assumptions.

I: You mean, **we should try to avoid stereotyping**?

S: Well, I'm not saying stereotyping is a good thing, but it *does* fulfil an important psychological function. It makes us feel we understand a confusing situation; it helps us believe we are in control. But when we stereotype, we oversimplify an observation about someone else's behaviour, then make a generalisation from just one or two isolated examples about the cultural norms of an entire society. It's a place to start, but we need to know that stereotypes are more often wrong than right. So **we must be prepared to continue observing people's behaviour** and to reconsider our views with each new observation.

I: Are there any useful techniques to help us do this?

S: It begins with admitting that ours is not the only way. Keeping an open mind is important, as is developing an empathy for others – considering each situation not only from our perspective, but also from their point of view. When we communicate, **we'd be better off finding ways to make it work** rather than worry about whose fault it is when it breaks down. A very effective technique is what we call 'active listening'. It involves listening carefully, then restating the other speaker's statements in your own words to check you both understand them the same way. As well as rephrasing statements, you also need to ask frequent questions to ensure none of the intended meaning is lost.

I: Yes, I can see how that would help mutual understanding. Is there anything else to watch out for?

S: Yes, communication is about much more than just words and phrases. Facial expressions and gestures, of course, also carry meaning, but something that people don't always think about is the fact that we also communicate by how loudly we speak, by where we stand or sit in relation to one another and how much space we keep between us.

I: What do you mean exactly?

S: I'll tell you about my own experience at the university. A couple of years ago, a new colleague, Julia, joined us from Malta. Her first language is English, as is mine, so **I couldn't imagine her having any communication problems with me**. Sure enough, there were no language problems, but each time we spoke, I felt something was just not working right. Then I noticed that whenever we started a conversation in the middle of a room, we always finished with me standing with my back to a wall or my desk. And **that led me to discover the problem was with** our differing sense of personal space. For Julia, who was from the Mediterranean, it was natural to stand closer during an informal conversation. But where she felt comfortable, I had to step backwards to ease my own discomfort because I always felt she was standing too close. And both of us were doing this, completely unaware of what was going on – which is why I always ended up against the wall. The experience made me realise communication was much more than just the language we use.

I: So this means that when I speak to anyone from the Mediterranean, **I should remember to stand a bit closer**?

S: No, you've just fallen into the trap of stereotyping. It's worth bearing in mind that, whatever the cultural norms are, they may not apply to any particular person. Our cultural background is only one of the many factors that influence our behaviour and attitudes – we are all much more complicated than simply representing the place we come from. What I'd advise you to do is to keep your eyes open. Use what you now know about personal space, or whatever else you discover in your interactions, to understand the other person better and adjust your own expectations about how to communicate more effectively.

I: Thank you, and now …

Unit 4 Living in the past

Listening Part 2: Sentence completion

🔊 1.12

Dr Natasha Drake

OK in today's lecture I'm going to discuss how we remember and retain experiences in a human brain which has a finite capacity.

As we all know, a good deal of the memorable events in our lives occur when we're children – our first day at school, the first time we ride a bike. One would assume that such significant events would be retained or at least extremely difficult to forget. But they're not. In many ways childhood memories fall into predictable patterns, becoming more like an anecdote than an actual experience.

Canadian researchers at the University of Toronto have conducted experiments to understand why this is. They looked at the formation of new brain cells and how they impact on our memory. Neurogenesis – the formation of neurons in the region of the brain crucial for learning and remembering – reaches a peak prior to birth and in the very early stages of childhood development. After this peak, there is a steady decline during the remainder of childhood. And what the study has shown is that as neurons grow, memory formation decreases.

Before the age of five, scans show that this area of the brain is constantly changing as children learn how to do new things. A consequence of this dynamism is that memory storage is unstable. Certain memories will become really vague, many others forgotten altogether. The young brain, as it learns new skills, erases memories that are no longer of any use to it. This process of forgetting is referred to as 'infantile amnesia'. In the past, psychologists believed that the reason for vague memory was directly linked with verbal development. The assumption was that a speaking child could discuss, and therefore better retain memories. However, the new research suggests that memory loss is utterly inevitable as the brain develops.

One result of the scans conducted during the research is we now have a better picture of how we remember. For each of our memories to be recalled, we use a range of brain cells in different combinations. This may explain why memories are not static, but constantly evolve. As we think about a memory, we may make minor changes based on our current emotional state. In remembering, we 're-record' the past, and that can result in people creating thoroughly believable false memories.

The new research may also have practical results. Psychologists have long suggested that many phobias are caused by a memory of an event being given prominence over others. These memories could be described as 'jumping the queue' during stressful situations, overloading the parts of the brain which reason and consider consequence. By removing the memories that trigger the phobia, it would no longer be able to take control.

However, engineering our pasts should be approached with caution. Any change to a neural pathway can have an unexpected effect on other interactions and thought processes. While your fear of flying might be cured, you may not be able to find your way to the airport in the first place!

Language focus 1: Adverbs of degree
Exercise 1a

🔊 1.13

1 One would assume that such significant events would be retained or at least extremely difficult to forget.
2 Certain memories will become really vague, many others forgotten altogether.
3 However, the new research suggests that memory loss is utterly inevitable as the brain develops.

Listening Part 1: Multiple choice

🔊 1.14–1.16

Extract One

You hear part of a film review show.

Jake: So, that covers cinema releases. Amy, any suggestions for the small screen over the next seven days?
Amy: Well Jake, my recommendation would have to be Michel Gondry's classic *Eternal Sunshine of the Spotless Mind*. A real gem, with superb performances from a star-studded cast and Charlie Kaufman's whip-smart script.
Jake: That's quite an endorsement! Not seen it myself. What kind of film is it, and why should I watch it?
Amy: It's a bit tricky to pigeonhole – there are elements of sci-fi and psychological thriller in there, but at the end of the day it's your standard non-linear narrative exploring the nature of memory and love.
Jake: Oh right, one of those. So what's the plot?
Amy: Most of the film takes place in the mind of one character who's undergoing a procedure to have his memories of a failed relationship erased. As this happens, another part of his brain works to hide the memories away – changing events to preserve those valuable recollections. The story jumps around and changes as time goes on. There are a number of scenes which we see repeatedly, from different perspectives. It's very clever and tremendously poignant.
Jake: So it reflects the idea that we reconstruct our memories?
Amy: Yes, I suppose it does …

Extract Two

You hear a radio interview about how the past is used to sell products.

Tim: From the resurgence of old TV shows to retro fashions – the past is a powerful tool when it comes to selling. My guest today is Elena Mitchell, author of *The Art and Commerce of Nostalgia*. Elena, can you shed any light onto what's happening?

Elena: Well Tim, there are lots of factors at play; but take advertising and its careful use of soundtracks and visual cues. Early experiences evoked by a song or an image suggestive of simpler or happier times can unconsciously influence consumers' buying habits.

Tim: I can see why – music is so emotive. Like when you hear something on the radio and suddenly you feel that you're young and carefree again.

Elena: Right. And with that return to the past some companies go even further. In recent years branding and packaging reminiscent of that seen decades ago has been revived by businesses hoping to tap into our cultural memories.

Tim: So what's the advantage of doing that?

Elena: Well, it results in what we call 'associative branding' – something we're seeing more frequently. Consumers are manipulated into identifying a modern product with something that is historically more established. Loyalty to a brand can be promoted as we identify these products with those we bought and used in the 'good old days'.

Extract Three

You hear a brother and sister talking about their childhood home.

Brother: Did Mum and Dad tell you that they're thinking about selling the house?

Sister: No, they didn't mention it when I saw them last month. I guess now it's just the two of them it makes sense to downsize – they certainly don't need such a massive place. To be honest I've never been very fond of it, far too minimalist for my taste and I only lived there for a year before going off to uni. I much preferred our old house in Cornwall. After all, that was where we grew up.

Brother: The fact it's contemporary doesn't bother me but I know what you mean, you're always going to feel more sentimental towards somewhere that holds so many memories. Though I have to say your recollection of it is a bit hazy. Don't you remember how cramped and cluttered it was? There wasn't room for us all. And the plumbing was an absolute nightmare! The water was either freezing or scalding.

Sister: None of that really mattered – even you didn't really mind at the time. You've just got too used to living the high life in your fancy open-plan apartment. I'll never forget the spectacular views down to the beach and how warm and cosy it was. If I could, I'd move back there in an instant.

Unit 5 Pushing the limits

Listening Part 4: Multiple matching

🔊 1.17–1.21

Speaker 1
My friends often point out how ironic it is that while my job is going round giving talks on how to minimise stress at work, I'm one of the most stressed out people they know! They just don't understand the pressure that comes with being self-employed. I don't have all the perks that my friends enjoy like 30-days paid holiday, health insurance and long lunches. I can never guarantee where my next pay cheque is coming from so I often end up biting off more than I can chew. If I were to work any longer hours, I'd go crazy. The only thing that helps me unwind is a good, long workout. It helps me to shake off all my worries and clear my mind. Knowing my luck, I'll overdo it and end up getting injured which is the last thing I need.

Speaker 2
I've been with the company a while and used to get on well with everyone. We all used to socialise and help if someone was particularly snowed under or off sick. When I was made supervisor that all changed – no one listens to me at all. There's one guy, Darren, who's particularly causing me trouble. It's difficult because he is good at what he does but his way of talking to me just isn't on. I've found reading a book at lunchtime helps me to take my mind off it all and I go back to my desk feeling more positive. But I guess that won't solve things in the long term. I think the time's come to face this head on. If I happen to see him later today, I'll ask him out for a coffee and we can have a chat.

Speaker 3
I'm pretty well-respected in the world of health and fitness and give presentations all over the globe. Whilst it would sometimes be nice to spend a bit more time at home, I appreciate how lucky I am to have seen so much of the world. Standing in front of really big audiences is something I really struggle with. When I tried to talk to my friends about it they just said 'Oh, you'll be alright'. I realised this was something that I had to overcome alone, after all, it was my reputation that was on the line. I did a bit of research – some of the advice I found was a bit odd – go for a run an hour before, don't drink any coffee for a week beforehand … eventually I stumbled across something … close your eyes and think positive thoughts. I know it sounds a bit daft but it works for me!

Speaker 4
I've only got one more year left until I get my law degree … provided I complete my dissertation on schedule. And I have to say the end can't come soon enough. A classmate of mine is so competitive and always comparing her grades to mine. Last summer I made the mistake of telling her about the internship I was interested in doing – well of course she applied for it too. And guess who got it? She did! If it hadn't been for me, she wouldn't have even heard about it! In the past I always used to meet up and talk through everything with my friends but they all live back home and talking on the phone just isn't the same. Luckily, I do have my housemate – she can always make me laugh and listens to me patiently as I get everything off my chest.

Speaker 5
My grandmother was a ballerina, so it was perhaps inevitable somebody in the family would follow in her footsteps. I've always loved everything about it: the sensation during the moves, the exhaustion after practice,

even getting up on the stage in front of hundreds of people doesn't faze me. It's the constant injuries that are getting me down. If I don't perform, I won't get paid. But that's not really my main concern. It's the risk that if the director won't wait for me to recover, I'll lose my part in the productions. Experts recommend exercise to cope with stress but my life's pretty much a workout already! What helps me is to get out of the city. When I come back home, I always feel much more upbeat.

Language focus 1: Conditionals: Exercise 2b

🔊 1.22

1 If I were to work longer hours, I'd go crazy.
2 If it hadn't been for me, she wouldn't have even heard about it!
3 If I happen to see him later today, I'll ask him out for a coffee.
4 I've only got one more year left until I get my law degree … provided I complete my dissertation on schedule.

Unit 6 Changing times

Listening Part 3: Multiple choice

🔊 2.01

(I = Interviewer; L = Lisa Jones; A = Andy Mitchell)

I: Hello, and welcome to the programme, where this week we're discussing trends and changes in an industry which is worth more than $110 billion globally. With us to share their opinions and predictions, are two gaming enthusiasts, Lisa Jones and Andy Mitchell. Lisa, **it's so easy to get lost amongst all the newly developed products.** Would it be right to say that we're going through a transition time in gaming?

L: Well, I think that you could say that, yes. In the last few years games have dropped in price, so we're seeing more and more people being able to play them. The fact that hand-held devices and smartphones are more widespread these days has certainly impacted on the industry too. But for me, the biggest influence of change has been demographic. We're now seeing gamers whose parents played games too. This means that there's a lot more understanding and interaction around gaming, as parents are better equipped to select appropriate content, or play alongside their kids. What's really impressed me is the way that the industry has responded to this.

I: Andy, do you agree with that assessment? How will it impact on gaming?

A: It's a very interesting point. A lot of people have pointed out that in a society where the pace of life is frenetic, cross-generational gaming can provide an opportunity for families to share experiences positively. But I'd argue that interactive gaming of any kind will develop as it mirrors our needs to communicate, build relationships, and collaborate with people over a range of digital networks.

I: Are there any specific developments we should be looking out for?

L: Sure. Picking up on Andy's point, there's a lot going on with simulations at the moment. It was with the success of games like *Minecraft* that this idea really took off. There you had a platform where friends could meet and talk while working collaboratively. And that is set to grow – I think the industry is definitely pushing the notion of games as a place for socialising … sharing … connectivity. There's a big move to make games more about the social experience rather than the gaming experience. Sharing is going to be integral to the design of many forthcoming games. Tying in with that, there'll be a lot more connection with social networks, so games can connect to players' accounts in real time.

I: I see. Are there any other ways game design is changing?

A: Yes, I suppose there are. A lot of these tend to be focused around the processes of development, rather than the look or feel of games. Traditionally, the model has been for developers to keep their games secret and build up to a big-budget release with short trailers – a bit like the way the film industry works – but there are some interesting developments occurring. Initiatives like preview programs have allowed users to buy games before they're finished and even have a say in how the development process pans out. It's only a matter of time before that model becomes more mainstream and we see studios live-streaming the development process. Probably charging a subscription fee. Audiences could interact and make suggestions for plots, characters and mini-games within the game. It could radically change the user/developer relationship.

I: Is that concept likely to be popular with most gamers?

L: I think so. **We might not see a time when individuals have games created for them specifically, but developers are expected to involve gamers in content creation** much more in the future. There are already PC games where players can construct their own levels and share them online. **This process will probably be replicated in the console sector by developers.** We may even see a new era where new content is outsourced to dedicated fans and gamers sell their own creations to one another.

I: And what about the technology that we play games on? Are there any big changes set to occur there?

A: Certainly for game developers, VR … um that's 'virtual reality' … has provided a welcome shot in the arm. Most of the major corporations are paying a lot of money for VR applications. So, in terms of investment into gaming, there are benefits. With regards to game-playing though, I think that the jury is still undecided. For your average gamer it's a lot of money to pay out. The technology still needs improvements before these kinds of games become a mass consumer phenomenon.

L: I tend to agree with that. I think in many ways gamers would like to see the experience of playing improved, rather than having to commit to buying costly VR that can rapidly date and impede the flow of a game. What we need are technological developments that improve upon what we've already got. Sometimes a relatively simple advance can bring the biggest gains.

I: Well, thank you both.

Unit 7 Brave new worlds

Listening Part 4: Multiple matching
🔊 2.02–2.06

Speaker 1
In the past twenty years or so technology has just escalated beyond anything we could have ever imagined. I'm not bothered about fitness gadgets, social media or the development of machines which will run our households for us. What I do keep an eye on is the advancement of smartphones; it still amazes me that what is essentially a computer can fit neatly and easily into my back pocket. I'm a business consultant so I'm often on the road – visiting different companies, checking in and out of hotels. I'm hardly ever at the office and don't have time for much of a social life either to be honest. So without my phone I'd be completely out of touch in my professional life.

Speaker 2
All of my mates have become obsessed with binge-watching TV series on streaming services like Netflix. We used to go to the gym every weekend. The equipment they have there is state of the art – it can monitor your heart rate and you can set it to a marathon training profile. But they don't take advantage of it – their fitness levels have really taken a knock. All they do is watch episode after episode. And on the all-too-rare occasions when we do go out, they spend the journey there staring at their smartphone screens replying to messages … it's ridiculous. Don't get me wrong – I do appreciate that we live in an age of technological advancement, but it shouldn't come at the expense of real interaction and relationships.

Speaker 3
So many people criticise social media but they just need to accept this is the age we live in. It's not like I'm obsessed with it or using it to replace real friendships with virtual ones but I do appreciate how versatile it is. It's just so convenient for inviting people to events. My friends and I set up a group on a social network to organise our training schedule for a half-marathon we were all taking part in. We could also keep a record of the routes we'd taken and share our personal bests. So the argument for it making young people lazy doesn't really stand up. If I didn't use it, I'm not sure my mates would go to the effort of calling me or messaging me separately.

Speaker 4
My girlfriend bought it for me for our two-year anniversary. At first I thought it was a smartphone watch so initially I was quite disappointed. But it's changed my life. It really made me face up to the fact that I had let myself go a bit. Basically it's a gadget which measures how active you are throughout the day. For me it's much more effective than going to the gym as I just don't have the willpower to get up and go there every morning. I used to dutifully pay my membership, full of the best intentions, and then would inevitably choose to push the snooze button on my alarm. So not only am I looking and feeling much better, I'm better off too!

Speaker 5
I moved to the countryside a few months ago. And in many ways it has been great … the wi-fi and network signal are pretty intermittent, which is a bit of an inconvenience, but it means I've started to lead a more active lifestyle and work doesn't follow me home. The one drawback is that it's very cut off. My friend was coming to stay for the weekend and commented on how it was like something out of a horror movie! She told me about this app that allows you to turn on your lights and TV remotely, so I would always come back to a bright, inviting home. Well, it's not quite worked out that way… my saved TV shows blast out across the fields and the lights flick on and off … my neighbours must think I'm absolutely insane. I wish I'd left well alone!

Listening Part 1: Multiple choice
🔊 2.07–2.09

Extract One
You overhear a conversation between two people about recycling.

John: Have you heard what's going on with this selective recycling project, Fiona? The city council was going to introduce it from January, but apparently there's been some resistance. I heard that the council was already considering dropping the scheme altogether.

Fiona: That's ridiculous! Why would they just cancel something that's in everyone's interest? Did they give any reasons, John?

John: Well, they're suddenly worried about the extra cost of three different bins per household. According to their claims, they were also hoping to increase the capacity of the recycling plant near Whitefield. It was due to have been completed by September. But that didn't happen – unforeseen circumstances, they're saying. I guess it would have been a reasonable explanation for a delay, but what's really annoying is that they're no longer talking about a postponement now.

Fiona: You know, I wonder what our local representative thinks about all this. And why aren't local residents involved in making a decision of this magnitude? What could we do? Do you think starting a petition might help? I'd certainly be ready and willing to take that on! I'm convinced most people will side with us and put their name to it.

Extract Two

You hear two researchers talking about their work.

Sally: So, Mark, I've just heard you're one of the people going to the Milan conference on the 15th. Will you be presenting something or are you just going there to watch?

Mark: No presentations for me this time, actually. But hang on a minute, Sally. You were supposed to be going too, weren't you? Or did I get my wires crossed somewhere?

Sally: No, you're right, I was. But Nick found me just as I was about to leave work last night, and he's given me responsibility for that new project that's been in the pipeline for so long. Essentially, he offered me a promotion, so I'd have been an idiot not to accept. But I'll now have to put together a detailed plan for the research phase, including budget projections, resourcing … you know, the works. And that's before things get going in earnest. No time for conferencing, no time for fun. And of course, no one yet to delegate all these tasks to!

Mark: Well, I'm not sure if I should congratulate you or sympathise with you. It's certainly a very big step up the ladder, though and I couldn't think of a better person for the job. You deserve it!

Extract Three

You overhear a conversation between a customer and a shop assistant in a technology store.

Customer: I was going to buy a new laptop, but now I'm looking at these tablets you've got. I can't decide. Do you think I'd be better off getting one of those instead? Are they a better deal do you think?

Assistant: That depends. Laptops are more flexible, portable versions of desktop computers. These days they are capable of everything bigger machines can do. I'd say they've caught up in computing power and performance already. On the other hand, tablets are essentially mobile devices with some computing features. They are lighter, more compact and often cheaper. They're just as good as laptops for functions like browsing the internet, electronic communication, viewing documents and watching or listening to media.

Customer: Would you recommend a tablet for work? I'm looking for something I could use to do my PhD dissertation.

Assistant: I usually recommend tablets for people whose jobs involve lots of travelling and only limited amounts of desk-based work. Tablets aren't really suited to delivering presentations, substantial research or processing longer documents – they simply run out of storage capacity. Of course, if you're doing a lot of field research, portability is more important – so a tablet may be your best option. As I said, it all comes down to what your priorities are.

Unit 8 Getting through

Listening Part 2: Sentence completion

🔊 2.10

Ben Frost

While there is obvious interest from the academic research community about the potential of Artificial Intelligence, in financial terms it is also big news. Companies exploring the technology are often backed by multimillion dollar investments. AI is already being used in the banking sector for trading and making financial decisions, and no doubt will become even more widespread in the future. In the last couple of years, systems have been developed that can learn from data and make rational decisions based upon it.

Although AI has started to make inroads on 'reason', understanding emotion is a greater challenge. Emotional intelligence plays a massive role in understanding how other people are feeling. We rely upon it to recognise emotions and use these to guide our behaviour. So, how can inert objects made of plastic and wiring hope to learn this aspect of our everyday interaction? Well, the answer seems to be 'affective computing'. By analysing hundreds of facial expressions, computers that recognise a range of subtle human emotions and respond accordingly, could in theory be built.

Globally, scientists in different fields of research have joined forces with engineers to establish whether this can be made a reality. Initially, projects attempted to analyse data such as someone's heart rate. Now computers are also studying vocal pitch, basic facial expressions and even our body language and muscle movements when we interact with digital content.

Research has shown that over a long period of time individuals display consistent patterns in how they respond to emotions. Provided they are displayed consistently, wearable computers can be taught to recognise those patterns. In a small step, a computer with a camera can start to learn how to take lots of different data points from your face, and map it to a smile or a frown. The human face has 45 different muscles. These constantly contract and convert to facial movements. The computer uses an algorithm to match these with known emotions so that it can tell if you are statistically happy, tired or anxious.

Over the next few years we'll see a whole range of companies utilising this technology. It's already being used to test audience response to new TV shows, music and film trailers, and the potential for use by advertisers is vast. For instance, your smartphone might detect that you are feeling sad or frustrated. Consequently it'll direct you to information about holidays or a change of job. But the applications are not only commercial – for example affective computing could be used by healthcare companies to create emotion-sensing wearables – potentially your laptop could contact your doctor if it became concerned with your emotional well-being, or identified prolonged periods of stress.

Unit 9 To the market

Listening Part 3: Multiple choice

🔊 2.11

(I = Interviewer; L = Lucy Francis; S = Simon Ryder)

I: Hello, my guests today are Simon Ryder and Lucy Francis, both consultants in the advertising industry. With the growth of digital media this is a turning point for the industry, right Lucy?

L: Things are definitely going through a transition right now, yes. The online world has had considerable impact, but we can't underestimate changes in consumers. Traditionally, advertising used a lot of techniques derived from persuasion studies conducted in the 1960s, but consumers nowadays may not believe the superlative claims about a product's qualities. The same old slogans and annoying tunes that get stuck in your head all day, can actually turn a lot of people off. Arguably, consumers are more sophisticated these days or at the very least most people like to think that they have refined tastes. This shift in perspective has meant that advertising companies have changed how they advertise in order to reflect consumer preferences.

I: Simon, what's your take on that?

S: I'd say that adverts that can make people laugh are, and I think always will be popular. Advertisers just have to make sure they pitch the comedy at the right level. However, I do think Lucy makes a good observation and I tend to agree that advertising has been affected by increased critical thinking in consumers. More traditional approaches to selling, which often appealed to buying habits or generated peer pressure, no longer hold as much influence. Fundamentally, we've become so accustomed to the language of advertising that we see right through it. As a result, it has had to make changes in order to keep working effectively.

I: So, how are we seeing these changes?

L: We've recently seen more sophisticated central messages. Millennial parents account for upwards of 40% of households. They tend to require quite targeted advertising. On the other hand, research suggests 25% of parents learn about new products from their kids. So advertisers need to strike a fine balance and consider the viewpoints of both the buyer and consumer. Consider 'stealth-health', where companies brightly package products as child-friendly, while pushing the nutritional value to parents. In this sector there's also a tendency to tap into the real food movement. You notice lots of emotionally-charged language such as 'local', 'fair' and 'organic'. There's also been a move to use more creatively engaging advertising. Some of the guerrilla marketing campaigns, mixing conventional advertising and conceptual art, have had incredible success … mainly as they get posted on social media, or retweeted.

I: Is this a trend which you see continuing?

S: Guerrilla advertising has certainly grabbed a lot of headlines and I think advertisers will continue to push the envelope and challenge expectations. An area I think we will really see a lot of growth in is the notion of targeting consumers directly. We're moving from a position where brands knew relatively little about their consumers' specific needs to a place where personal and publicly available data are used to influence marketing. I think we're much closer to the point where generic adverts are customised and directed at one consumer – anticipating their needs. Programs which have access to income and usual spending habits will fill your online grocery shop. Using a device which has been programmed to assess your mood, products could be ordered automatically, to improve your health or well-being.

I: So, what kind of impact does this have on big, established brands? Are they changing their approach?

L: Well, the implication for many brands is huge. Consumer expectations have moved on. Just having a great product or a big ad campaign is no longer enough. Consumers may respond to both but they also want to be talked with, not talked at. Sometimes this means recognising that, rather than featuring sports stars and celebrities in adverts, companies will be more successful focusing on ordinary people. The technique of showing people how the rich and famous live doesn't have the same effect as it did in previous decades. In realistically depicting users, a brand can create a sense of understanding and empathy. Showing that you've listened to your audience is really important to ongoing success.

I: Interesting. Simon, what do you think?

S: Over the last few decades, consumer trust has been gradually worn away. In one respect, this is a problem for advertisers, but it presents opportunities in another. There's lots of attention being paid to the power of brands to positively influence social change – whether that's supporting good causes or paying workers a living wage. People want to buy from brands that are authentic and do what they claim to do. I think that companies can gain attention by not making false claims and clearly telling consumers what they stand for, and then delivering on those promises.

I: Thank you both for coming in today, that's all we have time for. Next up …

Language focus 1: Determiners and pronouns: Exercise 1

🔊 2.12

1 So, what kind of impact does this have on big, established brands?
2 Well, the implications for many brands is huge.
3 Consumers may respond to both but they also want to be talked with, not talked at.
4 Over the last few decades, consumer trust has been gradually worn away. In one respect, this is a problem for advertisers, but it presents opportunities in another.
5 There's lots of attention being paid to the power of brands.

Unit 10 School of thought

Listening Part 4: Multiple matching

🔊 2.13–2.17

Speaker 1
I seemed to spend a good deal of my childhood with my head in a book, looking up facts and figures and the traditions and customs of far-flung places. But after I left school, work and family took over. When I retired I finally had the time to become an avid reader again. A friend suggested doing an online course in Cultural Studies. At first I found it a bit daunting, but the syllabus was very accessible and the tutors were incredibly supportive. Since completing the first modules I've signed up for more. As a result of all this, I'm actually considering taking a degree course. There's no reason why not, despite my age.

Speaker 2
After graduating I started working for an IT firm in the capital. Initially there was so much to learn and everything was very fast-paced. We were developing a system that analysed trades in stocks and shares, and made predictions about emerging trends. Soon it became very repetitive though, and I needed a bit more stimulation. So I decided to attend pretty much every professional development course the company ran. Banking and finance had always seemed like a foreign language, but within a few months I was able to understand most of what was going on. Anyway, I started looking at other avenues and there were certainly a lot of well-paid jobs out there. Interestingly enough, there's a lot more to be made in finance than IT.

Speaker 3
When I spoke to the college about my plans to transfer here permanently, they suggested that I look into ways of improving my language proficiency – that was one condition that I needed to meet to carry on living here. One fairly affordable option seemed to be living with a host family. I really benefited from having the chance to converse with native speakers on a daily basis. Although at times it was incredibly frustrating not being able to follow everything that was going on. Fortunately, my result in the exam was good enough, so I could seriously look into getting permanent residency. Since then, I've had the confidence to do a lot more challenging things in life. Sure, they haven't all worked out, but you just have to take that in your stride.

Speaker 4
I suppose I'm the kind of person who thrives on setting themselves targets. I'd been working in the faculty for about six years and felt that the trip would be a great way to conduct a bit of field research. I thought it would be a good idea to learn a bit of the local language so I could get by on my own and get to know the way of doing things out there. I picked up some books from the library, and also started doing one of those online courses you see advertised. It turns out that I'm actually quite good at it! Although I'd always gone down the scientific route and been interested in that side of things, I learnt that languages seem to come to me pretty naturally. I'm still studying Malay, but in the end I didn't actually make it out to Malaysia as I couldn't get the funding.

Speaker 5
Throughout my studies I'd thought about whether to look for an internship near my home town, but after I graduated the idea of going back no longer appealed. I was enjoying life in a big city so I took a placement in a pharmacy there. A few months into the post, I was asked to help out in a rural practice as an important part of my ongoing training. Funnily enough, I ended up only a few miles from where I grew up. And I have to say it's been so worthwhile. I've learnt more here than I ever did at uni or at the pharmacy. Helping and getting to know patients from where I'm from, including some old school friends, has been amazing. Feeling part of something bigger than myself has really opened my eyes.

Listening Part 2: Sentence completion

🔊 2.18

Lesley Rankin
Urban schools face common challenges – a lack of space, high numbers of students and limited resources. These issues are often compounded by the fact that many urban schools draw pupils from low-income families, who may not have access to the technology often required by contemporary education. In some areas it's estimated that nearly 50% of high-school graduates from such schools feel they are not ready for study at university or college. So, what can be done to enhance learning experiences and ensure students are better prepared for ongoing education?

A good deal of research has focused on the impact of the immediate classroom environment on levels of concentration and attainment. Cluttered classrooms can actually reduce the chances of success. This is particularly evident with early learners, who can experience heightened levels of distraction. As teachers are faced with growing class numbers, they have to address this issue. While many schools like to ensure that pupils are engaged by bright posters, wall charts, and other stimulating content, there is growing evidence that children who are studying in low-sensory environments tend to be able to focus better on tasks.

Traditionally, teachers often place young learners in rows, with any computers being kept to the side of the classroom as it allows them to observe the whole class and maintain control. This classroom layout can also impact on educational success. Placing students in clusters, with one device per group, can help develop skills for life and work beyond the classroom. After one particular school had made this change to more collaborative designs, they saw an increase in levels of engagement and active learning. Basically, the school effectively turned conventional classrooms into learning studios, allowing students to move around and interact. This in turn should encourage collaborative problem-solving which is an essential skill for success.

Another key factor being explored is the role of the broader community in engaging learners. More and more urban schools are working in partnerships with businesses to ensure that industry figures can provide a positive influence. Studies have shown that if role models encourage positive growth by highlighting the importance of cooperation, then learners tend to work better together. Since they started the partnerships, schools have seen a marked improvement in exam results. Alongside programmes like 'Getting Ahead', where urban school leavers are supported in work experience placements, such approaches can provide a meaningful and successful link between the classroom and the workplace.

Language focus 2: Participle clauses: Exercise 1a

🔊 2.19

1   As teachers are faced with growing class numbers, they have to address this issue.
2   Children who are studying in low-sensory environments tend to be able to focus better on tasks.
3   After one particular school had made this change to more collaborative designs, they saw an increase in levels of engagement.

Answer key

Unit 1: Aspire and inspire

Vocabulary and Speaking: Inspiration and success page 6

2
1 make, get 2 encounter, achieving
3 following 4 overcome
5 Set, keep 6 pushing, reach

Reading and Use of English Part 8: Multiple matching page 6

2
1 B   2 A   3 C   4 B   5 D
6 D   7 A   8 C   9 A   10 C

Language focus 1: Past and present perfect – simple and continuous page 9

1a
1 *had been*   past perfect simple
2 *you haven't been using*   present perfect continuous
3 *'d been reading*   past perfect continuous
4 *have read*   present perfect simple

1b
1 b   2 a   3 d   4 c

2
1 has worked
2 have/'ve been painting
3 has/'s known
4 had/'d been living
5 had not/hadn't taken off
6 had/'d visited
7 have/'ve been taking
8 had been watching
9 had/'d checked
10 have not/haven't eaten

3
1 c   2 b   3 d   4 a

4
1 C   2 B   3 A   4 C   5 B
6 B

Word formation: Adjectives page 10

1a
voluntary – volunteer
energetic – energy
restless – rest
memorable – memory

1b
1 imaginary, complimentary, necessary
2 scientific, dramatic, specific
3 breakable, likeable, knowledgeable
4 countless, doubtless, careless

2
1 significant   2 risky
3 unsatisfactory   4 cooperative
5 apparent   6 cautious

Listening Part 1: Multiple choice page 11

2
1 B   2 A   3 C   4 B   5 C
6 C

3
3 It really wasn't what I'd expected. You can say that again!
4 The whole idea that how a town baker … preposterous
5 I'm not quite sure how to do that
6 my research ran into a dead end there

Language focus 2: Inversion page 12

1a
1 didn't know
2 would never choose
3 don't often come

1b
Suggested answer
The emphasised phrase or clause is moved to the start of the sentence. In the main clause, the order of the auxiliary and the subject is inverted. If the phrase we emphasise is negative (*not until*), the verb in the main clause is changed from negative to affirmative to avoid double negation.

2
1 negative   2 subject   3 auxiliary
4 more   5 formal

3
1 Only when she/Vanessa tried to take out her purse to pay did Vanessa/she realise it had been stolen.
2 On no account should you share the contents of this document with anyone else.
3 Not only is he really clever (but) he is also incredibly funny.
4 At no time have you (ever) mentioned (any) reservations about getting married.
5 Had I known Jared was allergic to nuts, I wouldn't have made that satay dip.
6 Seldom do we see players with such natural ability.
7 No sooner had I arrived home than they called me back to the office.

Reading and Use of English Part 2: Open cloze page 12

3
1 (comparative) adverb
2 preposition
3 preposition
4 determiner
5 negative word used for contrast
6 part of an expression
7 part of an expression
8 part of a phrasal verb

4
1 more   2 as   3 from   4 whose
5 Not   6 in   7 all   8 out

Writing Part 1: Essay page 13

1
Suggested answers
1 your tutor
2 two of the factors in the notes
3 Each opinion relates to a factor in the notes (here the related opinions are in the same order as the factors in the notes). No, you do not have to use the opinions in the essay. (You can but you should use your own words as far as possible.)

2
Suggested answers
Two factors included: limited choice of possible careers; fame and wealth as goals
Paragraph 2: Focus on the first factor: professions shown by the media; other influences on young people
Paragraph 3: Focus on the second factor: fame and fortune seen as same as success and happiness
Paragraph 4: Conclusion: summing up of opinions

3

a

Giving your opinion
it should be pointed out …
A much more significant aspect … is …

Stating other people's views
Some would argue …
The main reason for this opinion …

Widely held beliefs
few people would dispute …
The main reason for this opinion …
This has led many … to view …
this seems to be a widespread belief

Providing sources
Statistics show that …
upon the basis of viewing figures
A recent survey …
substantial coverage in the media

b
Firstly; as a result; However; On the other hand; The main reason for this; This; Consequently; In conclusion; A much more significant aspect

4
Sample answer
Recent research suggests that young people only truly begin to think about their futures once they enter college. There are many aspects of college which help to determine these ambitions, some of which have a far greater influence than others.

Firstly, one must consider the courses on offer. As much as you may want to study medicine if this class is not available or requires certain grades that you have not attained, then this field of study is closed to you. As such it would be extremely difficult to ever imagine becoming a doctor. In this subtle way whole doors to potential careers are closed to students forever. On the other hand, nowadays young people are much more open to commuting or living away from home so they could find a college that is better suited to their needs.

Some people would argue that a more significant factor is the way in which exams are conducted. Many young people dread being tested for a variety of different reasons. One thing is certain though, if you do badly in an exam, your confidence can be affected. This can have a huge impact on shaping ambitions as it could put off students from pursuing careers which require high grades in exams.

Taking everything into consideration, whilst you can find a college that teaches subjects you are interested in, there seems to be little way around not being good at exams. Consequently, this has considerable influence in shaping ambitions.

Unit 2: Working together

Vocabulary: Relationships page 15

2a
1 B   2 A   3 A   4 A   5 C
6 B   7 C

3a
1 committed   2 nuclear   3 close
4 sheltered

3b
Suggested answers
1 committed relationship
2 nuclear family
3 close friend/relationship/family
4 sheltered upbringing

Listening Part 2: Sentence completion page 16

3
1 negative impact
2 opportunities
3 (constant) interaction
4 powerful positions
5 confidence
6 shared interests
7 objectives
8 (huge) rewards

Language focus 1: Modals page 18

1
1 must have, would
2 needn't
3 shouldn't have, Haven't you
4 can't, can

2
1 logical deduction (must have), willingness (would)
2 lack of obligation/necessity (needn't)
3 criticism (shouldn't have), annoyance (Haven't)
4 inability (can't), request (can)

3
1 B   2 B   3 B   4 B   5 A
6 A

Reading and Use of English Part 1: Multiple-choice cloze page 19

1
1 D, a
2 A, c
3 C, b

3
1 C   2 D   3 C   4 A   5 C
6 D   7 A   8 B

Reading and Use of English Part 7: Gapped text page 20

2
Suggested answers
Subject – relationships between humans and animals

4
1 C   2 E   3 B   4 G   5 D
6 A   not used = F

Language focus 2: Relative clauses page 22

1
1 c   2 b   3 a   4 d

2
The pronoun can only be replaced with *that* in Sentence 1. *That* can only be used in defining relative clauses to replace *who* and *which*.
The relative pronoun cannot be omitted from sentences 1, 3 and 4. Relative pronouns can be omitted in defining relative clauses if the relative pronoun is the object of the verb in the relative clause.

3
1 whom, where   2 which, whose
3 which, which   4 who
5 why, which   6 who, which, where

4
a
3 … is something which/that we haven't …
4 … a woman who/that said …
5 … reason why/that so many …; it's a city which/that offers a lot …
6 … the town that she had grown up in …
b
3 … is something we haven't done for ages.
5 … reason so many …
6 … the town she had grown up in …

Answer key

Listening Part 4: Multiple matching page 22
1 G 2 E 3 A 4 F 5 H
6 E 7 D 8 H 9 B 10 F

Writing Part 2: Letter/email page 23
1
Correct options:
1 reference
2 Whilst
3 In addition
4 Aside from
5 I feel I must also point out
6 also
7 hope
8 faithfully

2
Suggested answers
Paragraph 2: describing candidate's work experience
Paragraph 3: describing candidate's personal skills and qualities
Paragraph 4: closing comments, request for action, summarising main point(s) of the letter, final recommendation

3
a *I feel; I have no doubt; I very much hope; I am certain; would not hesitate to recommend; I had the pleasure*
b *which was essential when working …; when it came to showing tour groups …*
c *driven; have an affinity for; will go that extra mile; personable; diplomatic*

5
Sample answer
Dear Dr Schmidt,
I am writing in response to your letter asking for a reference for Nathan Fallon. I worked with Nathan for five years at the Antarctica Climate Research Centre and it is a pleasure to recommend him for the role of Conservation Research Assistant at your centre.

Firstly, I would like to state that Nathan is an ambitious and intelligent individual, who is always there to lend a helping hand to his colleagues. He has the confidence to work alone but is also very friendly and works well within a team. Furthermore, he often helped to resolve conflicts and disputes within the team with his calm and reasonable manner. He has a real passion for protecting the environment and has dedicated his career to this.

In terms of experience, I doubt whether you will find another candidate as highly qualified. Nathan graduated from Harvard University with a Masters in Environmental Studies. In addition to this, he has ten years' work experience in Antarctica and in Sarawak, Borneo. Whilst we were working together, Nathan led a small team investigating the causes and effects of climate change.

I trust that you will make the right decision and hire Nathan. You could not ask for a more professional employee. If you have any further questions please do not hesitate to contact me.

Yours sincerely,
Matthew Higgins

Review Units 1 and 2

Reading and Use of English Part 4: Key word transformation page 24
1 no account should you
2 sooner had I finished than
3 no need for Tom to make
4 does not/doesn't/will not/won't allow pupils to
5 no circumstances are you/do I want you
6 had known each other for

Reading and Use of English Part 3: Word formation page 24
1 significant
2 civilisations
3 modification(s)
4 innovative
5 alterations
6 enable
7 inaccessible
8 interactive

Vocabulary page 25
1 close knit, obstacles
2 hit it off, get
3 after, failure
4 set, quarrel
5 brought, follow
6 make, drifted apart
7 see eye to eye, driven
8 reach, rubbing shoulders

Language focus page 25
1
1 ~~could~~ may/might
2 correct
3 ~~have to~~ might/could
4 ~~won't~~ can't
5 ~~shouldn't~~ must
6 correct
7 ~~need~~ have
8 correct
9 ~~would~~ must
10 ~~must~~ can/could

2
1 has (just) become
2 have had
3 has been
4 had been beating/had beaten
5 had been driving
6 has been living/has lived
7 has said
8 has been planning/has planned

3
1 which   2 whom
3 who/that   4 which
5 who/that   6 which
7 when   8 whose

Unit 3: A sense of wonder

Vocabulary and Speaking: Travel page 26
2
1 b 2 a 3 c 4 b 5 b

Word formation: Nouns 1 page 27
1
1 shortage: -age
2 wisdom: -dom
3 hardship: -ship
4 proficiency: -cy
5 neighbourhood: -hood

2
1 cancellation/publication
2 confusion/collision
3 procedure/signature
4 senator/investigator
5 punctuality/diversity
6 fairness/tidiness

3
1 boredom   2 packages
3 selfishness   4 efficiency
5 likelihood   6 applications
7 depth   8 membership

Answer key

Reading and Use of English Part 3: Word formation page 27

1
1 enjoyable
2 universally
3 departure
4 unforgettable
5 vastness
6 lasting
7 strangers
8 familiarity

Listening Part 3: Multiple choice page 28

1
Suggested answer
There is a miscommunication in the best way to greet a colleague. Perhaps because the people come from different cultural backgrounds.

2
Suggested answers
2 failure, cross-cultural communication, uncertain, cultural values, attitudes, unaware, rules, correct behaviour, incapable, viewing, perspective, others, own beliefs, strange
3 feel, cultural stereotypes, accepts, serve role, understand, another culture, concerned, people in power, misuse, undecided, more beneficial, harmful, confused, complex situations
4 key, active listening, who, responsible, communication breakdowns, translate, one's own language, eliminate misunderstanding, summarise regularly, all possible perspectives
5 Julia, example, communication breakdown, misinterpreted gestures, lack, awareness, preferred distances, English proficiency, different sensitivity, how loudly
6 advice, never, stereotypes, inform, behaviour, closer, Mediterranean, let, understand, better, review, assumptions

3
1 B   2 C   3 A   4 C   5 B
6 D

Language focus 1: Gerunds and infinitives page 29

1a
1 to view
2 stereotyping
3 observing/to observe
4 finding, work
5 having
6 to discover
7 to stand

1b
2 continue observing/to observe: no change in meaning
7 remember to stand/remember standing: different meaning (infinitive with *to* = reminder for future action; gerund = recalling past experience)

2
1 ~~to visit~~ visiting
2 ~~To watch~~ Watching
3 ~~trying~~ to try
4 ~~to look~~ looking
5 ~~to research~~ researching
6 ~~to check~~ check
7 ~~to go~~ going
8 ~~trying~~ to try
9 ~~spend~~ spending
10 ~~going~~ to go

Vocabulary: The senses page 29

2
1 tasty   2 subtle
3 overpowering 4 rich
5 delicious   6 foul
7 appetising   8 mouth-watering

Reading and Use of English Part 6: Cross-text multiple matching page 30

2
B

3
1 D   2 B   3 B   4 C

Language focus 2: Reported speech: Tense changes and reporting verbs page 32

1
I → he
can't remember → couldn't remember
is → was
it's become → it had become

2
present continuous → past continuous
present perfect → past perfect
past simple → past perfect
past perfect → no change
will → would
be going to → was going to
can → could
should → no change
must → had to

3
The interviewer asked her:
1 what the most unusual thing was about her visit the previous day/the day before.
2 if/whether being offered chocolate in a gallery had surprised her.
3 if/whether she thought young people would enjoy the experience.
4 how often she visited museums or galleries.

4
Suggested answers
1 argued (that) (of course) galleries needed to be 'overwhelmingly visual'.
2 offered to pick her up from the airport.
3 demanded to know what he had been doing all day.
4 reminded everyone (that) whatever they had decided the week before could not/couldn't be changed then.
5 stressed how important the next few months would be.
6 predicted (that) this/it might turn out to be the best year for all of them.
7 queried whether Alice would be able to get to the interview on time.
8 admitted (that) they/he/she had made some mistakes during the reform process.

5
1 on   2 for   3 to
4 against/about   5 of
6 from

Writing Part 2: Review page 34

3
Suggested answers
1 the unusual concept and sculptures
2 negative (The writer says the experience wasn't an enjoyable one.)
3 The writer would recommend it to Banksy fans and people looking for a unique experience.

4
Suggested answers
Paragraph 2: what made it memorable
Paragraph 3: describing their experience/opinion
Paragraph 4: giving a recommendation/summarising

Answer key

5
1 strangely compelling; impressive; truly unique and unforgettable experience
2 the experience wasn't an enjoyable one; gloomy; rather unsettling; too cynical for my taste; not one I wish to repeat anytime soon
3 a definite must-see for …; highly recommend it to …

6
Sample answer
Invisible Exhibition
The Invisible Exhibition in Budapest is a unique experience which provides visitors with a first-hand experience of what life is like for visually impaired people. A visit is just under an hour, most of which you spend in complete darkness.

The first gallery is the only one with lighting, and here you can try various devices that visually impaired people use, including a Braille typewriter or a specially designed chess board. Later, small groups of visitors are accompanied by a blind or partially sighted guide. In each dark gallery, visitors are given the challenge to perform everyday actions, guided only by sounds, smell, touch and the voice of the tour guide.

For me, it was an incredibly moving and humbling experience to try crossing a simulated street or walk up a flight of stairs without using the sense of sight. It has certainly helped me empathise more with people who face these challenges every day of their lives. What had the biggest impact on me was the realisation that visually impaired people lead lives just as full and joyful as my own.

The whole exhibition is very well designed to give as complete an experience as possible within the limited timeframe. The main strength of the tour is the personal attention you receive from your guide, who gives you a fascinating insight into a world you might not otherwise know. When you next visit Budapest, I would strongly advise you to book a tour and experience it for yourself.

Unit 4: Living in the past

Vocabulary and Speaking: Memory page 35

2a
1 brings
2 jogged
3 stuck
4 has
5 reminisces, share
6 spark
7 haunted

2b
Suggested answers
1 makes me remember (often forgotten experiences)
2 reminded me about something
3 stayed in my memory
4 has a tendency to forget things easily
5 talks about enjoyable experiences in her past, have the same memories as someone else
6 suddenly make a forgotten memory come alive
7 troubled by remembering something – I want to forget it, but I can't

4
1 clear   2 unclear   3 unclear
4 unclear 5 clear

Listening Part 2: Sentence completion page 36

2
1 (predictable) patterns
2 birth
3 memory (formation)
4 forgotten
5 verbal development
6 false memories
7 stressful situations
8 unexpected effect

Language focus 1: Adverbs of degree: *extremely, very, absolutely, completely, etc.* page 37

1a
1 extremely   2 really   3 utterly

1b
1 and 2 are gradable adjectives, 3 is non-gradable

2
1 usual   2 gifted
3 unnecessary   4 qualified
5 inadequate   6 clear

3
1 extremely hard/difficult/challenging
2 utterly ridiculous
3 severely damaged
4 enormously influential/powerful
5 perfectly understandable
6 terribly boring
7 badly hurt/injured

quite page 37

4a
1 to a particular degree (= fairly)
2 to a large degree (= really)

4b
1 to a large degree (= really)
2 to a particular degree (= fairly)
3 to a large degree (= really)
4 to a particular degree (= fairly)

Listening Part 1: Multiple choice page 38

2
1 B   2 C   3 A   4 C   5 B
6 A

3
1 It's a bit tricky to pigeonhole – there are elements of sci-fi and psychological thriller in there, but at the end of the day it's your standard non-linear narrative …
2 The story jumps around and changes as time goes on. There are a number of scenes which we see repeatedly, from different perspectives.
3 Early experiences evoked by a song or an image suggestive of simpler or happier times can unconsciously influence consumers' buying habits.
4 … packaging reminiscent of that seen decades ago has been revived by businesses hoping to tap into our cultural memories. Loyalty to a brand can be promoted as we identify these products with those we bought and used in the 'good old days'.
5 The fact it's contemporary doesn't bother me …
6 I much preferred our old house in Cornwall. After all, that was where we grew up.
I know what you mean, you're always going to feel more sentimental towards somewhere that holds so many memories.

Vocabulary: Rooms and spaces
page 39

3
1 A, B   2 D, A
3 B, C   4 C, D
5 A, B

Reading and Use of English Part 5: Multiple choice page 40

3
1 C   2 B   3 D   4 A   5 C
6 A

Language focus 2: Comparisons page 41

1a
1 The, of   2 more, more
3 The, the   4 now, ever

2
1 d   2 c   3 b   4 a

3
1 ~~out of~~ in
2 ~~as~~ like
3 ~~not nearly~~ considerably/far/much/a lot/a great deal
4 ~~a great deal~~ easily/by far
5 ~~like~~ as
6 ~~best~~ most
7 ~~most~~ more
8 ~~a bit~~ the
9 ~~little~~ slightly

Writing Part 2: Report page 42

3
Content: Yes, the information given is relevant to the task and all the points are covered. (The report evaluates the accommodation in a number of different ways, and identifies both suitability and areas for improvement. There is a very concise recommendation for next year's event.)
Communicative achievement: The register is appropriately formal. It communicates both straightforward and more complex ideas effectively.
Organisation: The report is logically ordered with an overview, description of positives/negatives and evaluation/recommendation.
Language: Language is of the appropriate level. There are a number of phrases for describing accommodation.

4
a Additionally, Furthermore
b Firstly, Secondly
c However
d In conclusion

5
Outlining the purpose of the report
The main purpose of this report is to … recommendations … will be outlined
Evaluating
+ *simply furnished; comfortable; roomy; spacious; wholly positive; well-suited*
– *not quite right; dark; impacted on students' well-being*
Making recommendations
to best address the concerns raised … it may be worthwhile considering … … should perhaps also be … It is felt that …

6
Sample answer
Introduction
The aim of this report is to give an overview of the facilities used by the college during last year's leisure break. I will provide evaluation and make recommendations for the future.

Accommodation
The property chosen by the college was incredibly well-situated, with fantastic views across the bay. This appealed to most of the students as such an attractive location was extremely relaxing. Students also benefited from the spacious living areas. All in all, the house had a well-furnished, up-to-date feel.

Transport
However, there were some major drawbacks. A limited bus service and relatively poor transport links made it challenging to get to and from the house. Some students felt that they would have liked to be able to travel into the nearby town during their stay, but were unable to without difficulty.

Sports facilities
Furthermore, the sports facilities offered could have been better. In comparison to the tennis courts and playing surfaces at the college, these were rather disappointing. Many students felt that their enjoyment of games was greatly affected by the poor conditions. If the facilities are to be used in the future, there will have to be considerable investment made by the owners to bring them up to standard.

Recommendations
In conclusion, due to the concerns raised in the above report, it would be worthwhile considering a different location for future leisure breaks. These could be based somewhere that is easier to reach and with better facilities. As the emphasis is on leisure, this factor is perhaps even more important to get right than the accommodation.

Review Units 3 and 4

Reading and Use of English Part 4: Key word transformation page 44
1 congratulated Mary on doing
2 from going there on my
3 she ended up paying
4 nothing like as impressive
5 she ('d/had) had in mind
6 was not/wasn't nearly as interesting as

Reading and Use of English Part 1: Multiple-choice cloze page 44
1 C   2 A   3 B   4 A   5 D
6 D   7 B   8 A

Vocabulary page 45

1
1 f   2 d   3 a   4 h   5 g
6 e   7 b   8 c

2
1 cosy, fragrant
2 lavish, mouth-watering, vile
3 dimly, spectacular, aromatic
4 conveniently, cramped, old-fashioned
5 dingy, pungent, delicious

Language focus page 45
1 analysing   2 find
3 to be   4 travelling
5 taking   6 to fulfil
7 standing   8 photographing
9 to set   10 feeling
11 to complain   12 doing
13 applying   14 checking
15 to make

Unit 5: Pushing the limits

Vocabulary and Speaking: Work page 46

2
1 running   2 fill, get
3 under, on 4 go   5 out

Answer key

Listening Part 4: Multiple matching page 47

2
1 E   2 C   3 B   4 D   5 H
6 G   7 C   8 H   9 F   10 A

Language focus 1: Conditionals page 47

1
1 a   2 b   3 e   4 c   5 d

Other uses of conditionals page 47

2a
1 to   2 for   3 happen   4 provided

3
1 were to
2 wouldn't be playing
3 hadn't
4 Provided
5 would
6 happen

Word formation: Verbs page 49

1
social**ise**
streng**then**
captiv**ate**
intens**ify**
endanger

2
Suggested answers
1 again
2 not; the opposite
3 badly or wrongly
4 not; the opposite
5 reversing or removing; reducing
6 more so

3
1 rehydrate/hydrate
2 straighten
3 re-energised/energised
4 purify
5 destress
6 Minimise
7 disconnect
8 enrich

Reading and Use of English Part 1: Multiple-choice cloze page 49

2
1 A   2 D   3 A   4 C   5 C
6 B   7 D   8 A

Reading and Use of English Part 7: Gapped text page 50

2
Suggested answers
1 She runs longs distances.
2 People want to challenge themselves and move out of their comfort zones.

3
1 F   2 C   3 A   4 B   5 D
6 G   not used = E

Language focus 2: Unreal time, wishes page 52

1
1 and 2 both refer to a past situation. The past perfect is used.
3 refers to a present situation. The past simple is used.

2
1 perfect infinitive (have + past participle)
2 gerund
3 *if* + clause with past verb form

3
Suggested answers
1 I wish I'd learnt to ski properly.
2 I'd sooner take up an apprenticeship than go to university.
3 If only I could ride a motorcycle.
4 I'd rather not have visited Paris on a package tour./I'd rather I hadn't visited Paris on a package tour.
5 I would have preferred to learn Spanish (rather) than English at school.
6 My parents would like it if I exercised a lot more./My parents would like me to exercise a lot more.

Vocabulary: Health page 52

2
Suggested answers
under the weather = feel unwell
catch sth from somebody = get a disease or illness
run-down = so tired that you do not feel well
worn out = extremely tired
on the mend = getting better after an illness

3
a torn
b broken, fractured
c blistered, swollen
d twisted, sprained
e dislocated
f sore

Writing Part 2: Proposal page 53

2
Suggested answer
increase investment, health and fitness, proposals, facility, service, outlining, benefits

3
Suggested answers
Increase investment: increase spending, to invest in, increased investment, spreading the investment, justify the investment
Health and fitness: benefits, physical activities, physical exercise, well-being, families spend more time actively together
Proposals: I believe, undertaking a larger-scale single project, initiatives
Facilities and services: new facilities, existing facilities, generous green spaces, several playgrounds, outdoor facilities, outdoor gym, gym equipment, gym facilities, indoor facilities
Outlining: outlines, I am putting forward my proposal
Benefits: attract more attention, would encourage more people, would facilitate, contribute positively, we could encourage, setting a good example, would also appeal

4
Suggested answer
Yes, the model answer answers the points in the task. However, as the word count is only around 240 words, there would be 'room' for the writer to add more benefits, for example: reduced maintenance costs because playground and gym could be repaired simultaneously; no need for advertising the new facilities as there are already several existing users of playgrounds; increases the amount of time people spend in public parks, etc.

5
Introducing points
Firstly, I believe
I (strongly) feel that

Making a comparison
much less significant   larger-scale
more … than

Introducing a contrasting idea
Although

Adding a new idea or example
also   as well as   Furthermore

Summarising
In conclusion

Making a recommendation
putting forward (my proposal) for your consideration
I believe it would be to our advantage
should mostly focus on
… would encourage ….
I strongly feel (that)

6
Sample answer

Introduction
Our college is planning to organise a sports event for young people. My proposal outlines an event which could allow us to attract a significant proportion of the target age group.

The event
First of all, in order to provide our event with a strong identity, we could set it up as a regular trophy event with a memorable name, like 'The Athletes' Cup'. Furthermore, including a wide range of different types of sports within the same event would allow us to attract more participants, and potentially more spectators, rather than focusing on a single sport with a league format.

Suitable activities
Apart from the most popular and most commonly practised sports like running, swimming and football, we should aim to include some less obvious sports contests, to broaden our appeal. Research with a brief online questionnaire should provide us with information on what other sports may appeal to students at our college. The decision could then be made on the individual events by the organising committee.

Encouraging participation
Besides promoting the event through posters, leaflets and an email campaign, the inclusion of students' particular favourite sports will also help us attract a wider range of participants. Offering valuable or unusual prizes rather than simple trophies may also encourage more people to join in.
I believe that the combination of a familiar multi-sport event format with the inclusion of less obvious competitions will appeal to more young people than more conventional tournaments.

Unit 6 Changing times

Vocabulary and Speaking: Change
page 55

1
Suggested answers
1 3-D printing
2 mobile phone technology; the rise of digital technology; how a lot of very young children can use technology
3 virtual reality
4 genetically modified food; popularity of organic food

2
1 significant = very large or noticeable (the other two mean 'nice' or 'welcome')
2 subtle = not obvious (the other two mean 'important' and 'extensive')
3 radical = very different (the other two mean 'small' or 'not very important')
4 unwelcome = unpleasant or annoying (the other two mean 'happening very quickly and without any sign it is going to happen')
5 economic = relating to finance, the economy, business and trade (the other two relate to laws and rights)
6 rapid = very fast (the other two mean 'surprising')

3
a reform, adjust   b vary, distorting
c convert, remodel

Listening Part 3: Multiple choice
page 56

2
1 C   2 B   3 C   4 B   5 A
6 A

Language focus 1: Passives
page 57

1a
1 get   2 have   3 are   4 be

2
1 was decided (that) we would
2 was not believed to be/believed not to be
3 is estimated to be worth
4 are thought to be
5 appears to have been opened
6 need to have/get your car
7 been agreed (that) we will
8 should have been informed

Reading and Use of English Part 6: Cross-text multiple matching
page 58

2
1 B   2 D   3 C   4 A

Language focus 2: Passives of reporting verbs
page 60

1a
1 to be doubling (*continuous infinitive*)
2 to have written (*perfect infinitive*)
3 to help the brain (*simple infinitive*)

1b
1 b   2 c   3 a

1c
1 It is thought that the internet is doubling in size every five years.
2 It is known that Hunter S. Thompson wrote some of the most provocative journalism in modern America.
3 It is said that listening to music helps the brain to concentrate on tasks.

2a
1 It is expected that climate change will become an unstoppable phenomenon.
Climate change is expected to become an unstoppable phenomenon.
2 It is claimed that illegal downloading is destroying the music industry.
Illegal downloading is claimed to be destroying the music industry.
3 It is thought that Jimi Hendrix was the greatest guitarist of all time.
Jimi Hendrix is thought to have been the greatest guitarist of all time.
4 It is said that life is changing faster than ever before.
Life is said to be changing faster than ever before.
5 It is said that crime levels are in decline.
Crime levels are said to be in decline.

Reading and Use of English Part 2: Open cloze
page 60

2
1 our   2 us   3 one
4 despite   5 what   6 take
7 to   8 on

Vocabulary: Figurative language
page 61

1
buzzing with excitement
wail of a siren
barking instructions
speakers groaned and began to shudder
swarmed over the stage
crowd who roared its appreciation

2
1 shudder 2 clap 3 wail 4 bark
5 roar 6 buzz 7 groan
8 swarm

3
1 swarmed 2 wailing 3 roared
4 shuddered 5 barking 6 buzzing
7 groaned 8 clap

Writing Part 1: Essay page 62

3
Content: Two factors have been discussed – with reasons given to support these choices. A decision has been made about the factor with the most impact, e.g. *while it is true that … we need to accept …*
Communicative achievement: Concise, clear topic sentences are used to introduce key points, e.g. *Another key factor is the emergence of the internet as a source of news.*
Organisation: A range of appropriate linkers are used, helping the text to be coherent, e.g. *However, as a result, According to*, etc.
There are clear paragraphs: an introduction; focus on the first factor; focus on the second factor; a conclusion.
Language: The language is sufficiently formal throughout, e.g. no contractions, formal linking words. A good range of vocabulary and grammatical structures are used, e.g. *The role of traditional media has long been in decline.*

4
1 Expressing an opinion
*this means that … cannot offer
Another key factor
… it is worth considering
while … is undeniable
… standards are not so high*
2 Referring to others' opinions
*Many people think that …
Supporters of this view believe …*
3 Referring to sources
According to recent statistics …
4 Concluding with a decision
To conclude, while it is true that … we need to accept that …

5
a 1 b 2 c 3 d 4/1 e 2
f 3 g 2 h 1/4 i 3 j 4

6
Sample answer
There can be no doubt that the entertainment industry is undergoing a period of considerable change. Traditional models are in decline as more and more people become used to accessing film, games, and music via online platforms. One area which has seen a large downturn is the music industry, where sales are consistently falling.

All the evidence suggests that younger people are likely to stream new music on handheld devices or their computers rather than purchasing it in physical forms. While it is true that many people may be using streaming services to sample music before going on to purchase it, they are doing this in smaller numbers.

Perhaps a more important factor causing problems for the music industry is direct competition from other forms of entertainment. Online gaming is a growth area which appeals to many young people. The communal nature of this kind of gaming means that social networks are often built around playing and discussing the games. They often provide a more immersive experience than other entertainment – many gaming platforms actually work alongside streaming services, which means you can hear new releases while you play. Sales of games are on the rise, meaning that people have less money to spend on other free-time activities.

In conclusion, while it is true that streaming sites and new methods of accessing music have impacted on sales, we need to acknowledge that the biggest reason for sales decline is the competition from other forms of entertainment.

Review Units 5 and 6

Reading and Use of English Part 4: Key word transformation page 64
1 unlikely event (that) enough judges vote/unlikely event of enough judges voting
2 Arno had arrived/been on/in time
3 regret not going/getting
4 would have someone clean/pick/clear
5 won't/will not be long until/before
6 was a steady rise in

Reading and Use of English Part 3: Word formation page 64
1 applicant
2 undeniable
3 supervision
4 invaluable/valuable
5 assumptions
6 Seemingly
7 obligatory
8 chosen

Vocabulary page 65
1
1 out, up
2 forward/together, on
3 up, in/to
4 down, under
5 into, toward(s)/to/in/about
6 between, in

2
1 swarmed, fractured
2 pulled, bruised, buzzing
3 dislocated, wailing
4 roared, sore
5 shuddered, sprained
6 clap, blistered

Language focus page 65
1
1 would/will; will/'ll
2 should/could; will/'ll/would
3 weren't; would have/would've
4 had not/hadn't; could have/could've/would have/would've

2
1 It is not known exactly when the first open-plan office was designed.
2 Your complaint is being dealt with.
3 It was initially thought that the fires were caused/had been caused by high summer temperatures./It was initially thought that high summer temperatures caused the fires.
4 His contract may (possibly) be extended for another few months.

5 I'm having/getting my car serviced soon. I get/have it done every six months./It is done every six months.
6 Peter's car window was smashed with a brick.
7 Our main accounts have been taken over.
8 A lot of people are thought to have been affected by this change.

Unit 7 Brave new worlds

Listening Part 4: Multiple matching page 66

2
1 F 2 C 3 B 4 E 5 D
6 H 7 B 8 C 9 G 10 D

Language focus 1: Future forms (review) page 67

1a and 1b
'm going to – to talk about plans and arrangements based on intentions
it's (on) – to talk about timetables and schedules
is coming – to talk about plans and arrangements
it'll – to make predictions about the future

2
1 c 2 b 3 a

Other ways of expressing the future page 67

3a
1 a 2 b 3 a 4 a 5 b
6 a 7 b 8 a 9 b

3b
Suggested answers
1 telephone operator
2 climate change
3 the new office
4 a hotel
5 an abandoned building
6 the champions league final
7 an important letter
8 a film
9 a cake

Speaking Part 3: Collaborative task page 68

1a
1 Ecofuels
2 Irrigation
3 Recycling
4 Reforestation
5 Renewable energy

Reading and Use of English Part 1: Multiple-choice cloze page 69
1 C 2 D 3 A 4 A 5 B
6 D 7 B 8 C

Vocabulary 1: Verbs with *up-, down-, over-* and *under-* page 69

1a
1 d 2 c 3 e 4 f

1b
5 a 6 h 7 b 8 g

2
1 overruled   2 to downsize
3 to uphold   4 underperforming
5 update   6 to overcome

Listening Part 1: Multiple choice page 70

1
1 C 2 A 3 A 4 B 5 B
6 C

Language focus 2: Future in the past page 71

1
1 No, he was distracted by looking at tablets.
2 No, she was promoted and couldn't go to the conference.
3 No, due to unforeseen circumstances.

2
1 interrupted   2 intentions
3 happen   4 perspective
5 happen   6 predictions

3
1 would be exploring
2 were going to
3 was to be
4 wasn't
5 were going
6 were to be
7 was supposed to
8 was about to

Reading and Use of English Part 5: Multiple choice page 72

2
1 B 2 D 3 A 4 C 5 C
6 B

Vocabulary 2: Science and research page 73

1a
1 improvise   2 converts
3 development   4 procedures

3
1 criteria   2 determine
3 dissolves   4 proposed
5 relevance   6 principles

Writing Part 2: Review page 74

3
Suggested answers
Paragraph 2: characters, some plot details
Paragraph 3: narrative technique, writing style, the reviewer's assessment, the key strengths of the book
Paragraph 4: critical remarks, the reviewer's recommendations

4
1 eventful; (not) wholly convincing
2 believable; the vivid depiction of the central character; intriguing
3 a masterpiece; distinct style; elegant; effortless; expertly balances; keep readers intrigued; particularly enjoyable; complete unpredictability; incredibly well-thought-out
4 What makes this such a fascinating read is …; Readers will want to keep on reading long into the night; you are guaranteed to have fun; (such) a joy to read

5
Sample answer
Women Behind the Counter: a look back into history

Women Behind the Counter is a television drama series, made in 1977 in what was then Czechoslovakia. The series focuses on a number of shop assistants working in a large supermarket in Prague. The main character is Anna, whose relationship with her colleagues as well as with her husband and teenage children is at the centre of the story. Each episode presents the events of a month, vividly depicting everyday conflicts and turning points in Anna's life.

What makes the series a fascinating watch, especially for those who never had a chance to visit the country in the 1970s, is the detailed look into the everyday lives of a different generation living in different times. Visually, there is nothing really that sets the series apart from its contemporaries. However, the writing is strong and the characters are not only believable, but easy to relate to. As they are all everyday people shown in everyday situations, most viewers will be able to find elements reminding them of their own experiences.

There is also a gentle sense of humour throughout, which keeps the viewers not only interested but also entertained. The writers demonstrate a real sensitivity to small-scale human dramas – which also helps viewers to care about and take an active interest in the characters.

Apart from those interested in the history of Central Europe, the series may also appeal to viewers who enjoy soap operas in general. *Women Behind the Counter* is a different, more down-to-earth approach to the genre than usual, and as such, a joy to watch in itself.

Unit 8 Getting through

Vocabulary 1: Expressing feelings page 75

2
1 astounded, livid 2 frustrated
3 elated, smug 4 indifferent
5 wary, petrified 6 devastated
7 troubled, lost 8 disgusted

Listening Part 2: Sentence completion page 76

3
1 financial
2 (rational) decisions
3 behaviour
4 heart rate
5 (consistent) patterns
6 movements
7 (audience) response
8 healthcare

Language focus 1: Conjunctions page 77

1
1 c 2 a 3 b

2a
Suggested answers
1 Provided you pay me back by next month, I'll lend you the money./I'll lend you the money provided you pay me back by next month.
2 Marko and Amy should have a back-up plan in case their original plan doesn't work out./In case their original plan doesn't work out, Marko and Amy should have a back-up plan.

3 We have to get this computer fixed, otherwise we can't do any work.
4 Even though they had been in the area a long time, they still didn't know the quickest way to the hospital./They still didn't know the quickest way to the hospital even though they had been in the area a long time.
5 Although he wasn't a fan of social media, he had to admit it was sometimes very useful./He wasn't a fan of social media although he had to admit it was sometimes very useful.
6 After I finish work at 5, I'll pick up the kids from their swimming lesson./I'll pick up the kids from their swimming lesson after I finish work at 5.
7 Joe was messaging Danilo whilst the lecturer was talking./Whilst the lecturer was talking, Joe was messaging Danilo.

2b
0 making a contrast
1 giving a condition
2 giving a condition
3 reason and result
4 making a contrast
5 making a concession
6 sequencing actions
7 making a contrast/referring to two things happening at the same time

Vocabulary 2: Onomatopoeic words page 77

1
Suggested answers
ping – correct answers on a game show, microwave, cooking timer
buzz – bee, wasp, doorbell, alarm clock

2
Suggested answers
1a drip, patter
1b roar, gush
2a croak, hiss, growl
2b shatter
3a whisper, chatter, hum
3b whoosh
4a crackle, rustle
4b pop, bang
5a howl, sigh, whistle
5b swoosh
6a screech, shriek, snarl
6b sigh

3
1 pattered 2 whistled 3 hum
4 rustling 5 whooshing 6 roar

Reading and Use of English Part 7: Gapped text page 78

3
1 D 2 G 3 A 4 C 5 F
6 B not used = E

4
1 slight mismatch
2 practical implications
3 tallies with
4 acute
5 general consensus
6 identifying errors

Word formation: Nouns 2 page 80

1
1 psychologists, development
2 participants, performance
3 mismatch, assessment
4 content, disposal
5 development, society

2
1 disappearance 2 refusal
3 acknowledgement 4 variety
5 environmentalist 6 contestants

Reading and Use of English Part 3: Word formation page 81

1
1 emergence
2 similarities
3 communication
4 updating
5 approval
6 tendency
7 fascination
8 unavoidable

Language focus 2: Discourse markers page 82

1
a **Adding information/Developing a point:** Furthermore, Accordingly
b **Contrast:** However
c **Cause and result:** Owing to
d **Generalising:** on the whole

2
a **Adding information/Developing a point:** in addition to, besides, what's more, moreover, in fact, not only … but also
b **Contrast:** besides, having said that, nevertheless, conversely, in fact, on the contrary
c **Cause and result:** consequently
d **Generalising:** by and large, in fact

3
1 By and large
2 Likewise
3 Consequently
4 What's more
5 Furthermore
6 Having said that

Writing Part 2: Letter/email
page 82

3
Persuading
I can't recommend it highly enough.
You'd get so much out of it.
I think … would be a marvellous opportunity
I'd say that there's no better way
When you compare it with …
I know you'd love to …

Advising
Whatever you do, make sure that …
There's not much point …

4
Reasons for writing
Remember that … I told you about?
I'm getting in touch to let you know about …

Persuading
Just think of …
I'm convinced that you'd …
Just imagine how it would …, not to mention …

Advising
You'd be much better off …
I wouldn't … if I were you

5
Suggested answers
I'm considering taking some advanced exams.
you build on what you've learnt
you also meet up with so many diverse people
I've added so many more people to my social network
Being part of a household … helped me to build on my listening skills.
I had to become more fluent, as clear pronunciation …
people end up just using their native tongue
Apart from the costs, …
the financial side of things probably balances out
you'd love to see a bit more of the world.

Review Units 7 and 8

Reading and Use of English Part 4: Key word transformation page 84
1 expert in the field of
2 makes no difference to me
3 was due to be published
4 has no intention of giving
5 come under criticism in recent/ come in for criticism in recent
6 on the verge of losing

Reading and Use of English Part 2: Open cloze page 84
1 that
2 what
3 from
4 of
5 all
6 while/whilst/although
7 on
8 this/their

Vocabulary page 84

1
1 d 2 h 3 e 4 i 5 k
6 f 7 b 8 a 9 g 10 l
11 j 12 c

2
1 undervalue, relevance
2 overemphasise, criteria
3 downsize, proposed
4 oversee, determine
5 underestimated, improvise
6 overperform, investigating
7 upload, convert
8 upgrade, development

3
1 growls
2 sighed
3 screeching
4 chatter/chattering
5 crackle/crackling
6 dripping

Language focus page 85

1
1 Even so
2 Provided
3 long, that
4 otherwise
5 although
6 so as to
7 Having said that
8 By and large

2
1 always going to be
2 the verge of
3 bound to
4 to be
5 on the point of
6 not to be

Unit 9 To the market

Listening Part 3: Multiple choice page 87

2
1 C 2 A 3 C 4 D 5 B
6 D

3
1 Lucy states that advertising nowadays
A is much more persuasive than in the past.
Not stated *The online world has had considerable impact, but we can't underestimate changes in consumers.*
B relies solely upon research.
Not stated *Traditionally, advertising used a lot of techniques derived from persuasion studies conducted in the 1960s …*
C has adopted different techniques to those used in the past.
Correct answer *This shift in perspective has meant that advertising companies have changed how they advertise in order to reflect consumer preferences.*
D often makes exaggerated claims about products.
She implies advertisers would avoid doing this: *consumers nowadays may not believe the superlative claims about a product's qualities*

2 Simon believes the principal challenge facing advertising is that people
A are not fooled by the methods being used.
Correct answer *Fundamentally, we've become so accustomed to the language of advertising that we see right through it.*

Answer key

B no longer have any trust in it.
He says that people are more critical of advertising and are more aware of advertising techniques, but not that they no longer trust it:
… *advertising has been affected by increased critical thinking in consumers.*
C place too much emphasis on each other's opinions.
He says peer pressure no longer holds as much influence.
… *generated peer pressure, no longer hold as much influence.*
D have changed the way they make decisions.
Not stated

3 Lucy says that in order to appeal to families, advertisers need to
A have a clearer message.
Not stated (she mentions there is a tendency towards this but she doesn't say if advertisers need to)
We've recently seen more sophisticated central messages.
B promote healthy living.
Not stated (she gives this as an example but doesn't say all advertisers need to do this)
C take into account a range of opinions.
Correct answer *So advertisers need to strike a fine balance and consider the viewpoints of both the buyer and consumer.*
D be more realistic in their expectations.
She says advertisers are getting more creative: … *a move to use more creatively engaging advertising.*

4 In Simon's view, future advertising will be
A based online.
Not stated (he only mentions online shopping)
B affected by privacy laws.
He anticipates that companies will have access to a lot of your personal information
Programs which have access to income and usual spending habits will fill your online grocery shop.
C much more influential.
Not stated … *personal and publicly available data are used to influence marketing.*

D tailored to individuals.
Correct answer … *customised, and directed at one consumer …*

5 Lucy says that large, well-known companies need to
A use well-known people to promote their products.
She says the opposite of this: … *rather than featuring sports stars and celebrities in adverts, companies will be more successful focusing on ordinary people.*
B reflect their customers more closely.
Correct answer
In realistically depicting users, a brand can create a sense of understanding and empathy.
C offer the public a luxurious lifestyle.
She says the opposite of this: *The technique of showing people how the rich and famous live doesn't have the same effect as it did in previous decades.*
D respond to criticism more quickly.
Not stated. (The speed of response is not mentioned.) … *they also want to be talked with, not talked at.*

6 Simon believes that brands can win back public support by
A advertising on social media.
Not stated
B consulting with customers.
Not stated. Lucy says this not Simon.
C reducing costs to consumers.
Not stated. (Ways a brand can influence society are mentioned.) … *supporting good causes, or paying workers a living wage.*
D honestly expressing their purpose.
Correct answer *People want to buy from brands that are authentic, and do what they claim to do.*

Language focus 1: Determiners and pronouns page 88

1
1 this   2 many
3 both   4 few, one, another
5 lots of

2
1 pronoun
2 determiner
3 pronoun
4 determiner, determiner, pronoun
5 determiner

3a
1 every, few, all, Much
2 one, several, all
3 Most, such, other, any

4
1 Incorrect: ~~Very little~~ Very few
2 Incorrect: ~~every days~~ every day/most days
3 Incorrect: ~~Every~~ Each/Either/Neither
4 Correct

5
Suggested answers
1 little   2 None/Few
3 Much   4 most, every
5 few, many   6 All
7 plenty

Vocabulary and Speaking: Money page 89

2
1 go, shopping/to shop
2 Sticking, fall
3 run, extortionate
4 break, going
5 make, tight, putting
6 impoverished, affluent

Reading and Use of English Part 8: Multiple matching page 90

3
1 D   2 E   3 C   4 E   5 C
6 A   7 C   8 B   9 C   10 A

Language focus 2: Reference, substitution and ellipsis: Reference page 91

1
1 edible currency
2 The M-Pesa system
3 The opportunity to control finances
4 Canadian Tire Money (CTM) notes
5 rai stones

Substitution page 91

2
1 nor   2 pair   3 so   4 those
5 ones 6 not

3
1 haven't, will (do)
2 hadn't, would
3 didn't
4 does
5 should

164

Ellipsis page 92

4
Suggested answers
1 They asked me to send a covering letter with my CV, but I already had ~~sent a covering letter~~.
2 There was a sudden increase in the sales of hats. I have no idea why ~~there was a sudden increase in the sales of hats~~.
3 He always comes to meetings in the afternoon, but ~~he~~ hardly ever ~~comes to meetings~~ in the morning.

5
Suggested answer
As most people find shopping a stressful experience, more are shopping online/doing it online. From 2008–2015, official statistics showed there was a 20% increase in online shopping among men and a 26% increase among women. Although we shop online, this only accounts for about 15% of all retailing.

Reading and Use of English Part 1: Multiple-choice cloze page 92

2
1 B   2 A   3 D   4 A   5 C
6 A   7 B   8 C

Vocabulary: Describing trends page 93

1
a large increase – *an enormous surge of interest, significantly boosted*

2
1 enormous, steady
2 significant, moderate
3 disappointing
4 moderate, substantial
5 spectacular, slight
6 substantial

4a
1 on   2 at   3 up   4 in
5 off   6 up   7 up   8 between

4b
1 d   2 g   3 h   4 c
5 a   6 f   7 b   8 e

Writing Part 2: Proposal page 94

1b
1 generally speaking   2 Obviously
3 undoubtedly   4 Frankly
5 Personally

2
Proposals should include: 1, 2, 4, 5, 7, 8

Unit 10 School of thought

Speaking: Learning page 95
1 True
2 False (it takes place between the ages of two and eleven)
3 False (German mathematician Karl Witt earned his PhD in Philosophy at Hessian University at the age of twelve)
4 True
5 True

Listening Part 4: Multiple matching page 95

2
1 H   2 C   3 E   4 G   5 B
6 G   7 E   8 A   9 F   10 C

3
Suggested answers
1 online course
2 professional development course
3 college, study abroad, living with a host family
4 book study, online course
5 internship, ongoing training

Vocabulary: Academic language page 96

2
1 f   2 g   3 a   4 e   5 c
6 d   7 b

3
Suggested answers
A Bachelor's degree is a first university degree; a Master's degree is one you can study after your Bachelor's degree. An undergraduate is a student studying for a first degree at a college or university; a postgraduate is studying for an advanced degree.
A lecturer gives presentations at a college or university; a tutor teaches a student or small group of students at a college or university through discussions of a subject.
An academic major is a student's primary academic discipline at college or university; an academic minor is the secondary discipline.
A lecture is a talk at a college or university to a large group of people; a seminar is a class at university in which a small group of students discuss a subject with a teacher.
A semester is one of the two periods of about 18 weeks that an academic year at a university or college is divided into in some countries; a term is one of the periods of time into which the university, college or school year is divided – in the UK there are usually three terms.

Writing Part 2: Report page 97

1
current educational opportunities:
state-funded education, private schools
challenges:
cost, class sizes
future developments:
online study (although this doesn't particularly relate to 'in your area')

2
1 Yes, but quite briefly. The last bullet point talks about future developments, but not specifically for people in the writer's area.
2 The writer talks about opportunities in his/her country, rather than their own area. There is some material which is unnecessary, e.g. after saying that private schools and colleges are expensive, the writer says 'reducing costs … would be better' even though this is fairly obvious. There is also some material which repeats what has already been said – 'There are far too many people in each school' just repeats the sentence before: 'classes are so busy'.
3 No evaluative language is used in the first two paragraphs. The third paragraph does use evaluative language – 'significant', 'this would be better' 'far too many', as does the fourth paragraph: 'many very good', 'the best education'.
4 Yes.
5 No, it mainly repeats the same wording.

Answer key

6 It makes one recommendation – 'I would strongly recommend'.
7 The conclusion is quite weak as it just says that more money will provide more opportunities but this does not really reflect the content of the report or the task itself. There is no clear recommendation in the conclusion.
8 Sometimes the report is too informal – 'This is my report about …', 'On top of this'.

3
Sample answer

Introduction
The aim of this report is to illustrate findings on the current educational opportunities for young people in south-west Spain and the challenges they may face. Additionally, predictions on future developments will also be presented.

Current opportunities
The local authorities ensure that all children have access to free schooling from the ages of six to sixteen, ensuring that students attain a certain level of education. Furthermore, there has been a substantial number of private language schools and vocational colleges opening in the area in the past five years. This has resulted in many young people choosing to study in their free time.

Challenges facing students
A significant issue that causes problems for many students is cost. Tuition fees at private schools and colleges are increasingly expensive, restricting the number of children to whom these are available. Another concern is that the popularity of such institutions, coupled with limited spaces in classes has led to many being unable to sign up for courses and being left disappointed.

Future developments
The hope in the area is that the local government will continue to invest in expanding existing educational facilities as this will allow more young people to attend classes. Consequently this should enable the institutions to lower their tuition fees and guarantee that young people from all different economic backgrounds will have access to further education.

Vocabulary and Speaking: The mind and brain page 98

1b
1 b 2 a 3 c

2a
1 thinking
2 thought/been thinking
3 thinking
4 think
5 think
6 thinking
7 thoughts
8 think

3
1 brains   2 mind
3 head, mind   4 mind, brains
5 sense   6 unknown, intellect

Reading and Use of English Part 6: Cross-text multiple matching page 98

2
1 D 2 C 3 A 4 B

Language focus 1: Emphasis with cleft sentences page 100

1a
1 … the reason he is such a leading light in the field of psychology became very clear.
2 … they just have to picture it.
3 I was genuinely moved by his story of how the power of thought helped him to resolve a quarrel with an old school pal.
4 O'Rourke's research could make real changes when the doubters in the field come round to this alternative way of thinking.

1b
1 The phrase *what became very clear* is given prominence. This stresses the importance of what it was that became very clear.
2 The use of *all* suggests that picturing success is more important than any other factor being discussed.
3 The phrase *It was the story of how* emphasises that it was this story, rather than any other, which moved them.
4 The use of *It's only when* emphasises a period of time, and a condition.

1c
A an action/actions, a noun
B *the only thing that*
C a prepositional phrase, a certain time

2
Suggested answers
1 What can really change the course of your life is a university degree./It's (only) a university degree that can really change the course of your life.
2 It's her lectures that always confuse me.
3 What you have to do first is decide on your goals in life.
4 What you should consider doing is taking an IQ test.
5 What annoys me the most is their lack of concentration./It's their lack of concentration that annoys me the most.
6 What the government should do is help out with the cost of studies./It's the government who should help out with the cost of studies./All the government should do is help out with the cost of studies.

Listening Part 2: Sentence completion page 101

2
1 contemporary education
2 cluttered classrooms
3 maintain control
4 active learning
5 essential skill
6 industry figures
7 cooperation
8 'Getting Ahead'

Language focus 2: Participle clauses page 102

1a
1 As 2 who 3 After

1b
Suggested answers
1 Word order has changed. In the second sentence, the verb phrase has replaced the clause using *as*.
2 Word order has changed. There is no relative clause in the second sentence. The verb is singular in the second sentence. 'Low-sensory environments' is given more prominence than 'children' in the second sentence.
3 Word order has not changed. The conjunction *after* has been omitted. There is more emphasis in the second sentence on the change itself.

2
begin, written, conjunctions

3
1 Realising (that) there was nobody home, they left the parcel with a neighbour.
2 Opening the cupboard, I found it was empty.
3 Shrieking and screaming, the children jumped into the pool.
4 Having acquired the business as a young woman, she was reluctant to sell.
5 Having been criticised by his boss, he was asked to resign.
6 Not wanting to wake the children, we left the house quietly.
7 Looked after carefully, this laptop should last until you leave university.
8 Having no money and no phone, I didn't know how I was going to get home./Not having any money or phone, I didn't know how I was going to get home.
9 Taken a long time ago, the photo was of my grandfather and his best friend.
10 Driving home, Danny realised he had left his wallet at the shop.

4
1 speaking
2 Judging
3 Taking
4 considered

Word formation: Affixes review page 103

1
verb: compete(s)
nouns: competition(s), competitor(s), competitiveness
adjective: (un)competitive

2a
1 adjective
2 adjective – with negative meaning
3 noun – plural
4 verb
5 noun
6 verb

2b
1 studious   2 unscientific
3 failures   4 broaden
5 dedication   6 visualise

Reading and Use of English Part 2: Open cloze page 103

3
1 which   2 Could/Can/Might
3 less/not   4 another
5 rather   6 this/much
7 if   8 too

Review Units 9 and 10

Reading and Use of English Part 4: Key word transformation page 104
1 been highly thought of by Christopher
2 cannot/can't stand not being told
3 was only after I (had)/was only when I
4 not to/to not let her children spend
5 did was (to) apply for/to university
6 has every chance of getting

Reading and Use of English Part 3: Word formation page 104
1 unavoidable
2 Designers
3 necessarily
4 attractive
5 undertaking
6 repetitive
7 acknowledge
8 influential

Vocabulary page 105

1
1 e   2 d   3 c   4 b   5 g
6 f   7 a

2
1 think twice
2 thought long and hard
3 right in thinking
4 think straight
5 having second thoughts
6 think nothing of

Language focus page 105

1
1 This/It, It, it, These, this
2 It/This, This/That, it, those
3 this, it, those, it

2
1 too many *different suggestions* for me to mention
2 'so' replaces *the rise of Bitcoin will mean an end to traditional banking*
3 but it can *be trusted*
4 'one' replaces *new way of paying*
5 'others' replaces *other systems*

Macmillan Education
4 Crinan Street
London N1 9XW
A division of Macmillan Publishers Limited

Companies and representatives throughout the world

ISBN 978-1-786-32566-2 (with Answers)
ISBN 978-1-786-32667-6 (without Answers)

Text, design and illustration © Macmillan Publishers Limited 2017

Written by Richard Storton and Zoltán Rézműves

The authors have asserted their right to be identified as the authors of this work in accordance with the Copyright, Designs and Patents Act 1988.

First published 2017

All rights reserved. No part of this publication may be reproduced, stored in a retrieval system, or transmitted in any form or by any means, electronic, mechanical, photocopying, recording, or otherwise, without the prior written permission of the publishers.

Original design by Macmillan Publishers Ltd
Page make-up by emc design Ltd
Illustrated by Atsushi Hara (Dutch Uncle) pp9, 28, 65

Cover design by Macmillan Publishers Ltd
Cover photographs by Alamy/Andrew Shlykoff (background), Alamy/Chin Yao Chew (tigers)

Picture research by Thomas Bonsu-Dartnall

Authors' acknowledgements
Richard Storton would like to thank the editor, Jane Coates, and the in-house team for doing such a great job. Also a big thank you to my family for their support and patience. Zoltán Rézműves would like to thank Roy Norris for his invaluable input and the team at Macmillan for their support, as well as his co-author, Richard Storton – I hope we will have a chance to work together again in the future.

The publishers would like to thank Roy Norris, Imelda Maguire-Karayel, Mark Harrison, Andy McNeish, Hugh Podmore and Laura Villiger.

The authors and publishers would like to thank the following for permission to reproduce their photographs: **Alamy**/Blend Images p39(br), Alamy/Bill Cheyrou p56(bl), Alamy/Marjorie Kamys Cotera/Bob Daemmrich Photography p70, Alamy/Benedicte Desrus p91, Alamy/Hauke Dressler p39(tr), Alamy/EPA european pressphoto agency p19, Alamy/Philippe Hays p87(bl), Alamy/Jim Holden p18(t), Alamy/Craig Holmes Premium p36(b), Alamy/Eduardo Huelin p108(bl), Alamy/Imagebroker p18(b), Alamy/Image Source Plus p83, Alamy/Arif Iqball Photography – Japan p75(1), Alamy/Gunter Marx p68(bl), Alamy/Mauritius images GmbH p94, Alamy/National Geographic Creative pp46(t), 50–51, Alamy/Grant Rooney Premium p33(r), Alamy/Jay Shaw-Baker p59, Alamy/South West Images Scotland p48(t), Alamy/Zoonar GmbH p75(4); **Getty Images** p55(2), Getty Images/Carlo A p80(b), Getty Images/Colin Anderson p26(rm), Getty Images/Stuart Ashley pp95(t), 113(tr), Getty Images/Astronaut Images p89(br), Getty Images/Matthew Baker p34, Getty Images/Peter Beavis p36(tl), Getty Images/Brand X Pictures p8(tr), Getty Images/Vishal Bhatnagar/NurPhoto p33(bl), Getty Images/Andrew Brookes p85, Getty Images/Gary Burchell p111(tl), Getty Images/David Clapp pp35(t), 45, Getty Images/Paolo Cordelli pp15(tr), 24, Getty Images/Robert Daly/OJO Images p48(m), Getty Images/Artur Debat p80(t), Getty Images/Digital Light Source p104, Getty Images/Digital Vision p106(b), Getty Images/Erik Dreyer p95(b), Getty Images/Sam Edwards/Caiaimage p103, Getty Images/Evirgen p39(bl), Getty Images/Franz-Marc Frei pp26(t), 33(tl), Getty Images/Mitchell Funk p86(bl), Getty Images/Georgijevic p53(r), Getty Images/Leon Harris p15(mr), Getty Images/Michael Heffernan p36(tr), Getty Images/Hero Images p101(b), Getty Images/Hill Street Studios p113(tl), Getty Images/Image Source p37, Getty Images/Johner Images p53(l), Getty Images/Mark Jones/Roving Tortoise Photos p20, Getty Images/Rick Kern/WireImage pp6(r), 13(r), Getty Images/John Lamb pp75(2), 76, Getty Images/Chris Mansfield p42, Getty Images/Maremagnum p40, Getty Images/Tony May pp86(t), 89(tr), Getty Images/Mint Images p29, Getty Images/Kali Nine LLC p96(b), Getty Images/Michael Ochs Archives p66(l), Getty Images/Lori Adamski Peek p110(br), Getty Images/Jose Luis Pelaez Inc/MNPhotoStudios p52, Getty Images/Paul Piebinga p111(b), Getty Images/Bill Pierce/The LIFE Images Collection p13(l), Getty Images/Christopher Polk p6(l), Getty Images/Thomas Roetting/LOOK-foto p106(tr), Getty Images/Quinn Rooney p86(br), Getty Images/George Rose/Getty Images News p87(br), Getty Images/Saro17/E+ p106(tl), Getty Images/Daniel Schoenen p68(br), Getty Images/Shaw Family Archives p35, Getty Images/The Asahi Shimbun p56(t), Getty Images/skynesher pp75(2), 97 Getty Images/Sylvain Sonnet p108(t), Getty Images/Stone pp6(t), 8(tl), Getty Images/Sturti p64, Getty Images/Justin Tallis/AFP p31, Getty Images/Trond Tandberg p39(tl), Getty Images/Mark Thompson p25, Getty Images/Alex Treadway p44, Getty Images/Todor Tsvetkov pp78, 113(b), Getty Images/Klaus Vedfelt pp46(br), 111(tr), Getty Images/VCG p105, Getty Images/Jerry Wachter/NBAE p12, Getty Images/Andrew Watson p26(rb), Getty Images/WIN-Initiative p108(br), Getty Images/Thanasis Zovoilis p15(tr); **NASA** pp66(t), 71; **Photoshot** p68(tl), Photoshot/Cultura pp8(b), 81, Photoshot/Imago p55(3), Photoshot/Mint Images p21, Photoshot/UPPA p48(b); **Plainpicture**/NTB Scanpix/Stig Tronvold p110(t); **Rex/Shutterstock**/20th Century Fox/Courtesy Everett Collection pp67(l), 72, Rex/Shutterstock/Bruce Adams/Daily Mail p55(1), Rex/Shutterstock/Environmental Images/Universal Images Group p68(tm), Rex/Shutterstock/C.Focus/Everett p38, REX/Shutterstock/Juergen Hasenkopf p6(m), Rex/Shutterstock/Jonathan Hordle p67(r), Rex/Shutterstock/Mint Images p75(3), Rex/Shutterstock/Monkey Business Images p96(t), Rex/Shutterstock/View Pictures p89(tl); Science Photo Library/CAIA p62, **Science Photo Library**/Coneyl Jay p55(4); **Marina Shacola** p93; **Shutterstock** pp15(br), 17, 26(rt), 46, 55(t), 60, 68(tr), 89(bl), 101(t), 110(bl)

The authors and publishers are grateful for permission to reprint the following copyright material: p31 Abridged material from 'Review: 'Tate Sensorium'' by Anna Zanetti, copyright L.C. Broad 2012-2016. First published in The Oxford Culture Review 24.09.15. Reprinted by permission of the publisher.

p30 Abridged material from 'Sensorium, Tate Britain, review: 'less than the sum of its parts'' by Mark Hudson, copyright © Telegraph Media Group Ltd 2015. First published in The Telegraph 25.08.2015. Reprinted by permission of the publisher.

p40 Abridged material from 'Beautiful urban architecture boosts health as much as green spaces' by Sarah Knapton, copyright © Telegraph Media Group Ltd 2015. First published in The Telegraph 28.12.2015. Reprinted by permission of the publisher.

p7 Abridged material from 'How my year of tidying up changed my life and family' by Angela Buttolph, copyright © Telegraph Media Group Ltd 2016. First published in The Telegraph 01.01.2016. Reprinted by permission of the publisher.

p31 Abridged material from 'Review: 'Maybe it works: José da Silva on Tate Sensorium' by José da Silva, copyright © 2016 The Art Newspaper. First published in The Art Newspaper 17.09.15. Reprinted by permission of the publisher.

p7 Abridged material from 'The Hitchhiker's Guide taught me about satire, Vogons and even economics' by Ha-Joon Change, copyright © Guardian News & Media Ltd 2016. First published in The Guardian 07.08.15. Reprinted by permission of the publisher.

p30 Abridged material from 'It all smells a bit fishy' by Waldemar Januszczak, copyright © News Corp UK & Ireland Ltd 2016. First published in The Sunday Times 06.09.15. Reprinted by permission of News Syndication.

p59 Material from the article 'News gathering has changed, news values haven't': BBC editorial director on the last 25 years of international reporting', published on www.mumbrella.asia 15.03.16, copyright © 2008-2016 Mumbrella Asia Pte Ltd. All rights reserved. Reprinted by permission of the publisher.

p19 Adapted material from 'GPS vultures swoop down on illegal dumps in Peru' by AFP, copyright © 1994-2016 Agence France-Presse. First published in The Daily Telegraph 12.01.16. Reprinted by permission of Agence France-Presse.

pp20–21 Material from 'Ecotourism can put wild animals at risk, scientists say' by Kendall Morgan and UCLA Newsroom, published on newsroom.ucla.edu 09.10.15, copyright © 2016 UCLA All rights reserved. Reprinted by permission of the publisher.

pp50–51 Adapted material from 'Lizzy Hawker: What you can learn from Britain's greatest ultra marathon runner' by Sophie Morris, copyright © The Independent 2016. First published in The Independent 15.01.16. Reprinted by permission of the publisher. www.independent.co.uk

These materials may contain links for third party websites. We have no control over, and are not responsible for, the contents of such third party websites. Please use care when accessing them.

Printed and bound in Thailand

2021 2020 2019 2018 2017

10 9 8 7 6 5 4 3 2 1